PRISONERS of HOPE

How Engineers and Others
Get Lift for Innovating

Lanny Vincent

WEST BOW
PRESS
A DIVISION OF THOMAS NELSON

ISBN: 978-1-4497-2826-7 (sc)
ISBN: 978-1-4497-2825-0 (e)
ISBN: 978-1-4497-2827-4 (hc)
Library of Congress Control Number: 2011918061

WestBow Press books may be ordered through booksellers or by contacting:

WestBow Press
A Division of Thomas Nelson
1663 Liberty Drive
Bloomington, IN 47403
www.westbowpress.com
1-(866) 928-1240

Printed in the United States of America
WestBow Press rev. date: 12/28/2011

for
the next generation of engineers, designers and scientists
innovating for the next generation of adopters, their children.

The reasonable man adapts himself to the world;
the unreasonable one persists in trying to adapt the world to himself.
Therefore all progress depends on the unreasonable man.

George Bernard Shaw
"Maxims for Revolutionists,"
Man and Superman (1903)

Contents

Foreword

A baby gasps for air. A cry for remedy ensues.

It is attending midwife or nurse who first "tends" to the newborn, with few exceptions. Mother then continues her ever-evolving nurture, now as mindful as it is emotional and physical.

Mother and child in mutual trial and error, at times tedious, form a continuum with an uncertain future. Yet, far from obligation or duty, this relationship is inspired by two inherent human traits—selfless love and faith.

Some say that these are acts of God. I agree with the author; these faithful relationships transcend religion. Beyond Christian, Judaic and Islamic faiths, these faithful interactions between midwife, mother and child require no element of proof to warrant action.

All that goes into birthing and parenting are pure "leaps of faith." And while scientists may account for specific brain functions and hormonal dynamics manifesting this relationship, still no neuroscience can account for "why" each relates to one another as they do. Similarly, scientific knowledge can account for the sequence of forces causing an apple to fall to the ground—and even predict its force of impact. But *why* this governing force called gravity is there remains unanswered. Nevertheless, apples fall and children are nurtured, both to points of independence.

This is the same "act of faith" that enables scientist and engineer to give birth to innovations—unplanned collisions of experience and possibility. Without the selfless love that promotes these acts of faith, both newborn and invention face perilous futures. Exact steps must be taken to ensure both child and innovation are nurtured and fully prepared to endure amidst the inherent instability of human nature and society.

Prisoners of Hope likens these acts of faith—moments of innovating—to an airfoil producing lift. For the first time, and brilliantly, the following chapters complete this metaphor. Competitive and corporate atmospheres either promote or inhibit the foil's successful take-off and landing in the market place. Deft scriptural references reveal universal human traits that support or impede the entire process of innovative flight.

Those who will benefit most by reading *Prisoners of Hope*, in the quiet of humility, will realize their own business atmosphere requires a careful reassessment. And even experienced innovators may want to re-examine their wings one more time, prior to take-off.

Douglas M. Gilmour
Advertising / Brand Maker August, 2011 San Anselmo, California

Introduction

When driving in a densely populated area, you learn to simply get off the freeway at peak traffic times and find your way home on side streets. Despite slower speeds, these local avenues promise relief. The side streets refresh the eye and the mind. They take you away from "rush hour."

A "rush hour" of books and articles on innovation has emerged. Some are worth reading; others are not. Most treat innovation as an entrepreneurial verb or an economic noun. Few look at what innovators as people believe and do. So, instead of adding to that congestion, this book offers a "side street" to innovators and their managers—a street that runs through the largely ignored intersection of faith and innovation.

By "faith" I mean a dictionary definition of a nonreligious "confidence, reliance, or belief, especially without evidence or proof."[1] Innovators believe in what they are doing *before* they have evidence or proof. That's faith.

Faith is largely ignored in studies of innovation and innovators, partly because faith is mistakenly confined to the religious or spiritual realm. Some have it. Others don't. Faith is also avoided in innovation literature because it is not receptive to analysis; empirical, economic, or scientific. However, faith is what makes innovators who they are and enables them to do what they do. (I define faith more completely in Chapter 2.)

The inspiration for this book came from patterns observed in the expressions and actions of innovators with whom I have collaborated for over 30 years. Years ago, I found myself working in the bowels of a Midwestern R&D organization. Surrounded by engineers and scientists—many deeply skilled and experienced in their respective specialties and disciplines—I began recognizing patterns in how they were thinking and acting, especially in their collaborative attempts to innovate. These patterns were strikingly similar to patterns of faith I had studied in seminary and preached from on Sunday mornings in my previous profession.[2] What I noticed both in the lab and in the field were acts of confidence and belief without sufficient evidence or proof. Sometimes just a hunch launched a flood of activity. The willingness to act without evidence or proof was striking. I was seeing faith in action.

At first I said nothing, since one should honor the unspoken boundary between personal matters of faith and organizational matters of business. But then I began to discuss my observations with a few of these innovators. I was told that what I was seeing was not only interesting but helpful—and new. Back then I was a social forecaster, small-group facilitator, and trainer of technologists in creative problem-solving techniques. I had the chance to rub shoulders with innovators while they were in the process of innovating. I eventually developed my current practice as an innovation facilitator, coach and "midwife," a practice of over 30 years, still rubbing shoulders with the real innovators in the midst of innovating.

For three decades since those first inklings, the associations between narrative patterns conveyed in the Old and New Testaments and the patterns of faith scientists and engineers demonstrate when engaged in innovating kept getting stronger and strongr. This book attempts to describe a few of these associations. For this purpose, the Old and New Testaments are regarded as collections of faith patterns—more descriptions than prescriptions. Patterns of faith, of course, are not confined to the ancient stories that codify them but are alive in the minds, hearts and hands of innovators today. However, by extracting the architecture of these faith patterns from these old stories and then comparing these patterns with how innovators do what they do today, both innovators and managers can see the power of faith at work in their innovating, every step of the way. And seeing is believing, and a step toward improving innovating capability and the management of it.

Just as faith is mistakenly confined to matters of religion, the Bible is often shackled to spiritual, even doctrinal matters. When the Bible is understood, however, as a potent source of *practical* wisdom, relevant to all matters of human affairs, it can be seen as the remarkable resource that it is and has been for centuries. It is only in the past hundred years or so that the Bible has been misused as a battering ram to defend against what some consider doctrinal heresy, forcing from its varied literature a precision it never intended in the first place. That the Bible must be re-interpreted anew in every age is an underlying assumption in the following pages. I do not ascribe "inerrant authority" to the Bible, though I do recognize the "authority" that a large community over the centuries has attributed to its wisdom. Put another way, innovators and innovating can be better understood when viewed through the lens of faith, and where better to look for that lens than in the stories of faith caught (and released when read) in the pages of the Old and New Testaments.

Understanding what makes innovators tick is this book's obsession. Successful innovators work *through* the uncertain twists and unforeseen turns of parenting innovations into reality. They work *through* their fears. Timing and circumstance play large roles in every successful innovation effort, for sure. Relationships too: innovator-to-innovator and with non-innovators. But faith is what enables innovators to work *through* the headwinds of resistance and fear. And this faith manifests in recognizable patterns when innovators innovate.

The familiar biblical story of David and Goliath is a perfect example of the intersection between faith and innovation. The innovator in this case is David; Goliath, a robust symbol of what and who innovators face. David's faith makes all the difference. It reminds us that innovators live with hope for the future. They are "prisoners of hope," with all the fear, irony, grief, and even humor that come with the innovator's way. Chapter 1 sets innovators in the context of innovating viewed through the lens of faith.

Part 1 is about who innovators are, what their faith is, and how innovators use their faith to meet the challenges they face. It describes the innate character traits of innovators, traits that emerge. Like wings, faith "lifts" innovators *through* their fears. It is their faith that propels, energizes, and sustains innovators through their many challenges.

Part 2 identifies the five faith patterns that innovators use as they work through the predictable challenges of innovating:

1. Awe and wonder for discovery.

2. Inspiration and appreciation for invention.

3. Forgiveness and persistence for reduction-to-practice.

4. Submission and humility for the introduction.

5. Acceptance and gratitude for the integration of the innovation in daily life.

These patterns are unmistakable. The longer I have worked with innovators, the more recognizable these patterns have become. You'll recognize them as you read the stories about the firsthand experiences of innovators and as they appear in some ancient stories, many of them familiar.

Innovators become self-imposed exiles for a time in journeys that are remarkably unique and remarkably similar. They go from being *a part* of a group to being *apart* from the group and back again. Each journey is unrepeatable, tied to the specific needs of the market and the technological means to address them. Yet each journey shares a similar fabric, woven together with fear and the pattern of faith that overcomes it.

Successful innovation always looks different in hindsight—inspired, brilliant, clever. But when innovators are in the midst of innovating, they exhibit what appears to be a much more chaotic reality, at least, until you recognize the patterns. And these patterns—the innovators' thoughts, attitudes, and behaviors—all point to the central theme of this book:

Successful innovators work *through* fear. Their wings of faith give them the crucial "lift" they need.

Without that faith, the only other choice is to give up.

* * *

Finally, three notes to the reader:

First, I have included selective chunks of narrative from the Old and New Testaments. Selective, yes, but chunks nonetheless. I did so to allow you to see firsthand how a specific pattern appears in the biblical narrative so you can make your own decision just how it compares to the patterns of innovators' thoughts and actions. It also saves you from having to look up the Bible passage.

The second has to do with metaphors. The faith of innovators is so intangible, metaphors are a useful vehicle for describing faith and its dynamics. Because of my extensive use of metaphor, I ask you to indulge my imprecision and to interpret the metaphors in the same sense of play in which they are intended.

The third has to do with whom I have in mind when I use the word "innovator." Engineers, designers and scientists—technologists employed in commercial R&D organizations—are the people with whom I have the most experience. This does not mean to imply that innovators are confined to people with these kinds of credentials and experience. Innovators can emerge from marketing, sales, logistics and manufacturing or other functions. Having technologists in mind when I use the term innovators may be a semantic artifact of my experience more than a prescriptive requirement for innovators.

Chapter 1

A Parable for Innovators

Innovators change the world around them. In doing so they change themselves. What defines the innovat*or* is inseparable from their innovat*ing*, successful or not. Innovators derive their identity from the innovations they create.

Each innovators and his or her respective innovation are both an original mix of characteristics. This makes any generalization about innovators difficult at best. Another challenge to defining who innovators are derive from the fact that they are not fixed, static beings. They emerge and evolve. Nor are they solely the product of genetic fate or a peculiar kind of parenting, or of a particular position in birth order. Whether innovators are born or made, it is more important to recognize that they are shaped into innovators from and by their innovation and their innovating. Innovators are living, emergent "systems" who adapt to conditions around them. Sometimes these conditions are inviting, sometimes threatening. Normally, they're a mix of both. Regardless, the true innovator develops and emerges, just as does the innovation itself.

Regardless of the inherent and pervasive "originality" among and between innovators, one thing all innovators have in common is faith. In fact, the following pages are based on the premise that faith is *the* distinguishing characteristic of innovators. Faith is there at the beginning with the innovator's initial vision. It is in the middle, amidst all the challenges and problem solving. It is there in the end as well when they let go. Their faith is secular—nonreligious. It is demonstrated when innovators push ahead with an idea they believe—without proof and often without evidence—will work. Innovators tend to rely on a set of behaviors and attitudes that grow and evolve into an increasingly sophisticated and more fine-tuned capability. Faith is the heart of this capability. The faith of innovators gives them the crucial "lift" they need to work through their doubts and fears.

The faith of innovators is of the same character and type as the faith canonized in the various writings found in the Old and New Testaments and I am assuming in scriptures of the world's other great spiritual traditions. Many stories in the Old and New Testaments have been providing people with wisdom for centuries. It really shouldn't surprise us that some of this wisdom is relevant to innovators. Yet few innovators have thought to look to this ancient source for guidance in innovating. However, this source—the prophetic tradition especially—is replete with stories that reveal patterns of innovation in general and the faith of innovators in particular.

To put some flesh on the skeleton of this hypothesis, take a closer look at what might be considered an archetypal biblical story of innovation— the story of David and Goliath. Most of us have at least some familiarity with what happens. The story comes down to an epic match between two rival armies facing off against each other—the Israelites against the Philistines.

The conflict has some starring roles. First, there is David. He's the upstart, a virtual unknown shepherd who comes to the attention of an increasingly unstable and anxious King Saul. Years later, David succeeds Saul as king largely because of his victory over Goliath, a victory David finessed by means of a disruptive innovation Clayton Christensen might call "just-good-enough."[3]

Next, there's Goliath. He's the larger, more technologically sophisticated warrior sent forth by the Philistines to taunt, frighten, and otherwise intimidate Israel. This intimidation strategy actually worked for a while. It created a stalemate, not unlike what happens when two big rival companies reach product or brand parity (think Pepsi and Coke) and have to battle it out with overblown advertising budgets. Each tries to intimidate the other with a barrage of words and images.

Often forgotten in the David and Goliath story, however, is Samuel who plays a critical supporting role. Samuel is the prophet who, with God's guidance, selected David successor to Saul. Saul, it turns out, had already fallen out of favor with the Lord. Samuel knew it. Who else knew of Saul's impending decline and David's selection beforehand is not clear. What is clear, however, is that the succession was determined *before* the face-off between David and Goliath.

Read as a parable of innovation the story of David and Goliath can teach us a great deal about the elements present in every innovating effort: in other words, the conditions of necessity, positioning for serendipity, atmospheres of fear, experience reframed, permission to fail, motivations of love, and emergence. Here's the more familiar part of the story.

Now the Philistines gathered their armies for battle . . . . The Philistines stood on the mountain on one side, and Israel stood on the mountain on the other side, with a valley between them. And there came out from the camp of the Philistines a champion named Goliath, of Gath, whose height was six cubits and a span. He had a helmet of bronze on his head, and he was armored with a coat of mail; the weight of the coat was five thousand shekels of bronze. He had greaves of bronze on his legs and a javelin of bronze slung between his shoulders. The shaft of his spear was like a weaver's beam, and his spear's head weighed six hundred shekels of iron; and his shield-bearer went before him. He stood and shouted to the ranks of Israel, ' . . . Choose a man for yourselves, and let him come down to me. If he is able to fight with me and kill me, then we will be your servants; but if I prevail against him and kill him, then you shall be our servants and serve us.' And the Philistine said, 'Today I defy the ranks of Israel! Give me a man, that we may fight together.' When Saul and all Israel heard these words of the Philistine, they were dismayed and greatly afraid.

Now David was the son of . . . Jesse, who had eight sons . . . The three eldest had followed Saul to the battle; the names of his three sons who went to the battle were Eliab the firstborn, and next to him Abinadab, and the third Shammah. David was the youngest; the three eldest followed Saul, but David went back and forth from Saul to feed his father's sheep at Bethlehem. For forty days the Philistine came forward and took his stand, morning and evening.

Jesse said to his son David, 'Take for your brothers an ephah of this parched grain and these ten loaves, and carry them quickly to the camp to your brothers; also take these ten cheeses to the commander of their thousand. See how your brothers fare, and bring some token from them.'

. . . David rose early in the morning, left someone in charge of the sheep, took the provisions, and went as Jesse had commanded him. He came to the encampment as the army was going forth to the battle line, shouting the war cry . . . . David left the things in charge of the keeper of the baggage, ran to the ranks, and went and greeted his brothers. As he talked with them, the champion, the Philistine of Gath, Goliath by name, came up out of the ranks of the Philistines, and spoke the same words as before. And David heard him.

All the Israelites, when they saw the man, fled from him and were very much afraid. The Israelites said, 'Have you seen this man who has come up? Surely he has come up to defy Israel. The king will greatly enrich the man who kills him, and will give him his daughter and make his family free in Israel.' David said to the men who stood by him, 'What shall be done for the man who kills this Philistine, and takes away the reproach from Israel? For who is this uncircumcised Philistine that he should defy the armies of the living God?' The people answered him in the same way, 'So shall it be done for the man who kills him.'

His eldest brother Eliab heard him talking to the men; and Eliab's anger was kindled against David. He said, 'Why have you come down? With whom have you left those few sheep in the wilderness? I know your presumption and the evil of your heart; for you have come down just to see the battle.' David said, 'What have I done now? It was only a question.' He turned away from him towards another and spoke in the same way; and the people answered him again as before.

When the words that David spoke were heard, they repeated them before Saul; and he sent for him. David said to Saul, 'Let no one's heart fail because of him; your servant will go and fight with this Philistine.' Saul said to David, 'You are not able to go against this Philistine to fight with him; for you are just a boy, and he has been a warrior from his youth.' But David said to Saul, 'Your servant used to keep sheep for his father; and whenever a lion or a bear came, and took a lamb from the flock, I went after it and struck it down, rescuing the lamb from its mouth; and if it turned against me, I would catch it by the jaw, strike it down, and kill it. Your servant has killed both lions and bears; and this uncircumcised Philistine shall be like one of them, since he has defied the armies of the living God.' David said, 'The Lord, who saved me from the paw of the lion and from the paw of the bear, will save me from the hand of this Philistine.' So Saul said to David, 'Go, and may the Lord be with you!

Saul clothed David with his armour; he put a bronze helmet on his head and clothed him with a coat of mail. David strapped Saul's sword over the armour, and he tried in vain to walk, for he was not used to them. Then David said to Saul, 'I cannot walk with these; for I am not used to them.' So David removed them. Then he took his staff in his hand, and chose five smooth stones from the wadi, and put them in his shepherd's bag, in the pouch; his sling was in his hand, and he drew near to the Philistine.

The Philistine came on and drew near to David, with his shield-bearer in front of him. When the Philistine looked and saw David, he disdained him, for he was only a youth, ruddy and handsome in appearance. The Philistine said to David, 'Am I a dog, that you come to me with sticks?' And the Philistine cursed David by his gods. The Philistine said to David, 'Come to me, and I will give your flesh to the birds of the air and to the wild animals of the field.' But David said to the Philistine, 'You come to me with sword and spear and javelin; but I come to you in the name of the Lord of hosts, the God of the armies of Israel, whom you have defied. This very day the Lord will deliver you into my hand, and I will strike you down and cut off your head; and I will give the dead bodies of the Philistine army this very day to the birds of the air and to the wild animals of the earth, so that all the earth may know that there is a God in Israel, and that all this assembly may know that the Lord does not save by sword and spear; for the battle is the Lord's and he will give you into our hand.'

When the Philistine drew nearer to meet David, David ran quickly towards the battle line to meet the Philistine. David put his hand in his bag, took out a stone, slung it, and struck the Philistine on his forehead; the stone sank into his forehead, and he fell face down on the ground.

So David prevailed over the Philistine with a sling and a stone, striking down the Philistine and killing him; there was no sword in David's hand. Then David ran and stood over the Philistine; he grasped his sword, drew it out of its sheath, and killed him; then he cut off his head with it. When the Philistines saw that their champion was dead, they fled.

—I Samuel 17

Conditions of necessity

For incumbents, innovators can be a threat. This is precisely what Peter Chernin, former COO of Fox News Corporation, meant when he said, "Success is the enemy of innovation."[4] From Goliath's point of view, the innovator David and his innovation (slingshot) were both unwelcome and unexpected. From David's perspective, however, the innovation was more than a path to success; it was a matter of survival.

One clear lesson from the David and Goliath story is that innovation and innovators emerge under conditions of necessity. Imagine competing companies occupying different mountains with a valley of uncertainty between them. Consider the recent experience of the consumer electronics industry. Sony, Panasonic, Philips, and others were occupying one mountain. Facing them on the opposing mountain was the computer industry—with Dell, HP, Apple, Intel, and Microsoft. In the valley of uncertainty between them was the market with all its existing technology.

Each had the same opportunity. Who would be the first to go down into that valley, into that available stream of MP3 players and cell phone technologies? Who would emerge successful in this face-off? Like David picking up five smooth stones, Apple picked up a few "stones" laying in the stream of existing technologies and "smoothed" them with elegant product and service design and gave us the iPod, iTunes, iPhone, and iPad.

Conditions of necessity emerge in different ways. Two of the most reliable, according to Peter Drucker, in his classic book *Innovation and Entrepreneurship*, are an incongruity that emerges (reality as it is versus reality as it should be) and a process need (a deficiency in how something is done).[5] Other conditions to pay attention to are the emergence of an unexpected failure or success and a change in the market or industry structure. One or more of these always precedes the bright idea of innovation.

Where there is unresolved conflict something is likely to happen. My former mentor, Bill Wilson (a highly regarded Samuel of innovation at Kimberly-Clark during the '80s and '90s) had a favorite technique for predicting where innovation was likely to occur. Wilson's formula was simple. Identify the two leading experts in any field. Ask them what they are arguing about. It could be dramatic or subtle. While the answer will not tell you *what* the outcome will be, it is a reliable method for indicating *where* change is likely to occur and innovation likely to emerge.

Atmosphere of fear

Innovators grow in an atmosphere of fear. That's another innovating lesson of the David and Goliath story.

> When Saul and all Israel heard these words of the Philistine, they were dismayed and greatly afraid . . . . All the Israelites, when they saw the man, fled from him and were very much afraid.

As the incumbent on the battlefield and a true giant, Goliath was someone to be feared. Today, incumbents are wrapped in superior technology and garnered with the privileges of sheer size, scope, and scale. They present a formidable force. However, whenever their arrogance spews forth with disdain for their seemingly weaker opponent, as Goliath's did for David, conditions may be ripe for a stunning reversal.

Fear for the upstart David, the innovator, was real. Today fear for innovating upstarts is just as real, no matter how large the upstart.

In 2009 as Toyota was about to surpass GM as the largest manufacturer of automobiles in the world, the company publicly voiced anxiety over *its own* temptation of arrogance. That public introspection spoke volumes about the wisdom of Toyota's leaders at that time.[6] Most in a Goliath posture, as GM was then, fail to acknowledge the precarious position they are in. Pride gets in the way. Arrogance blinds them. GM, which had been the world's largest automobile manufacturer for years, fell to number 2 in 2010 when Toyota, like David, overcame fear and toppled the giant, moving up into the top spot. Jim Collins has documented examples of this in his recent book *How the Mighty Fall*.[7]

One of my early experiences with how innovators struggle to overcome their fears occurred in the early 1980s. I was on a team that developed what became a very successful product—the first disposable training pants, called Pull-Ups®. For the product's innovators, sponsors, and mentors in Kimberly-Clark, the fears came from both outside and inside. Patent filings from archrival Procter & Gamble (P&G) revealed that P&G also was poised to introduce a disposable training pants product of their own. Competing directly against the Goliath P&G had most at Kimberly-Clark convinced that P&G would be the first to introduce the product. But two innovators behind Kimberly-Clark's version, Glen Fleischer and Walt Perls, were not intimidated. Their challenge was not only to develop a great product. They also had to convince a reluctant and fearful management to introduce that product before P&G could introduce its new product. Going first was a decision the "Sauls" in Kimberly-Clark had a hard time believing was possible. They believed that the company had never done that before. As a result, there was unnecessary delay.

While the delay was excruciatingly difficult for the two innovators, their persistence paid off. A senior executive, Wayne Saunders, finally made the decision to launch. The launch was more successful than anyone had forecast—and the rest is history. P&G's eventual response was weak at best.

But there's more to the story of Pull-Ups®. Soon after the launch, Wayne Saunders became CEO, partly because of the success of Pull-UpsR®. His was an act of faith that changed the view Kimberly-Clark had of its own potential.

Fear can be revealed in different ways. Even a question can uncover fears. When David asked a seemingly innocent question, the reaction of his older brother Eliab revealed how saturated with fear and suspicion the atmosphere had become.

> David said to the men who stood by him, 'What shall be done for the man who kills this Philistine, and takes away the reproach from Israel? For who is this uncircumcised Philistine that he should defy the armies of the living God?' The people answered him in the same way, 'So shall it be done for the man who kills him.'
>
> His eldest brother Eliab heard him talking to the men; and Eliab's anger was kindled against David. He said, 'Why have you come down? With whom have you left those few sheep in the wilderness? I know your presumption and the evil of your heart; for you have come down just to see the battle.' David said, 'What have I done now? It was only a question.'

A question can often conceal unspoken fear that the idea will be rejected. By asking a question the one asking can often discover how receptive the environment is to a new idea. David did exactly that.

Positioned for serendipity

Innovators also put themselves in positions to see what others don't or won't. To increase the probability for serendipity, they need to hear and see for themselves.

Nothing grants advantage more than being in the right place at the right time. Louis Pasteur said it long ago: "Chance favors the prepared mind."[8] The serendipitous—the happy, accidental, and unexpected discovery that occurs when the discoverer is looking for something else—is at work in the actual circumstances of innovating more than many care to admit. This is another lesson in the David and Goliath story.

Initially David was far away from the front lines. He was clearly out of position, running supplies back and forth. Not until Jesse his father sent David to get news from the front about the welfare of his older sons did David have the excuse to get into a position to see for himself what was going on.

> Now Saul and all the men of Israel, were in the valley of Elah, fighting with the Philistines. David rose early in the morning, left someone in charge of the sheep, took the provisions, and went as Jesse had commanded him. He came to the encampment as the army was going forth to the battle line, shouting the war cry. Israel and the Philistines drew up for battle, army against army. David left the things in charge of the keeper of the baggage, ran to the ranks, and went and greeted his brothers. As he talked with them, the champion, the Philistine of Gath, Goliath by name, came up out of the ranks of the Philistines, and spoke the same words as before. And David heard him.

Before he could get himself in position, however, David had to find someone to leave in charge of his responsibilities. Twice, in fact.

Often successful companies—extending their success and profits with cost-cutting—unwittingly cripple their own well-intentioned innovating. Being so "lean" leaves no one to whom innovators can transfer their responsibilities so as to get themselves into position. As a result, innovators are at a disadvantage. In *Dealing with Darwin*, Geoffrey Moore describes the importance of freeing up the right people at the right time—people with the knowledge necessary to take an innovation to the next step.[9] Some call it "absorptive" capacity—having enough bench strength to redeploy experts when and where they are needed. Successful companies have an eye to the succession not only of the organization's executive leaders but of their innovators as well. They maintain some bench strength and are willing to move innovators to where they are needed, when they are needed there.

Successful innovators themselves have learned to get in position to take advantage of serendipity. Toyota's development system incorporates this approach. To thoroughly understand a situation, Toyota practices *genchi genbutsu*, "go see for yourself."

A good example of positioning for serendipity is the success of Mike Sinyard, founder of Specialized Bicycle, Inc. Sinyard was one of the first to see the commercial potential of the mountain bike (a form that turned the bicycle industry in the U.S. on its head). Because of his knowledge of, and relationships with, dealers and parts makers, he was the first to see the emerging opportunity for mass-producing mountain bikes, and he capitalized on it. His position as a parts distributor allowed him to see what others, like the incumbent giant Schwinn, were unable to see.

Another example is Paula Rosch, a senior product developer at Kimberly-Clark in the 80s and 90s. Paula was working on a project, the goal of which was to envision the ideal diaper product. During this project she commissioned all sorts of elaborate exploratory research with consumers. However, in the early stages of the project, Paula just happened to notice a problem at a public swimming pool. She saw how mothers were struggling to comply with rules preventing their diapered infants and toddlers from entering the wading pool without a diaper. However, when they waded in wearing a diaper, the diaper would absorb all the moisture it could, making it a challenge for little ones to move freely and enjoy their time in the pool. From this serendipitous moment was born Little Swimmers®—a very successful disposable diaper swimsuit.

A more famous example of serendipity is the work of Alastair Pilkington and Kenneth Bickerstaff, who invented a revolutionary method of producing high-quality flat glass, though it took several years to perfect the process for commercial application. Their invention came in part from the inspiration Pilkington had while helping his wife wash dishes after dinner. Pilkington and Bickerstaff were already working furiously against rivals in the glass industry to produce a high-quality glass, which required grinding and polishing plate glass to make it clear, a costly process. The suds in the dishpan reminded Pilkington that the surface of a liquid is perfectly flat. Pilkington had his "eureka" moment doing the dinner dishes in front of the kitchen sink. Taking this observation back to the plant, he tried floating molten glass on a bath of molten tin, and it worked.

David did the same thing. He got himself into position. He went to see and hear for himself what the threat was all about. He brought fresh eyes and ears to the stalemate that had stymied Saul and his warriors.

Experience reframed

Most would agree, it's always better to have experience. But applying this general rule to innovators is problematic. Direct experience with an innovation is impossible. Innovations are, by definition, originial. There is a "first-time-ness" to every innovation. As a result, the best experience we can expect from innovators is analogous experience in a similar field or situation. This is what David used in convincing Saul to give him a chance despite his lack of direct experience in fighting a giant.

> David said to Saul, "Your servant used to keep sheep for his father; and whenever a lion or a bear came, and took a lamb from the flock, I went after it and struck it down, rescuing the lamb from its mouth; and if it turned against me, I would catch it by the jaw, strike it down, and kill it. Your servant has killed both lions and bears; and this uncircumcised Philistine shall be like one of them, since he has defied the armies of the living God." David said, "The Lord, who saved me from the paw of the lion and from the paw of the bear, will save me from the hand of this Philistine." So Saul said to David, "Go, and may the Lord be with you!"

What's going on here? Is David trying to convince Saul that his experience fending off predators of his father's flocks qualifies him to take on Goliath? Perhaps. Innovators emerge *from* their formal expertise and their informal experience. When innovating they must go beyond both.

David's confident pledge to fight the giant Philistine is met with a healthy dose of skepticism from Saul. "Have you ever done this before?" This is *always* the question for an innovator. For every innovation, the honest answer is always, "Well, no, not exactly." Saul seems to know this, as does David. Saul points to the obvious difference between David with his lack of experience and the seasoned warrior Goliath. "Goliath has been a warrior from his youth. Not only do you lack experience, David. You are too young!" Clearly Saul did not share David's confidence to fight against the more experienced, not to mention more heavily armored and just plain bigger, opponent.

When it comes to experience, innovators are always found lacking. Innovators should expect this skepticism, as David did. Ultimately Saul gave in. Conditions of necessity overruled the normal rules of caution.

Years ago I found myself in the midst of changing careers from the ordained Presbyterian ministry to what, at the time, I had no clue, only imagination. I had the good fortune of conducting what Kenneth Bolles (*What Color Is Your Parachute?*[10]) calls an "informational interview" with the director of purchasing at Kimberly-Clark, Dick Loescher. At the time, I didn't even really know what purchasing was. But there I was, at the suggestion of a former parishioner, sitting on the other side of an imposing desk opposite this man who had been referred to me as "someone I should talk to."

Following Bolles' script for informational interviewing, I must have been visibly self-conscious. My complete lack of experience with the mysterious world of corporations left me uncertain, even a bit depressed about "throwing away" a promising career as a minister. In hindsight, I realized Dick Loescher undoubtedly sensed all this. In fact, as I came to know him later, his robust and empathetic capacity was fully engaged, unbeknownst to me at that moment. He leaned back in his chair, brought his hands down to rest on his rotund belly, and asked, "So, Lanny, tell me about what you really liked to do—what you felt you were good at—as a minister."

I remember saying something about preaching, especially how challenging it was to say something fresh, relevant, and meaningful with something very old and well known. I told him of the thrill I felt when I knew I was connecting with the congregation on those Sundays when the sermon worked.

Dick raised his eyebrows and said, "Oh. You're an *interpreter*. We need interpreters. They are in short supply. The only difference is that in this [corporate] world what we need interpreted is not confined to an ancient text of a thousand pages of wisdom. The text we need interpreted is much more varied than that." In that moment, it was as if Dick had reached across his desk, picked me up, dusted me off, and given me a new understanding of my experience and potential contribution. He had simply reframed my previous experience, liberated it from the confines of my own limited imagination, and placed it squarely into a new context. That moment gave me a sense of hope and promise, and actually did lead me to an entirely new career.

Experience, especially when canonized in an expert's sense of identity and self-worth, can be a blessing. It can be essential to fledgling innovation efforts. But it can also be a curse. It can just as easily disable these early efforts. Experience that remains in its original context may have a difficult time going beyond that area of expertise to forge the new and fresh connections so essential to any innovation.

Neurophysiologists speak of "long-term potentiation," which describes the neuronal pathways in the brain that develop from repetition. These neuronal pathways are the brain's way of creating "express" connections, particularly with frequently excited neurons. In other words, experts, by definition, have well-developed biases in their brains that are not merely attitudinal but anatomical.

David Kelley, the founder of IDEO and now head of the Design School at Stanford University, suggests that we should be on the lookout for people who are "T-types." These are people who have deep (vertical) expertise in one or more areas of a specialty *and*, at the same time, have a experience with a breadth (horizontal) of connections in other areas.

This is the dilemma of expertise. On the one hand, expertise from deep and extensive experience is needed if we are to avoid reinventing the wheel. On the other hand, our experience can be the very thing that causes us to reject the new, particularly when it has become part of our own sense of identity. Albert Einstein was fond of saying, "If an idea does not at first seem absurd, it is not worth pursuing." New ideas—as proof of their newness—are at first rejected.

I often counsel inventors to look for rejection instead of shying away from it, especially their own. When experts start to feel uncomfortable with the line of thinking being discussed, their discomfort can be a good sign. That felt rejection from an expert is an early signal that the innovator has entered a new line of thinking. The trick is to have the expert express rejection in such a way as to invite further thinking, not eliminate the idea or the messenger who delivered it.

Innovators benefit from the practice of taking what they know from experience and placing themselves and their experience into a new context.

David reframed his experience in successfully defending his father's flock and ultimately convinced Saul to give him a try. Was David overreaching? Was Saul out of options? Perhaps. In a sense, both took "leaps" of faith, but not without first some consideration of a reframed experience.

Permission to fail

Innovators need permission to fail—another innovating lesson from the David and Goliath story. This is the kind of permission we obtain from someone and the kind we give to ourselves.

The permission to fail precedes acts that may require forgiveness. It's a mental attitude that gives innovators freedom to try, to view the next step as an experiment that just might fail but is worth doing anyway because of what can be learned. Permission is something that innovators must give themselves and, at times, obtain from their sponsor. This is precisely what was going on when David approached Saul for permission to try.

> David said, "The Lord, who saved me from the paw of the lion and from the paw of the bear, will save me from the hand of this Philistine." So Saul said to David, "Go, and may the Lord be with you!"

David was seeking permission to fail—a license he had already given to himself. His risk-averse brothers and the cautious, anxious Saul were not able to give themselves this kind of permission. As a result, nothing was happening. There was a stalemate. Tension was building.

These conditions are reflected in many successful companies within which innovators emerge. Chris Argyris put it simply: "Because many professionals are almost always successful at what they do, they rarely experience failure. And because they have rarely failed, they have never learned how to learn from failure."[11] They also never give themselves permission to fail.

David goes to the front line to get a sense of the tension firsthand. It doesn't take much to imagine how David assessed the situation. Continue to do nothing, let the tension increase, and risk almost certain defeat. Or try something, almost anything. Wouldn't it be better to at least try something, even if it fails, than to do nothing at all?

Was it naïve youthful exuberance behind David's conviction that he could slay Goliath? Not entirely. If we read the story carefully, we find that David's experience was not without a method. David describes killing predators of his father's flock this way: "I would catch it by the jaw, strike it down, and kill it." Killing the predator came last, not first. First find the enemy's vulnerable point of leverage (the jaw of the predator) and concentrate the initial action there. David's confidence was born, at least in part, from his experience with a method that had worked for him in the past. He had an idea, with experience to back it up. All he needed was permission from Saul to try, even though his trying might fail. Not trying would leave Israel in this intolerable stalemate, eventually becoming subject to the rule of the Philistines. David not only gave himself permission to fail, he persisted in convincing Saul to give him permission to fail as well.

Stefan Thomke, in *Experimentation Matters*, has written convincingly of how important (and how difficult) it is for successful organizations to give in-house innovators—or any other employees for that matter—the permission to fail. Thomke writes, "A relentless organizational focus on success makes true experimentation all too rare."[12]

Years before, Tom Peters and Robert Waterman made a similar point in their classic *In Search of Excellence*. "Most big institutions have forgotten how to test and learn. They seem to prefer analysis and debate to trying something out, and they are paralyzed by fear of failure, however small."[13]

Many emerging innovators, embedded in the atmosphere of their host organization, decline to give themselves permission to fail. In the process they succumb to the fear around them. Hence, no one tries anything. No experiments are done. No one learns anything.

Successful innovators first give themselves permission to fail. They learn to resist the infectious temptation of their organizations to avoid failure. David certainly had this mental attitude and ability.

I can't help but wonder whether David's musical ability with the lyre might have had something to do with his ability to give himself permission to fail. I have worked with many innovator-engineers who maintained, on the side, an avocation for playing music. Musician-engineers represent robust inventive potential. Play itself—musical or otherwise—sculpts the brain, opens the imagination, and invigorates the soul, as Dr. Stuart Brown points out in his book *Play*. Brown introduces the emerging science behind play, citing evolutionary biologists Spinka and Bekoff. Brown tells us that play "prepares us for the unexpected."[14] Play occurs in conditions where failure's consequences are negligible.

David was clearly an experienced shepherd who had repeatedly given himself permission to try and to fail. He had a rich reservoir of experience from many "practice" rounds fending off predators preying on his father's sheep. David brought this attitude right into the big match with Goliath. When the permission to fail is brought out of practice rounds and into a context where performance counts, innovations and innovators emerge.

Some successful innovators were never given the permission to fail. They simply took it, and then sought forgiveness. Chuck House at Hewlett-Packard was told explicitly to stop working on a display innovation. He persisted and not only created a success but, several years later, inspired David Packard to present him with an award for "extraordinary defiance beyond the normal call of engineering duty."[15]

It's often tough for an innovator who is at the beginning of an idea for a new product to compete against rivals. In order to produce the needed evidence, the innovator needs permission to try, even to fail. Lacking that permission, the innovator must act, even if it necessitates an act of insubordination with hopes for some forgiveness in the future. Otherwise the innovator's promising idea will remain untried, abandoned in the realm of merely an interesting idea.

Heart of love

Closely associated with the mental attitude of the permission to fail is another characteristic of the innovator revealed in this classic biblical story. It is the source of the innovator's motivation—a heart of love. Where the permission to fail gives the innovator the freedom to try, the heart of love gives the innovator the conviction to commit, particularly in the face of uncertainty.

Champion was a word used twenty or more years ago to describe someone who felt strongly enough about a cause or a needed change to put themselves at risk of possible rejection, failure, or loss, or even merely looking naïve. Some organizations still use "champion," though it has lost much of the voluntarism found in strong motivations from the heart. Experienced managers, however, know to look for an inner passion in innovators that determines whether one has sufficient commitment to withstand the inevitable challenges and resistance to come.

Rewards are always promised to the one who succeeds, rewards even David was undoubtedly tempted to pursue ("The king will greatly enrich the man who kills him, and will give him his daughter and make his family free in Israel" [1 Samuel 17.25].) However, there is more going on here than lust after the rewards, whehter of freedom, the beautiful girl (none other than the king's daughter), fame, and money. This is an often over looked attribute of innovators—their intrinsic motivation.

In the chapter that precedes the David and Goliath episode, Samuel was coached to use selection criteria other than outward appearance to pick Saul's successor. Unlike what a resume can reveal, it's really about the ability to peer into the motivations of the innovator. For Samuel, the selection was based on what was on the inside—the heart of David.

> "[Most others] look at the outward appearance, but the
> LORD looks at the heart" (1 Samuel 16.7).

So at least we know where not to look—at outward appearances. Those are poor indicators of what really drives innovators to innovate. What motivated David? It was love—love for Saul (and at first, Saul's love for him); love for the nation of Israel; and certainly his love for his brothers and his father. David's heart was motivated by love.

Ascribing love as the root motivation of innovators may sound extreme or naive. *Passion* seems a more palatable, more politically correct, word. But love may be more prevalent and common in the heart of innovators, nonetheless. (Chapter 4 will examine this motivation more closely.) For now, it may be sufficient to draw from the work of Paul Lawrence and Nitin Nohria in their book *Driven: How Human Nature Shapes Our Choices.*

Lawrence and Nohria suggest that there are four independent roots for what motivates all of us to do what we do. These four basic drives operate in all of us. One or more of the drives may be dominant, while the others, like genes, are recessive, shaping not driving. The first two—the drive to defend and the drive to bond—are more biologically based, hardwired into our reptilian brain stems. The other two—the drive to acquire and the drive to learn—are more culturally based.[16] If there is even a wisp of truth to the hypothesis of Lawrence and Nohria, it is clear that David's innovation was stirred by both the obvious drive to defend and the not-so-obvious, but nonetheless evident, drive to bond: his love for Saul, his brothers, his father, his nation, not to mention his love for his God and his own freedom.

We could speculate as to David's other possible motivations: his professional ambitions, his lust for Saul's daughter, his desire to prove himself to be something other than the artistic geek and lowly shepherd boy many took him to be. But the more interesting motivation is something for which David is willing to risk his own life—love. Author Maya Angelou, on National Public Radio, described the difference between her mere interest in music versus her love of poetry. Asked why she became a writer and poet rather than a musician, she said, "I didn't love music the way I loved words. I wasn't willing to make the sacrifices I made for words and poetry. You sacrifice for what you love."[17]

Innovators have an inner clarity about why they are willing to make sacrifices for their innovation. This differentiates them from other, non-innovators. And this is where innovation and succession intersect.

There is currently a great deal of money, energy, and time being spent on what is called innovation. To discern which innovations are worth pursuing and who is worth investing in, look closely at the innovations for which the innovator is willing to make great sacrifices.

Emergence

Take a look at the more familiar part of the David and Goliath story. The narrative tells us much about how innovations and innovators emerge. It describes what actually happens to innovators in the midst of the process of innovating as opposed to what theorists want us to believe should happen but seldom does.

> Saul clothed David with his armor; he put a bronze helmet on his head and clothed him with a coat of mail. David strapped Saul's sword over the armor, and he tried in vain to walk, for he was not used to them. Then David said to Saul, "I cannot walk with these; for I am not used to them." So David removed them. Then he took his staff in his hand, and chose five smooth stones from the wadi, and put them in his shepherd's bag, in the pouch; his sling was in his hand, and he drew near to the Philistine.
>
> The Philistine came on and drew near to David, with his shield-bearer in front of him. When the Philistine looked and saw David, he disdained him, for he was only a youth, ruddy and handsome in appearance. The Philistine said to David, "Am I a dog, that you come to me with sticks?" And the Philistine cursed David by his gods. The Philistine said to David, "Come to me, and I will give your flesh to the birds of the air and to the wild animals of the field." But David said to the Philistine, "You come to me with sword and spear and javelin; but I come to you in the name of the Lord of hosts, the God of the armies of Israel, whom you have defied . . . ."
>
> When the Philistine drew nearer to meet David, David ran quickly towards the battle line to meet the Philistine. David put his hand in his bag, took out a stone, slung it, and struck the Philistine on his forehead; the stone sank into his forehead, and he fell face down on the ground.
>
> So David prevailed over the Philistine with a sling and a stone, striking down the Philistine and killing him; there

was no sword in David's hand. Then David ran and stood over the Philistine; he grasped his sword, drew it out of its sheath, and killed him; then he cut off his head with it. When the Philistines saw that their champion was dead, they fled.

What actually happens to innovators and their innovations in the making, unlike what is supposed to happen, goes something like this:

First, there is an agreement between innovators and a sponsor. Permission is given and received. Commitments are made and everyone plunges in without knowing for sure. Everyone takes a deep breath. Here we go. Here David and Saul reach an accord. Saul is willing to sponsor David in the attempt. And David is willing to fight the giant.

Second, all the conventional methods are brought out and tried on for size. And just like Saul's bulky armor, these methods were designed for a different age and an older generation of technology. The innovator is overburdened, cramped, and restricted. But we do this step anyway, perhaps to reassure ourselves that the old really is not going to work, especially with a new way of thinking. Here, clearly, Saul's armor doesn't fit or work with David's skinny physique.

Third, there is some conceptual improvisation, which involves both product and process. Both are conceived with the help of some previous experience, either simulated in practice rounds or learned from the "minor leagues." Untried and untested in the major leagues, the innovator, nonetheless, is convinced about the new approach, oftentimes the innovator's own invention. But what appears to be a product invention is really both product *and* process invention. For David it was not only five smooth stones and a slingshot (the product), it was also finding a vulnerable point of leverage—like a predator's jaw or the giant's forehead—to bring the larger beast down and then kill him (the process).

Fourth, there is a resource improvisation that converts the concept of the invention into a tool that can be used. David finds five smooth stones in the bed of a stream in the middle of the valley. This remarkable faith in "the process"—that more will be revealed and more will be provided—is a signature act of faith by innovators.

Finally, there is the try—the act. In this case the try succeeds on the first time. David was prepared for the possibility of failure. He had anticipated several more iterations of his technique and had four more stones for backup. His success surprised both the enemy (the incumbent) and David's own uncertain sponsors and allies.

This is the basic story line from which all innovators and innovations emerge. It can help us to understand how to spot the innovators among us, what makes them tick, and what contributes to their success.

The story of David and Goliath tells us that innovators and their faith emerge: fueled by the heart of love, lifted by the wings of hope, and shaped by the headwinds of fear. But where do they emerge *from*?

Take a look at what precedes David's encounter with Goliath. It has to do with the selection of the next king found in I Samuel 16.

> The Lord said to Samuel, "How long will you grieve over Saul? I have rejected him from being king over Israel. Fill your horn with oil and set out; I will send you to Jesse the Bethlehemite, for I have provided for myself a king among his sons.' Samuel said, "How can I go? If Saul hears of it, he will kill me.' And the Lord said, 'Take a heifer with you, and say, "I have come to sacrifice to the Lord." Invite Jesse to the sacrifice, and I will show you what you shall do; and you shall anoint for me the one whom I name to you.' Samuel did what the Lord commanded, and came to Bethlehem.
>
> When they came, he looked on Eliab [Jesse's oldest] and thought, 'Surely the Lord's anointed is now before the Lord.' But the Lord said to Samuel, 'Do not look on his appearance or on the height of his stature, because I have rejected him; for the Lord does not see as mortals see; they look on the outward appearance, but the Lord looks on the heart.' Then Jesse called Abinadab [Jesse's next son], and made him pass before Samuel. He said, 'Neither has the Lord chosen this one.' Then Jesse made Shammah [Jesse's third son] pass by. And he said, 'Neither has the Lord chosen this one.' Jesse made seven of his sons pass before Samuel, and Samuel said to Jesse, 'The Lord has not chosen any of these.' Samuel said to Jesse, 'Are all your sons here?' And he said, 'There remains yet the youngest, but he is keeping the sheep.' And Samuel said to Jesse, 'Send and bring him; for we will not sit down until he comes here.' He sent and brought him in. Now he was ruddy, and had beautiful eyes, and was handsome. The Lord said, 'Rise and anoint him; for this is the one.' Then Samuel took the horn of oil, and anointed him

in the presence of his brothers; and the spirit of the Lord came mightily upon David from that day forward . . . .

Now the spirit of the Lord departed from Saul, and an evil spirit from the Lord tormented him. And Saul's servants said to him, 'See now, an evil spirit from God is tormenting you. Let our lord now command the servants who attend you to look for someone who is skillful in playing the lyre; and when the evil spirit from God is upon you, he will play it, and you will feel better.' So Saul said to his servants, 'Provide for me someone who can play well, and bring him to me.' One of the young men answered, 'I have seen a son of Jesse the Bethlehemite who is skillful in playing, a man of valor, a warrior, prudent in speech, and a man of good presence; and the Lord is with him.' So Saul sent messengers to Jesse, and said, 'Send me your son David who is with the sheep.' . . . And David came to Saul, and entered his service. Saul loved him greatly, and he became his armor-bearer . . . . And whenever the evil spirit from God came upon Saul, David took the lyre and played it with his hand, and Saul would be relieved and feel better, and the evil spirit would depart from him.

—1 Samuel 16

As it turns out, the real story is less about the innovative act of a young unproven shepherd and more about succession. David's slingshot technique—the innovation—is actually a subplot to a more important narrative. Saul's loss of emotional stability, reliability, and confidence made succession to the throne *the* issue. The defeat of Goliath merely serves to confirm Samuel's divinely inspired selection of David as Saul's successor.

Most observers of innovation mistakenly believe that the overriding question is always, "What's next?" Wall Street investment bankers and Sand Hill venture capitalists all want to know, before their competitors, what will be the next hot market, product, or sector. Books are written about the next big thing. But as important as predicting what's next is determining *who's* next.

Venture capitalists have known this from the beginning. One of the first, Georges Doriot, said he preferred a class A entrepreneur with a class B idea over a class A idea with a class B entrepreneur. Doriot knew that *who* is more important than what. More recently, author Jim Collins emphasized the importance of making sure, before you get started on a new direction or initiative, to have the right people on the bus.[18]

Who is doing the innovating matters. And it's not just the Davids that count. There are many others who are part of the real story of innovating. Innovators don't innovate alone. Innovators operate with sponsors and mentors and in the context of rivals. All three—sponsors, mentors and rivals—and their relationships with each other provide the context from which innovators emerge with an innovation that succeeds.

But how do you become aware of innovators? Saul became aware of David because of David's musical talent. How often such serendipity contributes to the emergence of innovators is difficult to determine. That it happens often enough is clear. An innovation seldom develops in a straight-line orderly fashion. Instead, innovations often emerge from an innovator's observance of something odd, something different, something unexpected. We call that a lateral connection. Edward de Bono's popular "lateral thinking" codified this aspect of innovation decades ago.[19] The point here is that lateral connections are not only relevant to an innovation's development. They are relevant to emergence of the innovator as well.

David's seemingly unrelated lyric talent satisfied some of the needs of Saul, who was experiencing a growing paranoia. Saul was becoming less able to handle the pressures of his job as king of Israel.

Saul's relationship with David is complicated, not unlike an innovator's relationship with a host organization. That Saul became David's sponsor and "loved him greatly" sets up a tragic irony—the need of innovators for protection *from* sponsors. Saul, despite his great love for David, ultimately seeks to kill David. The unstable king came to see David as a threat.

Experienced innovators tell how they, during the course of working on an innovation, became a threat within their own organization. Innovators often need protection from the ire of the sponsor. The work may not be completed on the timetable set in stone by the corporate executives. The project may be running over budget. Clayton Christianson, in his *Innovator's Dilemma* and *Innovator's Solution*, points out how disruptive an innovation (and innovator) can be.[20]

Innovations are disruptive largely because of the invention at their hearts. How invention differs from innovation is important and Chapter 7 takes up it in more detail. For now it is sufficient to say that inventions, by their very nature, disrupt the status quo in the way they *solve* the problem addressed. This disruption causes friction—intellectual, political, even economic. Innovations, on the other hand, must **resolve** the very conflict caused by the invention if the innovation is to be adopted. Invention and innovation are not synonymous, and often the former is included in the later. Likewise for innovators and their sponsors.

David was a disrupter not only for Goliath but also for Saul. In fact, shortly after the David and Goliath story, the biblical narrative relates how Saul sets out to kill David, who has to flee. But David has a mentor-protector in Samuel, the Jesuit-like shaman of the tribe of Israel. Samuel is actually a peer to Saul, the king.

This set of relationships is not hard to find in many corporations today. While Saul's power is political, Samuel's is prophetic. Saul represents the power of the organization; Samuel represents the power of knowledge. Saul is atop the management ladder; Samuel is atop the technical ladder, so to speak, slightly out of step with the chain of command. The growing instability and insanity of the incumbent, Saul, necessitates someone to give David "top cover." This is what Samuel provides.

Innovators all need a mentor-protector to look out for them. Without an inside mentor—a Samuel-like shaman who has the power of knowledge—an innovator can't progress very far for very long. Emerging innovations and innovators—both are always emerging—are easily overwhelmed by competing and incumbent interests. Internal factions and groups all compete for the same limited resource pool. At first glance, there is little to gain and much to lose by continuing with an innovation effort that has become disruptive. Sooner or later immense political pressure gets put on the innovator's sponsor, and many abort the very effort (and sometimes the people) they originally sponsored. Without a mentor, or as some call them "innovation midwives,"[21] an innovator is likely to fail.

Saul himself is paradigmatic of many successful corporations today. After years of simply trying to extend the reign of a product or service in which much has been invested, a corporation can start to show wear and tear. Instead of looking ahead to what is needed, vested interests—financial, political, and career—prove to be a powerful mix of incentives to maintain the status quo. They drive attitudes and behaviors that seek to extend and defend the success of the old for as long as possible. When you take a good look at the situation, you find signs of paranoia, stress, arrogance, and just plain fatigue. All these are entirely understandable.

However, experience has shown that the revenue and profits generated from even wildly successful products and services will eventually plateau and even wane. Changes in external competition or market conditions eventually force innovations in product and process. Innovators must be looking for ways to improve the product (and process) to meet changing needs or even develop a new product.

Mentors are necessary to support an innovator's vision. They advocate for what's needed during development to keep funds flowing to pay for the work. Mentors like Samuel also help innovators deal with sibling rivalry. This rivalry comes in many forms: competition for the attention of customers, competition for resources from "sibling" products and solutions, or rivalry for the attention (and investment) of the "parent." Without a Samuel, innovators and their innovations risk losing out to the more data-endowed and cash-generating operations in a company. Without an effective mentor-protector, countless innovations suffer a premature death.

In the biblical story of David's selection as king, conventional practice would have selected one of the older brothers as the successor. This mirrors the practice of most corporations. They typically go for the safer, proven talent for the riskier projects. But older children are not always the best choice. Even Samuel had to be coached on the right criteria in picking the unconventional successor. "Do not look on his appearance or on [his] height . . . . [Look at] the heart" (1 Samuel 16.7). Rivals in a company are often older, more experienced, and seemingly more deserving of the corporation's investment and attention. What innovator has not encountered these formidable rivals in the drive to bring something new to market?

So how do you identify the genuine innovator? Innovators are not necessarily the ones with the most attractive resume. They may not even be the more "experienced". Frank Sulloway picked up on this as he studied the implications of birth order. In his book *Born to Rebel*,[22] Sulloway takes another look at the impact birth order and family dynamics have on an individual's openness to innovation. Sulloway's hypothesis suggests that "latter borns," in contrast to first borns, are more prone to innovation. The dynamics of sibling rivalry shapes them accordingly. While Sulloway uses large Victorian families from Darwin's era to illustrate his point, he could also have used Samuel's selection of David.

If we ignore what leads up to the story of David and Goliath, we get the impression there were only two characters involved—the innovator and the rival—David and Goliath. Instead, there were many others involved in this story of innovation: Saul, the sponsor; Samuel, the mentor-protector;

Jesse, the father; and Eliab, Abinandab, and Sahmmah, the elder brothers (sibling rivals). Each plays an essential role.

Yet the mistaken notion of the lone innovator persists, not only with the story of David but also with innovators today. It's understandable. But it's mistaken. Innovators do not operate, emerge, or succeed alone. Look more closely at a few of the more prominent ones, and you will find each has a key relationship—Bill and Dave (Hewlett and Packard), Steve and Woz (Jobs and Wozniak, who started Apple), Roy and Walt (the Disney brothers).

Innovation is as much about who is next as about what's next. And the signature characteristic of who is next is the presence and patterns of faith these individuals manifest in what they do, despite the odds.

How innovators' faith works—how its shape produces lift—is what the following pages are all about. But first we need to revisit what faith is before we examine what is special about the faith of innovators.

PART 1
Innovators and Faith

Who are innovators? How do they become that way? Are they born or made? Where do we find them and how can we recognize them, whether we are looking for them within our organizations, outside on the periphery, or even within ourselves?

Innovators are defined by the capacity and structure of their faith. "Faith" is used here to denote a nonreligious, a-spiritual capability available to all humans. (More is said about this understanding of faith in chapter 2.) For now, I make the following confession: My intent is to liberate faith from the tyranny of religious doctrine and spirituality. Too often, the word *faith* conjures up mental associations with specific religious traditions or spiritual practices. Faith is also disdained as a non-rational, even antiscientific, source of wisdom—two misconceptions exposed in chapter 2. Instead, faith, as used here, is the belief the innovator has in an idea for an innovation without any real proof that it will work, at least to begin with.

This section is about the innovators among us and for the innovator within us.

Chapter 2

Faith Revisited

If faith is the distinguishing characteristic of innovators, then what is faith? In what way do innovators rely on faith? How does faith work? And how does it work for innovators?

For innovators, faith takes on a particular form—a universal and common human capability. But first, it is important to understand what faith is not.

Faith is not

Revisiting faith is necessary but dangerous: necessary, because of persistent, pervasive misconceptions about it; dangerous, because of a myriad of volatile connotations associated with it. I fully realize the boiling waters I invite you to wade into here with me. My purpose is not to offer a philosophical or theological treatise on faith. Rather, my purpose is to get beyond two common misconceptions about faith—one spiritual, the other rational—and reconsider faith from a purely human, personal and practical point of view.

In most religious and spiritual traditions, faith holds a prominent, central place. The word *faith* is often used as a more politically correct word for "religion." This is particularly true for those espousing the "I am spiritual but not religious" posture. For some reason, using the word *faith* seems more palatable, less offensive, than the word *religion*.

Yet *religion* is really not synonymous with *faith* at all. Faith is the capability of an individual. Religion is a set of established traditions, practices, and doctrines that both inspire and hold together (more or less rigorously) the community of people who ascribe to them. Religion and spiritual traditions point participants toward the meaning, value, and practice of faith, true. In this respect, religion and spiritual traditions "carry" the message of faith. But like all carriers, they are subject to all sorts of imperfections, distortions, and corruptions. The signal they transmit is not without "noise." But to disregard faith because of its association with religious and spiritual traditions is to repeat the age-old mistake of confusing the message with the messenger.

In a religious or spiritual context, God is the primary *object* of faith. However, it does not follow that to have "faith" you have to believe in God or even believe that God exists. Even Jesus used the term *faith* in a nonreligious sense. For example, every account of Jesus healing someone reveals a nonreligious, even an a-spiritual, orientation. When the writers of the Gospels describe the aftermath of almost every miraculous healing, Jesus says, "*Your* faith has made you well." He didn't say, "My faith made you well." Nor did he even say, "God made you well." Rarely, if ever, did he take credit for being the healer. Nor is anything said about the religious, moral, or spiritual state of the one who is healed.

In other contexts, Jesus would lament, "Oh, ye of little faith," imploring his disciples and followers to have more faith. "If you had but the faith of a mustard seed you could move mountains" (Matthew 17.20). The implication is striking and inescapable: Jesus himself viewed faith as something everyone already has—religious and nonreligious alike. He thought too many of us have too little of it, however.

In fact, a person can believe there is a God, yet have little or no faith and experience much anxiety in their daily living. The opposite also is true. People who do not profess any particular religious doctrine or practice any spiritual tradition often demonstrate tremendous resilience and fortitude in how they handle difficult life circumstances. One couple, Joe and Sara Mascovich, lost their son Jay after twenty-two operations. At the age of six, Jay had a stroke that left him partially paralyzed. Neither Joe nor Sara is an active (or even passive) participant in any religious community or spiritual tradition. When asked how they were able to get through their difficulties and not give up, they said that, despite their grief (or because of what they were learning from it), "Life goes on, altered yes, but goes on." It is difficult not to ascribe their strength to some kind of unverbalized and implicit faith. Their faith continues inspire those who know them.

In contrast, faith held captive to religious or spiritual connotations becomes synonymous with religious doctrine and dogma. This may be meaningful and comforting to those within a specific religious community or a shared spiritual tradition. But when spoken outside that community, it often leads to misunderstanding and divisiveness and fuels all sorts of prejudicial, nonsensical, and bigoted behavior. Examples abound throughout history and continue today. What we call "fundamentalism"— Islamic, Christian, ecological, biocentric,[23] or political—bears witness to the unwillingness or inability of fundamentalists to think for themselves. Both fundamentalism and fanaticism in any form are actually more akin to fear than to faith.

Religion is not the only unintentional tyrant over faith. All too often faith is viewed as the opposite of science, the antithesis of rational thinking and understanding based on proof. Yet faith—as "confidence, reliance, belief especially without evidence or proof"[24]—is hardly absent from the mind of a scientist forming an initial hypothesis.

In fact, each of us every day, in matters small and large, exhibits confidence, reliance, and belief without complete evidence or proof. Without some degree of faith, it would be difficult to function in relationships with others, in learning something new, in facing some uncomfortable feeling, or in anticipating some positive outcome and working for it. If we are honest, we live by faith more than we realize. It is sewn into the fabric of our lives.

As a way of knowing or understanding, faith is too often mistakenly seen as the opposite of rigorous science or thorough analysis, as if faith and science oppose each other. In this view, faith is seen as the opposite of reason instead of its silent partner. Anselm, a twelfth-century Italian Benedictine monk and philosopher, challenged this mistaken juxtaposition of faith and reason. For Anselm, faith and reason were not opposites, but inextricably tied. Anselm asked, "Does faith seek or precede understanding? Or does understanding seek or precede faith?" Anselm did not leave the dilemma unresolved. Faith comes first, he said. "I do not seek to understand so that I may believe. Rather, I believe so that I may understand."[25] If Anselm was correct, the role of faith in knowledge creation is inescapable. And knowledge creation, it turns out, may be more essential to innovating then even new ideas.

In the work of innovators, this relationship between faith and understanding is essential. Isn't this precisely the first step a scientist takes in designing an experiment? When spoken of in the context of science, faith is strongly associated with knowledge and truth, real or perceived. In fact, in the scientific sense of evidentiary knowledge, faith is viewed as a way of knowing. The "object of faith" is that which is scrutinized or tested by the evidentiary discipline of the scientific method itself—a testable hypothesis.

Faith's resonance with knowledge—especially the creation and application of knowledge—is where faith becomes especially relevant for the innovator. Absolutely necessary is knowing and understanding what is true about the reality into which the new is being brought and must be made to fit. Casual observers of innovation believe innovation is founded on creativity and ideas. Serious students of innovation over the last decade have begun to recognize creativity and ideas as important but not the foundation supporting successful innovations. The foundation of innovation is knowledge and the ability to create new knowledge relevant to what is valuable and important to customers. How essential this knowledge creation is to innovation was stated by Al Ward, a student of one of the most consistent and successful innovation systems in the world (Toyota), who went so far as to describe innovation as "learning applied to creating value."[26] The role faith plays in the knowledge-creation foundation of innovation is a necessity for every innovator.

Faith is

Faith, removed from its religious and spiritual ties, is a human capability that we each have. Some have more of it than others. But all of us have faith and can access it. Like a muscle, faith gets stronger when it is used—when it's stretched, flexed, and exercised.

Think of faith as something akin to "potential energy"—a term in thermodynamics. Potential energy—coined by the nineteenth-century Scottish engineer and physicist William Rankine—is the energy stored within any physical system. Rankine called it "potential energy" because it holds potential to be converted into various other forms of energy to do work. For example, the energy that a coil spring stores in its coils when it is compressed or stretched is potential energy. When the pressure is released, this stored energy is converted into kinetic energy, and the spring snaps back with noticeable force and movement as it returns to its resting state. Likewise, when an object is lifted up, potential energy is invisibly stored in its lifted state and becomes visible when it is released. "According to the principle of conservation of energy, energy cannot be created or destroyed; hence this energy cannot disappear. Instead, it is stored as potential energy."[27]

Why faith is

Human beings, as physical systems, also have "potential energy." We use it in various ways, but it doesn't show up unless and until it is activated or converted. When it is, then we can sense it.

What gets even more interesting in looking at faith this way is that it helps us to understand why we have faith. Just as gravity works invisibly as the countervailing force to potential energy in a physical system, so an individual's faith works as a countervailing force to fear in social and economic ecosystems. Faith and fear are like light and dark, sound and silence. Like yin and yang, one serves in the context of the other.

Evolutionary biologists suggest that fear is hardwired in our subcortical brain stem. Some say fear is the inescapable neurological inheritance from our reptilian ancestors. It can show up as mistrust in the social dimension, anxiety in emotional contexts, disengagement in vocational matters, doubt and uncertainty in the intellectual dimension. Perhaps this is why new neuroses and anxiety-based syndromes are seemingly introduced every year, keeping psychotherapists billing and pharmaceutical firms profitable.

But fear is not always a bad thing. Fear can be triggered by some danger we sense, by a threat that is real. Fear arises from deep within the brain's amygdala—that part of our brain where fear is processed and instructions are sent out to the rest of the body to prepare for "fight or flight." These preparations involve not merely our emotional reaction to the threat but also our physiological response. Many evolutionary biologists suggest that our response to fear has contributed to the success and survival of our species.

When sufficient faith is activated, it can take the amygdala's "fight or flight" and transform it into "fight *and* flight," where the vector of flight is not *away from* but *into*. Our faith kicks in.

One of my first paying jobs when I was a boy was to deliver *The Washington Post*. The *Post* was a morning paper. Early in the dark stillness before dawn, I would make my rounds on foot, tossing papers onto the front stoops of homes in the Bethesda suburban development we lived in just outside Washington, D.C. One dark but quiet morning, the Great Dane of one of my customers suddenly confronted me. That particular morning he was angry (or was he frightened?). He probably had been let out of the house to take care of his "business." The Great Dane and I startled each other. Who scared whom first didn't matter. Instantly, our respective adrenaline systems took over. He saw me coming up the walk and started barking and pouncing aggressively toward me. I froze. All of my neuronal pathways were on high alert. My adrenaline, pumping.

Should I run? I somehow concluded that running was not an option, particularly with a canvas bag drooping with the weight of fifty-five copies of the *Washington Post* strapped across my shoulder. I knew the Great Dane could smell my fear.

But I had only one choice, to stand there, take an aggressive posture, make direct eye contact, and stare him down. I didn't know whether it would work. But like David, it was my own little version of a slingshot and five smooth stones as this canine Goliath lunged toward me.

It worked. The Great Dane stopped. His bark turned into a muffled growl as I stood my ground and maintained eye contact. The Dane's pause was all the time I needed to toss a folded copy of that day's *Post* up on his owner's stoop. I then started walking away, backwards of course, not taking my eyes off the eyes of the still grumbling Great Dane.

Was this some primal act of faith? Perhaps. It didn't seem so then. At the time my response seemed more like instinct. But that experience of turning into and facing a threat head-on left a lasting imprint on me, even all these years later. Instead of turning away to run, I turned toward the threat to face it head-on. And though my adrinal gland was pulsing with preparations for a fight response, I certainly didn't want to fight that Great Dane. So was my response actually a third option, somewhere between fight and flight?

President Franklin Delano Roosevelt, in his first inaugural address, on March 4, 1933, in the midst of the Great Depression, made one of the most eloquent statements on faith and fear—a statement that paved the way across the country for all kinds of initiatives and actions for recovery. "The only thing we have to fear is fear itself—nameless, unreasoning, unjustified terror which paralyzes needed efforts to convert retreat into advance." In his memorable radio address, he talked of how fear can spread—quickly and uncontrollably—and how it can be overcome through faith. That statement was the beginning of a remarkable era of prosperity for the United States, of faith overcoming fear.

Fear and faith. Yin and yang. Some unnamed but inspired observer defined fear by turning the word itself into an appropriate acronym—*F*uture *E*vidence *A*ppearing *R*eal. Faith was defined by the writer of the *Letter to the Hebrews* in the New Testament as the "substance of things hoped for, evidence of things unseen" (Hebrews 11.1).

Both faith and fear focus on future events. In his famous Sermon on the Mount, Jesus used as examples the birds of the air and the lilies of the field to suggest we be not anxious about tomorrow, "for tomorrow will be anxious for itself. Let the day's own trouble be sufficient for the day" (Matthew 6.25-34).

How faith works

Faith is, ironically, agnostic. It is a way of knowing (Greek: *gnosis*), not derived from certainty. It is a primal and basic ability present in all of us. We're born with it or grow into it very early on.

Faith is more than merely an emotional response. Faith is physiological—causing neurological and hormonal responses as well as changes in the muscles. William James recognized the physical nature of faith in his classic *The Varieties of Religious Experience.* He described faith as not only a psychological condition but also as "one of the most important *biological* functions of mankind."[28]

Use it or lose it, just like a muscle. The more we use our faith, the stronger it becomes. Innovators tend to be heavy users, and as a result, tend to have more faith than most.

Faith plays out in at least four dimensions—the social, emotional, vocational, and rational.[29] It is when we mistakenly confine faith to only one or two of these dimensions, or worse, relegate its relevance only for religious or spiritual matters, that we underestimate its potential and unnecessarily divorce ourselves from its power and energy.

In social contexts, we call faith "trust." In emotional contexts, faith is "confidence." And in vocational and mental contexts, faith shows up as "hope" and "belief," respectively. As I have observed over the years physicists, engineers, and scientists in the middle of innovating, I began to recognize each of these faith dimensions in their behavior and thought patterns. Scientists, engineers, and innovators constantly seek the *substance* of things hoped for and *evidence* of things unseen.

A conceptual model depicting this more complete picture of faith is shown in the following figures (see below). Figure 1 is intended to illustrate faith in its "resting" state, ready like a muscle to be stretched and flexed in at least four different dimensions.

In a social context, **trust** is the faith we have in other people. It is the basic currency of relationships. Trust is seldom, if ever, binary, even though we often think it is—living under the illusion that we either trust someone or we don't. Rather, trust is either building or declining. The rate at which it declines between people is always much steeper than the rate at which it builds.[30]

In the context of human emotions, faith as **confidence** describes how we are feeling. Professional golfers and other athletes at the top of their game know that while excellence in physical conditioning and skill is essential to their performance, confidence is essential as well. Like trust in others, confidence builds slowly and falls precipitously.

Figure 1: Conceptual Model of Faith in a "Resting" State

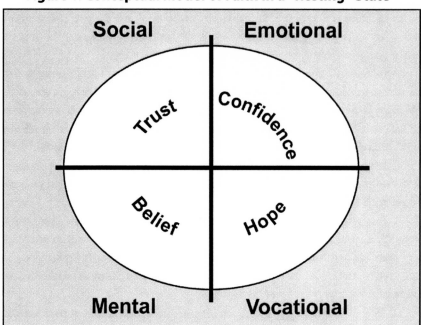

In our vocations, faith shows up as ***hope***. It is our positive anticipation of what will be and our role in bringing it about. This realm of vocational faith is often ignored or poorly understood. It has to do with motivations. Ultimately, motivations are grounded in what people value as important. How often, when we are engaged in something, do we ask ourselves, Why am I doing this? Why am I going to all this effort and taking on the risk? What is my motivation? Reasons range from the selfless to the selfish.

In an intellectual context, faith as a ***belief*** builds a mental model of what has yet to be fully revealed or fully understood. I first saw this faith years ago in innovators in a Midwestern industrial R&D organization. I observed scientists, engineers, product developers, and market developers trying to discover and articulate what they *believed* to be going on underneath the surface. As they attempted to make sense out of what they thought they knew and had experienced, they believed certain "truths," temporarily, until they could prove or disprove the belief. They did experiments in the lab and out in the field. This faith—believing—is at the core of both research and development, both never very far from innovating.

In short, faith is potential energy residing in the human system waiting to be released in concrete action. We can draw the following image of what the muscle of faith might look like in its more active state. When expending energy and put to work, faith strengthens or builds "muscle" in each of these four dimensions.

Figure 2: Conceptual Model of Faith in an Active State

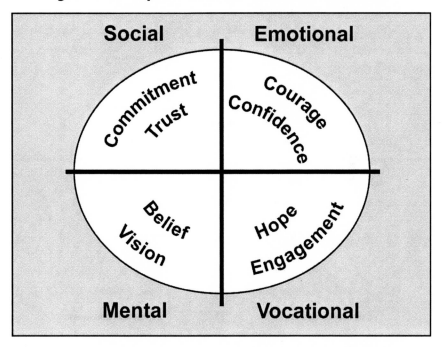

Faith doesn't work unless and until we put it to use. When faith is exercised, it expands in four different dimensions (see Figure 2).

1. Trust expands into ***commitment.*** When there is sufficient trust between and among participants, the commitment to do something becomes possible.

2. Confidence transforms into ***courage.*** When enough confidence builds up, we are encouraged, or able to encourage others, to do the next right thing.

3. Hope translates into participation or ***engagement.*** With sufficient hope, faith morphs into engaged and focused minds and hearts that become immersed in what needs to be done.

4. Belief extends into **vision.** And finally, when belief becomes conviction, our minds can envision where our intentions lead us.

In practice, these four dimensions interweave. Each dimension of faith can flex and contract independently, but seldom operates in isolation of the other. Strength in one dimension can compensate for weakness in another. For example, simply sharing an idea with another person we trust can compensate for the lack of confidence we may feel. Receiving input and feedback—sensing someone's visceral reaction to an idea—can encourage or discourage, depending on the response and our perception of it.

Figure 3: Conceptual Model of Faith with Love as Its Source of Fuel

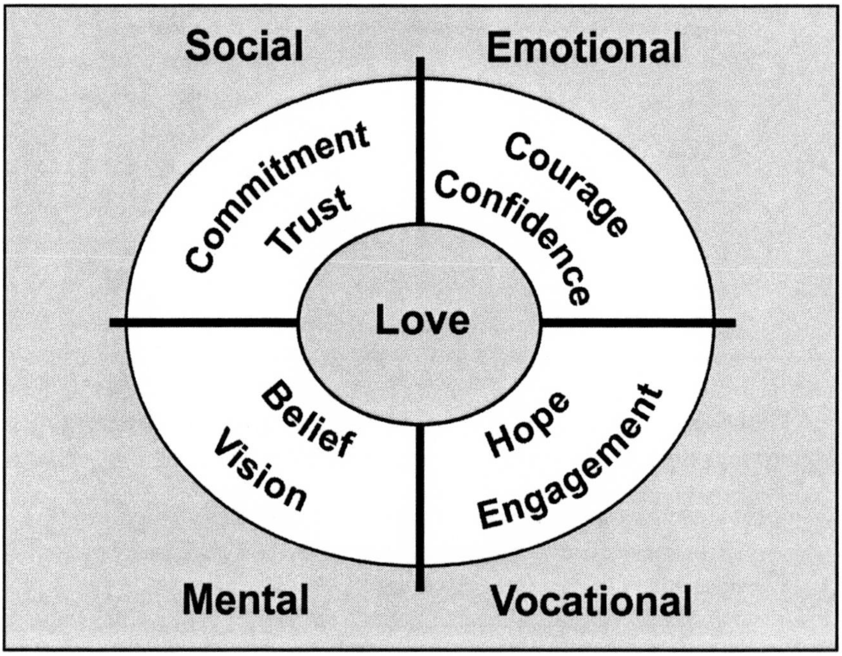

In order to work properly, faith requires a source of energy. Love is this energy. Love activates, animates, and sustains faith. Love provides the energy for trust to expand into commitment, for confidence to become courage, for hope to turn into engagement, and for belief to become vision. Without love, faith remains nothing more than potential energy. But with the fuel of love, faith comes alive and works. We take action.

Our model of the faith would remain incomplete without the placement of love in the center, at the heart of faith.

Converting the energy of love into acts of courage, commitment, engagement and vision depends in part on the kind or blend of love involved. Thermodynamics tell us that the efficiency of energy conversion depends, at least in part, on the inherent character of the fuel used. For instance, in heating our homes, gas is more efficient in the conversion process than is electricity. This holds true for the food we eat and the octane we select at the pump. So also with the love that fuels the muscle of faith. Unfortunately, the English language has but one word for love, making it more difficult in the English-speaking world to easily recognize the different kinds of love that we engage in all the time. Almost a half century ago, C. S. Lewis turned to the Greek language to help differentiate four basic kinds of love: affection, friendship, *eros*, and charity.

Affection (Greek: *storge*) is perhaps the most basic and universal love— one that both humans and animals experience and is likely hardwired in our subcortical nervous system.

Friendship (Greek: *philos*) is also universal but may be more conscious and intentional than affection, its more biological or neuronal cousin.

The ***erotic*** (Greek: *eros*) points to passionate and acquisitive love.

Selfless love (Greek: *agape*) is what Lewis refers to as charity.[31]

For now, it's sufficient to say that faith and love operate in all of us, but the faith and love operating in innovators takes a special shape and blend. The next two chapters are focused on how innovators shape their faith to find lift needed for innovating and the love that fuels them to keep innovating.

Chapter 3

The Faith of Innovators

Sometimes I end up in a window seat winging my way to or from a client assignment. Staring through the double-paned porthole, I secretly relish the forced serenity of my temporary confinement. Gazing at the slowly moving landscape below, my eyes drift over to the long span of the plane's wing, quietly extending into thin air.

At first glance, the wing appears to be perfectly still, even unyielding. But as glance glides into gaze, the wing reveals its flex. At certain moments its almost as if it is flapping. As I watch, this seemingly stiff, metal structure responds with fluid movement against the pure blue background, like some giant shock absorber, working overtime to handle the invisible potholes in the atmosphere. Sometimes the movement is subtle, sometimes pronounced.

This highly engineered wing system acts like a large living muscle, gracefully imitating a pelican's glide over beach-breaking ocean waves, or an egret's swoop as it zeros in for a soft landing on a coastal marsh. That each wing, designed by brilliant, yet anonymous, aeronautical engineers and constructed by unknown skilled craftsmen, is packed with more innovations and coordinated subsystems than I can even begin to imagine, is a wonder in itself.

But what is more wonderful, even magical, is how, on each flight, the pair of wings lifts and suspends, then gently lets down, hundreds of tons of metal, passengers, crew, and baggage. My father—a former Navy pilot and an aeronautical engineer—taught me the elementary physics of lift and drag first in sailboats and then in airplanes. The shape makes all the difference.

The faith of innovators takes the shape of wings, making their faith qualitatively different and quantitatively more potent than the faith of non-innovators. In this shape is the power that produces the lift so necessary for innovating.

Figure 4: Faith Muscle in the Shape of a Wing

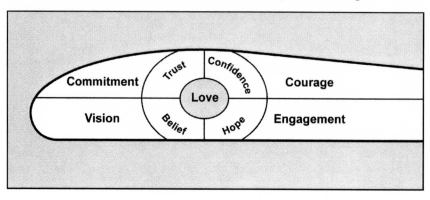

Lift is the force that carries innovators through the difficult segments encountered in the midst of innovating. It's built on a combination of trust, commitment, courage, belief, hope, and a vision. The Dutch-Swiss mathematician Daniel Bernoulli in 1738 may have been the first to work out the equations for lift, but it was the Old Testament prophet Isaiah who was first, thousands of years earlier, to use the metaphor of the wing to describe the potency and lift of faith.

> Have you not known?
>> Have you not heard?
> The Lord is the everlasting God,
>> the Creator of the ends of the earth.
> He does not faint or grow weary;
>> his understanding is unsearchable.
> He gives power to the faint,
>> and strengthens the powerless.
> Even youths will faint and be weary,
>> and the young will fall exhausted;
> but those who wait for the Lord
>> shall renew their strength,
> they shall mount up with wings like eagles,
> they shall run and not be weary,
> they shall walk and not faint.
>> —Isaiah 40.28-31

So, how does an eagle's wing—or any wing for that matter—work? Why is the wing such a revealing metaphor for the innovator's faith?

The answers are in the principles of fluid dynamics; it's in the wings of a bird or aircraft, the sails of a sloop, the curvature of a fish. They all operate on this same principle. This principle states that any object skewed at an angle (called an "angle of attack") that is moving through an atmosphere (air or water) will generate a force that is perpendicular to the flow of movement. This perpendicular force is called "lift." This lift makes flight possible for heavier-than-air objects like airplanes and birds. What started with the Wright brothers at Kitty Hawk, North Carolina, with a two-minute flight of an airplane at an altitude of a few feet in the early part of the twentieth century, is now a routine miracle as hundreds of tons are hoisted off the ground every day to transport people and goods across countries, continents, and oceans.

Lift implies up, though in some applications, the perpendicular force actually pushes down, like an airfoil on the back of a car to improve the car's traction at high speeds. The principle is the same and works because of the shape (See Figure 5).

The shape produces the needed lift in combination with the thrust, moving the wing through an atmosphere at a sufficient velocity and angle of attack. Atmosphere, velocity, thrust, angle of attack: they all play essential roles in producing lift.

Figure 5: Lift-Producing Forces

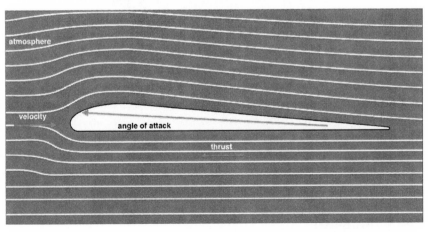

The lift that innovators seek when innovating is no different. Innovating atmosphere is typically filled with fear and incumbents' preference for the status quo. The velocity—both the direction and the speed of the innovator's progress—must be enough to defy the gravity of the traditional forces of drag that would otherwise keep the innovator and innovation grounded—criticism from peers, superiors, and even customers or the knee-jerk "that will never work" and "we've tried that before" reactions to new ideas. Thrust—the motivation of the innovator—can only partially be supplemented with extrinsic incentives. Finally, the innovator's orientationation to the future and clarity of vision—the angle of attack—determines how much of an innovator's progress will be transformed into lift when it hits resistance.

Lift is contagious. It improves the attitude and raises the spirits of collaborators. Lift can be seen in the way others are energized. Lift builds trust and catalyzes it into commitment. Lift grows confidence, encouraging both the innovator and collaborators to do something—try something. With lift comes hope. Lift turns belief into a vision of what is possible.

Atmosphere of fear

Fear disables innovators and kills innovation. In its many forms, fear often makes the air so thin that any liftoff is difficult, especially in the early stages when an innovation is most vulnerable. For example, back in the 1960s before the first disposable diaper had gained market acceptance, Jack Kimberly, then president of Kimberly-Clark Corporation, told Bill Wilson—the leader of the company's nascent but promising disposable diaper development efforts—to stop working on diapers. It was too risky, too uncertain, and too expensive. A direct order.[32]

Across the country in a completely different organization in a completely different industry, another direct order to stop working on a display innovation was given. This order was from David Packard to Chuck House to stop working on a monitor that House was already developing for Hewlett-Packard.[33]

Both men, Wilson and House, deliberately defied these direct orders. Success ensued, though not without much consternation. In both cases, innovations sentenced to death by executive order were kept alive despite the fear-induced directives from superiors whose names were on the front door. These deliberate acts of insubordination proved, in hindsight, to be more profitable than could have been imagined. In the end, the perseverance of Wilson and House created much value for consumers and richly rewarded both companies, despite the fears of company owners.

Conquering fear

What lies behind these acts of defiance is faith-induced courage and perseverance. Many years ago, W. Edwards Deming, the visionary American statistician whose theories paved the way for many Japanese companies to overtake their counterparts in the U.S., named fear as one of the first organizational conditions in need of correction. One of his fourteen principles—imperatives for leaders and managers who sought the benefits of continuous improvement—was to "drive out fear." Deming claimed that eliminating fear would enable workers to share ideas for improvements in their work process, ideas essential for improvements in both process and product.[34] According to some, Deming's point on fear is the first of his points that should be implemented.[35] "Fear will cause people to play defense. It will inhibit them from sharing with management a real view of the world. It will make them unwilling to risk new ideas."[36]

History has proven Deming correct. But despite the acknowledged success of Deming's principles, it is surprising fear has not received more attention, particularly in the literature on innovating. Do we believe nothing can be done about it? Deming's call to "drive out fear" assumed what most are relectant to admit: fear pervades the organizational climates of too many enterprises. Whether fear is visible or lying dormant just under the surface, it is seldom named as such. More socially acceptable terms like "risk," "unknowns," or "uncertainties" are stand-ins for what really is fear.

That fear constantly shows up for innovators and their sponsors shouldn't surprise us. Uncertainty is one of the consistent conditions in the climate in which innovators operate. Uncertainty is present for both organizations and for markets, like the permanent fog bank that sits off the west coast of northern California. Uncertainty cannot be wished away. Nor should we try.

Most of the time, innovators navigate through uncertainty's fog. It is simply a given that comes with the territory. But with feedback from customers, uncertainty's fog burns away with the light and clarity of feedback from the marketplace, whether it's hot and harsh or warm and friendly. What was unknown becomes clear. Fear of the unknown vanishes. The response from the market is trustworthy and purifying. Even if the response is rejection or failure. It is helpful. The innovator learns what doesn't work. Needed modifications are understood. With this new clarity and vision, innovators can either plow back into the fog of uncertainty to work through modifications or move on, knowing they are getting closer, perhaps even that they have a solution ready for customers to accept. But uncertainty's fog remains without acts of faith.

Fears from within

The fear of uncertainty is only one of the fears experienced by innovators. Fear of rejection from *within* the innovator's organization is another and a particularly virulent form, especially after there has been some positive evidence from the marketplace. It cripples the effectiveness of innovators, paralyzing their progress.

Fears from within are subtle and potentially more powerful than external ones. These fears can be harder to identify, more subject to denial. Left undiagnosed, they are lethal to innovation. Like flu or a common cold, this type of fear is highly contagious. Innovators can be infected with but a raised eyebrow from a colleague, a slightly off-key tone of voice from manager, or a misinterpreted whisper. These fears activate the innovator's own sense of insecurity, winding its way into consciousness when resistance is low and the innovator is vulnerable. Like an allergy, fear lies dormant until the right combination of conditions awakens it: "It doesn't fit with our business model." "We've never done it that way before." "We've already tried that before." "Yeah, but what's the size of the market?" "You'll never get enough people to buy it." It's fear that underlies the chronic not-invented-here syndrome.[37]

Many organizations have learned to insulate their innovators and innovation efforts. This protects them from these negative reactions within the broader organization to anything new.[38] A colleague Leo Shapiro, is fond of saying, "we are both predator *and* prey." Both are reflected in our thinking and our perceptions.[39] Accomplished innovators have become alert to both threat *and* opportunity and the proximity between the two. This is what the editor of Proverbs—a book of wise sayings in the Old Testament—intended when he named fear as the *beginning* of knowledge (Proverbs 1.7). Experienced innovators have learned how not to turn away from fear, but to turn *into* it.

The five forms of fear

Fear shows up in five different forms for innovators, each corresponding to the five challenges innovators face. Each challenge with its attendant fear shapes the faith pattern with which innovators fly *through* each fear. The five challenges innovators face:

1. **Discovery** of something new, whether technological, scientific, or about the end user's need;

2. **Invention** of something new and of value to the user or customer that addresses the need;

3. **Reduction-to-practice** of the invention to the point where it works for the user—both technically and economically;

4. **Introduction** of the new innovation so its fuller market potential is realized; and

5. **Integration (or diffusion)** of the innovation so that it finds a home in the lives of users and no longer is regarded as an innovation.

Each of these hurdles forms an atmosphere through which the innovator must move. Each of these challenges is encountered not in a general way but in a particular and very specific way. And each carries its own characteristic form of fear:

i. For discovery, it is the **fear of unlearning.**

ii. For the invention challenge, it is the **fear of rejection**.

iii. Reduction-to-practice is haunted by the **fear of failure.**

iv. Introduction is plagued by the **fear of loss.**

v. For the challenge of integration, it is the **fear of success.**

Each fear is not confined to its own particular innovation challenge. They often bleed through and influence a neighboring challenge. As one fear entangles with other fears, they become more difficult to overcome. But examining each separately can help innovators face each as it occurs.

Fear of unlearning in discovery

The fear that accompanies the challenge of discovery is not the fear of learning something new, but of unlearning what we thought we knew.

Before we can truly learn something new, we have to unlearn, at least to some degree, what we we already know. One of the first to recognize this in the context of corporate innovation was psychologist Edgar H. Schein, professor emeritus at MIT's Sloan School of Management. Schein described two kinds of anxiety associated with discovery: "learning anxiety" and "survival anxiety."

Learning anxiety comes from "being afraid to try something new for fear that it will be too difficult, that we will look stupid in the attempt, or that we will have to part from old habits that have worked for us in the past. Learning something new can cast us as the deviant in the group we belong to. It can threaten our self-esteem and, in extreme cases, even our identity." Schein goes on to say that "you cannot talk people out of their learning anxieties. Given the intensity of those fears, none of us would ever try something new unless we experience the second form of anxiety, survival anxiety. Survival anxiety is the horrible realization that in order to make it, you are going to have to change." This is why incumbents (e.g., market-share leaders) have very little incentive to innovate in any disruptive manner. They lack the "horrible realization" of survival anxiety. The basic principle, Schein says, is that "learning only happens when survival anxiety is greater than learning anxiety." Schein calls this the "fear of unlearning."[40]

Other expressions of the fear of unlearning can be found in Thomas Kuhn's *Structure of Scientific Revolutions*. Kuhn's thesis is that when evidence mounts which doesn't fit the prevailing paradigm, incumbents reveal their fear of losing power or status. Leo Shapiro likens this of fear to what he calls "infantilization" (becoming like a child again). The powerful and successful do not like to look foolish. Jesus told his disciples this was essential for entrance into the kingdom of heaven (Matthew 18.3). In a similar vein the late Steve Jobs of Apple counseled innovators to "stay hungry, stay foolish."

New evidence that does not fit the mental model of the business can make senior managers—sometimes lacking humility and seduced into omniscience projected onto them by subordinates—afraid of looking naïve, like a vulnerable infant. Those in power may be overly invested in an identity derived from their expertise, rank, power, and status—sometimes aided and abetted by the insulation accumulated wealth affords. As the ancient Greek Stoic philosopher Epictetus put it, "It is impossible to begin to learn that which one thinks one already knows."

The fear of unlearning is a killer of curiosity, awareness, inquiry, and, as a result, discovery—the very first challenge for the innovator.

Fear of rejection when inventing

The *fear of rejection* shows up in full force during in the midst of inventing, which shouldn't surprise us. Innovators fear not only having their idea rejected, but being themselves rejected by the organization or group with whom they identify. In this respect, innovators are no different than the rest of us.

Most of us consider the rejection of our *ideas* as a rejection of *us*. This builds up our fear of rejection and we start rejecting our own ideas even before we express them to anyone else. This slows, and can even kill, the ability to improve, which affects both individuals and companies. Why? Improvements and innovations require "new" ideas and "new" learning. When people are too afraid to express their new ideas because they fear rejection, the spigot of new thinking—both ideas and learning—gets shut off at the source. But one of the distinguishing characteristics of successful innovators is their attitude and response to rejection. Experienced inventors learn to listen for clues of where to improve the invention from the very rejections received.

Fear of failure when it's time to try out the new

We've all known people who seem to have an always-open faucet of creative flow. They are brimming with new ideas, oblivious to the rejection from others. But when it comes to doing something with those ideas, however, nothing happens. They seem paralyzed, nowhere to be found, or they're already on to the next idea. *Fear of failure* causes this shutdown that prevents trying out the new.

"Doing it right the first time" is a worthy goal, but doesn't happen often when you're innovating. Making something new work, both in a technical and a commercial sense, takes multiple trials and many errors to get it right. When the need for certainty and reassurance becomes more important than giving it the best shot at the time, innovators rob themselves of the experience that ultimately leads to the next iteration. When we label this experience "failure," we're discounting the value of what we can learn from the experience. ("Experimenting" is a much more receptive, even robust, way of putting failure into a healthier context.) Fear of failure can be so crippling that it slows the willingness to try something and learn from it. Paralysis of analysis is one form of fear of failure.

What innovators really want to do is experience failure in a safe and productive manner, and *learn* from that failure, as observed by Stefan Thomke in his book, *Experimentation Matters*. Thomke suggests we place special value on failures that come from experience which replicate actual conditions.[41] These are more productive for pointing us in the direction of what to do next. With another try and some adaptation based on what was learned from the previous try, innovators are bound to advance their learning and get closer to the goal. They are creating experience, which is perhaps *the* most trust worthy instructor. It's not failure that should scare us, but unwillingness to try. Turning off the flow of experiences turns out to be more lethal to innovation than turning off the spigot of ideas.

In contrast, a rule of thumb for many innovators is to fail quickly, frequently, and in the field. Some of the waste of relearning can be eliminated or reduced with this rule. This is the whole purpose of the lab bench, simulations, and development cycles—to gain experience and become aware of what cannot possibly be seen without these protected and purposeful failures.

Seasoned innovators know there is a gold mine of insights and feedback in observing users interacting with a fledgling innovation, irrespective of the outcome. When viewed as experience, the innovation-in-development can get stronger, healthier, and closer to being the tool the innovator wants it to be and the customer needs it to be.

Fear of loss when introducing the innovation

Another form of fear presents itself when an innovation is ready to be introduced, whether in the public marketplace or the private boardroom. This is the *fear of loss.*

Introducing an innovation takes innovators and marketers beyond the planning and theorizing, beyond the protyping and testing. Introductions require innovators to commit to the real. The loss feared is a loss of the ideal.

Up until this point, the innovation hasn't been proven. Innovators have no real assurance that what they have told themselves is true for others or not. The price for finding out this truth is the potential loss of expectations for the innovation, expectations that have been built into what has been sketched, designed, prototyped, and user-tested. All sorts of expectations—conscious, unconscious and complex—have become associated with the intended outcome. The fear is that something may have been missed in how the idea was executed, delivered, designed, or even described. It may not play out exactly the way the innovator envisioned. Or the innovation may not be received in the way it was intended. The market may not recognize its value, might use it in an unintended fashion, or might simply ignore it all together.

When introducing an innovation, innovators reveal their own expectations of how it will be received. It's like a parent launching a child off into the world as an adult. Parents have their own expectations of what choices their child can and should make. But in the end, the former-child-now-adult will make his or her own choices, which often are not what was in the mind of the parent. Most healthy parents accept this at some level, consciously or subconsciously. Unhealthy ones don't, hurting the parent and the child both.

Fear of success in integration

The fifth fear plaguing innovators shows up when the challenge is finding the innovation a sustainable home in the lives of end-users. Somewhat like the previous fear of loss, this is the fear of being unrecognized, forgotten or ignored for the contribution that has been made. This is a form of the *fear of success.*

The ultimate success of an innovation is when it becomes so fully assimilated in the lives of users that it loses its newness and even its distinctiveness. It becomes a part of daily life, no longer viewed as an innovation, but as a regular part of life. That which the innovator worked so hard to bring into being becomes absorbed, an anonymous part of the fabric of living. Innovators may fear in some way this loss of distinction applies also to them. At a deeper level, perhaps, it is the fear of losing a part of one's own identity.

For most of the innovation challenges innovators must maintain a passion and persistence for their vision—a fierce independence—to bring the new into reality. By the time they make it this far, the process itself will have revealed the degree and intensity of their resolve.

Unfortunately for some, the ambition that got them this far turns out to be less about the value of the innovation—the contribution it can make in the lives of customers—and more about the value of the innovator and the acclaim of a bigger bank account or a better resume. When this happens with innovators, it may be a symptom of the fear of losing themselves, being forgotten. This calls into question why the innovator is attempting to innovate in the first place. Is it for personal attention or to contribute something of value? Innovators who maintain their focus on contributing something of value accomplish so much more than those whose focus is on merely claiming credit.

Innovators work through these basic fears that saturate the atmospheres of innovating challenges. They work through these atmospheres with lift that comes from their wings of faith. Enabling lift is velocity—innovators' direction and speed.

Velocity: Innovators' direction and speed

Physicists and engineers know that velocity is more than speed alone. It is both speed and direction. Lift-enabled progress requires both. When there is little or no forward movement, such as when R&D budgets are cut and innovation projects are put on hold, or when development runs into a dead end, the momentum of progress slows, the direction becomes less clear, and the innovator ends up with more drag than lift.

Some innovators can make progress with only a little velocity, partly because of how they regard the future. Instead of seeing a wall of uncertainty, they look at the future as a reservoir of resources—a reservoir accessed by going into it and experiencing it rather than merely standing back and analyzing it.

The notion that the future can be regarded as a resource—though difficult to account for on a balance sheet—did not come from modern economic or entrepreneurial theory. It comes from ancient wisdom contained in the so-called "parable of the talents." This parable is an apt description and prescription for innovators.

> For it will be as when a man going on a journey called his servants and entrusted to them his property; to one he gave five talents, to another two, and to another one, to each according to his ability.
>
> He who received the five talents went at once and traded with them; and he made five talents more. So also, he who had the two talents made two talents more. But he who had received the one talent went and dug in the ground and hid his master's money.
>
> Now after a long time the master of those servants came and settled accounts with them. And he who had received the five talents came forward, bringing five talents more, saying, "Master, you delivered to me five talents; here I have made five talents more." His master said to him, "Well done, good and faithful servant; you have been faithful over a little, I will set you over much; enter into the joy of your master." And he also who had the two talents came forward, saying, "Master you delivered to me two talents; here I have made two talents more." His master said to him, "Well done, good and faithful servant; you have been faithful over a little, I will set you over much; enter into the joy of your master."
>
> He also who had received the one talent came forward, saying, "Master, I knew you to be a hard man, reaping where you did not sow, and gathering where you did not winnow, so I was afraid and I went and hid your talent in the ground. Here you have what is yours." But his master answered him,

"You wicked and slothful servant! You knew that I reap where I have not sowed, and gather where I have not winnowed? Then you ought to have invested my money with the bankers, and at my coming I should have received what was my own with interest. So take the talent from him, and give it to him who has the ten talents. For to everyone who has will more be given, and he will have abundance; but from him who has not, even what he has will be taken away."

—Matthew 25.14-30

No one can escape uncertainty. While the one-talent sponsor can always opt for a risk-averse approach, sooner or later, what looked like risk avoidance will turn out to be even more risky. Being quick to avoid an unknown future in exchange for continuation of the familiar may produce a temporary sense of security. But in the long run, the risk of taking no risk at all ends up being the greater risk of the two.

Take a careful look at the parable. First, consider the first two servants, for whom we might substitute the word *innovator*. Like these servants, innovators have been entrusted with "property." While the parable refers to the property as money the first two servants see something more. It could be some structural assets, intellectual property, technical capability or certain business assets.

Second, consider what a "talent" is. From a purely historical point of view, a "talent" was a standard denomination of currency weighing seventy-five pounds (mass) and equal to six thousand drachmas.[42] It is worth noting how meaningless this standard is to us today, a reminder that all money is really just a means of exchange rather than a measure of wealth.

"Talent," however, can suggest something more than a means of exchange. It can represent the knowledge and skill gained through education and experience as well as a person's natural abilities. The parable reminds us that innovators have varying types, depth, and degrees of talent, and no servant is without talent.

Next, consider what the first two do with their talents. They waste no time. They trade what they have and double the money they have been given. The parable is not specific about what this "trading" means, though it would seem that the point of the story is that the two did something more than just put their talents into an interest-bearing savings account. The first two servants were successful, doubling their money. The third servant, by contrast, was not an innovator. He was afraid of his master and afraid of losing the one talent he was given, so he buried it to keep it safe.

How often we all have seen resourceful companies behave like this third servant, hording and hiding their talents (their innovators), refusing to take on a risk of innovating out of fear, while another company moves ahead.

Direction

It is often said that leaders are led by a vision. This holds true for companies that are market-share leaders as well as for the senior executives of those companies. Companies that compete with a market-share leader have the "luxury" of aiming their innovation efforts at the target painted on the back of the leader. If they succeed in surpassing the leader, as they sometimes do, then they become the leader. But do they have vision? Thrust into this new position, they sometimes become directionless. They have lost their target, and with it, a sense of purpose. Executives face the same problem with direction setting. Their job is to keep the field of play fresh and compelling to the corps of knowledge workers in the organization they lead. To do this they must have a vision. Direction for innovators comes from their awareness and understanding of where innovation is needed and possible.

Over the past thirty years, I have heard many well-intentioned leaders say, in one form or another, "We need to be more innovative." While this may be true, it is insufficient and incomplete. All too often, senior, sponsoring executives are inarticulate in this regard or silent. What is needed is to state *where* innovations are needed and *why*. I have observed that when an executive *does* articulate where innovations are needed and why, innovators within the company willingly, vigorously, and effectively respond.

When direction for innovators becomes clear, clarity comes from the specifics in each of the five challenges every innovator faces:

- In the ***discovery*** challenge, direction can come from a proprietary insight regarding a need or pain of a customer, system, or society.

- In the ***invention*** challenge, direction can come from discerning where (and why) inventions are needed or from a technical problem that must be overcome in any solution that addresses the need.

- When making a conceptual invention work (***reduction-to-practice***), direction comes from what is learned in each attempt, success or not.

- In the challenge of **introducing** this new innovation and getting customers to try it, direction comes from an intimate knowledge of and empathy for customers' circumstances and conditions.

- Direction in the context of the **integration** challenge comes from tailoring the innovation in such a way that it is no longer regarded as an innovation, but as a routine necessity of the customers' world.

Innovators need direction. Many company leaders waste much time and money with the mistaken notion that all the innovators need to do is get the process right. But process is no substitute for a clear and compelling direction.

Don't get me wrong. Process is invaluable in coordinating any innovation effort. Process—a sequence of steps, activities, or procedures—is an important ingredient to getting things done in a timely manner. And when it works well, it is invisible. When it is not, process becomes very visible. The old adage, form follows function, or process follows content, still applies. Direction is content.

Innovating is like parenting. While parenting principles may be transferable from one child to the next, the actual applications of the methods, practices, and process itself is likely to vary, sometimes a great deal, depending on the needs of the child. In parenting, each child responds differently to discipline, love, and teaching moments.

The same is true with every innovation. Each innovation is unique, by definition. If we insist on applying the same sequence in the same way to every innovation, we are likely to escape the demands of learning, and unlearning, in a "repeatable process." When operating a manufacturing process designed to produce the same output over and over again it's appropriate to work to eliminate variabilities. However, when it comes to innovating, the variabilities and surprises in the results teach innovators where focus and what to do next. It's a matter of faith.

Peter Drucker made the observation decades ago in his book *Management* that the process one team used in its success is never exactly or directly transferable to another team. Each project team needs to work out its own process appropriate to the particularities, or content, of the project at hand.[43] This is not to say that one team cannot learn from the experience of another. However, direction (what the innovator works on) comes from content and results, not from process or framework (how the innovator does the work).

Many organizations are becoming more than "make and sell" execution machines. They are taking on the increasingly necessary "sense and respond" capabilities normally associated with living organisms. As a result, the art of clearly communicating where and why innovations are needed will become increasingly important and valuable. Stephan Haeckel from IBM's Advanced Business Institute wrote *Adaptive Enterprise*[44] in which he suggested that the traditional command-and-control leadership centered around "offers" was increasingly being complemented by a new kind of "context-and-coordination" leadership, centered in responses to customers more than offers to them. This kind of organization requires a clear, unambiguous, and shared understanding of where the organization is headed and why.

For innovators to be productive in creating new knowledge where it matters most, clarity about where the organization is headed and why is not optional. It is essential. It establishes context, and all value is context-based. Process may be important, but context and content trump process. Toyota's innovation management system is strikingly uncommitted to a particular process or method. Toyota sees the value in tools and methods but has no overall prescribed innovation process. What Toyota does insist on are stated principles and a clear sense of where it is headed. The sharper the "where" and "why," the clearer the direction. And Toyota's results in market-share gains speak for themselves. [45]

Speed

This brings us to the other factor in velocity lift requires—speed. Speed in the physical realm is a rate derived from distance traveled over a period of time. Speed in the innovator's world is also a rate, but it has more to do with knowledge created than distance traversed. For the innovator, the knowledge created is not that of the pure scientist, researcher, or academic. Rather, it is knowledge relevant to what will contribute to the satisfaction of another's need. The faster this kind of knowledge is created, the quicker innovators gain lift and the sooner both the innovation and innovator land at their destination, a satisfied customer.

If Al Ward's description of innovation—"learning applied to creating value"—carries even an ounce of truth, the implications for what speed means to innovating are subtle but significant. It is not simply getting to the market fast or first, though there may be advantages that accrue to the first mover. Speed for the innovator is as much about time-to-learn as it is about time-to-market. The first two servants were quick to invest the talents they had received and they doubled their initial investment. Not a bad return.

So, what was it that enabled these two servants to move so quickly in contrast to the third servant who moved not at all, burying his talent to keep it safe? The speed necessary to produce lift for the innovator comes from starting quickly, without permission if necessary, finding the compelling "pull" of the idea, and obtaining good feedback. Maverick innovators have adopted a general rule of thumb from the Jesuits: "It's easier to ask for forgiveness than permission." Asking permission before moving forward produces drag, not lift. Asking for resources (money, time, and people) before doing anything is an all too common way to seek permission. But it creates resistance.

Experienced innovators reverse the sequence. Instead of asking permission, they act first and, if necessary, ask for forgiveness later. While this may appear to be an act of insubordination, it is an act that is motivated out of empathetic interest in the customer, regardless of its misalignment with the chain of command.

My mentor, Bill Wilson, as vice president of exploratory projects at Kimberly-Clark in 1982, was approached by a group of employees looking for resources to fund an innvation project. They came to Bill with an idea. In his words, it was a "hell of an idea." After he heard them describe it, Bill asked them, "Why aren't you doing it?" They replied, "We don't have permission." Bill told them to go and talk with so-and-so. They said, "We did, and he turned us down." Bill suggested a few others, and they had struck out with all those as well. So, a little frustrated, Bill asked, "What do you want from me?" They said, "Permission."

So Bill said to them, "Fine. I give you permission."

They all laughed. "You can't do that, Bill. You can't just give us permission."

So Bill asked, "Why the hell not?"

The spokesperson for the group said, "We have to have a number. A cost center."

Without hesitation, Bill said, "Fine. You got a pencil? Write this down. Seven, nine, eight, six, three, four, two."

"Whose number is that?" they asked.

Bill responded, "What the hell do you guys care? You asked for permission and I gave you permission. You asked for a number and I gave you a number. What else do you want?" Before the group had spent no more than $2,000 or $3,000, the other vice presidents who had initially turned them down started fighting with each other for the chance to sponsor the idea and the project.

Three years later, Wilson was giving a talk about innovation to a group of employees at Kimberly-Clark and used this experience as an example. At a coffee break, the woman who runs the research budget came up to him and said, "You know, I was the one who got that number, and I couldn't figure it out. It looked legitimate. It had the right numbers in the right sequence. I tried to fit it in here and there and everywhere."

"So where did it end up?" Bill asked.

"In the president's discretionary fund. He never noticed a thing."[46]

Sarbanes-Oxley legislation's emphasis on increased transparency may make this form of giving permission a little more difficult, but not impossible. The point is still the same. Don't take no for an answer when you believe in what you are doing. Seek forgiveness rather than permission, because a prediliction to doing something to learn rather than relying on search and analysis alone may prove better stewardship when innovating. When conditions call for conforming, not innovating, finding permission may be the more prudent course.

Another source of speed necessary for lift can be found in the "pull"— what is compelling about the need. "Pull" may start out in the discovery phase as an emergent, even unmet, need—a "pain" for the end-user or consumer. As the rate of learning progresses, the particulars of the "pull" may evolve and morph. For example, the problems that need to be solved to make the solution work probably will need more than one trial-and-error cycle. But what is compelling will only grow when the need is real.

All too often companies seek innovations for the wrong reasons. They want innovation in their products or services so as to appear different from the competition. However, competitive differentiation as a reason to innovate is entirely different than a being attracted by the pull from a customer's unmet need and the possibility of satisfying that need.

Clif Bar & Company takes this "pull" principle seriously. Pull acts like an accelerator to their innovation efforts, counter-balancing all the "brakes" encountered along the way. Unlike many companies, the marketers and product developers don't even think they have an idea, much less a good idea, if it doesn't meet at least three qualifications. If there is an (complete) idea worth considering further, it must

- offer a viable solution to a pain of a consumer,
- "tell" a story that is easy for the consumer to hear and understand, and
- be clear where it will be easily heard and understood

Without all three, there is no idea. Requiring all three has the effect of causing discovery, invention, and reduction-to-practice steps to produce results sooner rather than later. Lewis Orchard, an innovator with whom we have collaborated for years, is fond of saying "Get to the 'no.'" The sooner you find the 'no' that turns out to be an absolute dead end, the sooner you can move on to work on something else that will produce results. If it turns out that you can't find the 'no,' then you just may have something. Of course Orchard's "no" also means "know."

High-fidelity feedback is also necessary for attaining the speed. Feedback alone is insufficient. It matters where that feedback comes from. Stefan Thomke defines this fidelity (coincidentally from the same Latin root, *fides*, for the English word "faith") as the degree to which the experiment replicates real-world conditions.[47] In the case of a new product innovation, does the feedback come from focus groups (low-fidelity), an in-home use test with consumers (medium-fidelity), or the actual placement of the innovation in live conditions in a market where people must find it and pay for it (high-fidelity)? In the case of a new process innovation, does the feedback come from verbal responses to the concept (low-fidelity), a discrete and limited trial with one or two users (medium-fidelity), or a more complete run of the process with a control running under the same conditions with which to compare results (high-fidelity)? High-fidelity feedback requires more upfront effort. But in the long run, it accelerates the overall progress.

Some innovators have recognized the meaning and importance of speed by practicing what is called "launch and learn." Instead of perfecting the innovation *before* releasing or launching it, many launch the innovation in order to learn. Launching early is not intended to test the waters and then decide whether to proceed or not. It is designed to learn what to do next for the sake of the innovation's development.

Angle of Attack: Innovators' future orientation

Innovators face the future more than the past. They lean forward, not back.[48] They have a bias for what is possible even more than for what is proven. By definition, innovators bend toward progress more than preservation. They're inclined to bring forth a needed solution where there is none. Innovators would rather suffer the pains of giving birth to the new, than seek the security of holding on to the familiar. As their muscle of faith flexes into the shape of a wing, the lift comes in no small measure from the "angle of attack"—their orientation to the future.

This is not to say that innovators have a disregard for the past. Successful innovators have a deeper-than-normal appreciation for what history and experience can teach them. Serial entrepreneurs build on prior successes and failures, theirs and those of others. Serial inventors build on prior art. Many, if not most, are very attuned to what has been thought of or tried before—particularly in their area of expertise. By paying close attention to the past, they have even found opportunities for innovation. Take, for example, Gary Erickson, who successfully brought a taste-*full* energy bar to an otherwise tasteless energy bar category with Clif Bar®. He is an astute student of the past, originally seeing opportunity in rival Power Bar®'s "tasteless" success in establishing the energy-bar category and then, finding opportunity to serve the underserved nutritional needs of women through the brand Luna®.

This is not to say that innovators don't live in the present. Many, if not most, have a deeper than normal appreciation for the demands and details of implementing what they are contemplating. They have an uncanny ability to differentiate between what needs their attention now and what can wait. They are at times extremely focused. However, if you look closely, you will see what occupies them today is that which is required to bring about a better tomorrow. Take the elegant criteria of Bill Hewlett and David Packard for choosing where to innovate next. They simply, but profoundly, asked themselves, "Can we make a contribution here?"[49]

That innovators are future oriented shouldn't surprise us. It could be merely a vocational predisposition. Just as historians are occupationally oriented toward the past and journalists are oriented toward the present, so innovators are focused on the future. What may be more interesting, however, is *how* innovators view the future.

Many believe that innovators and entrepreneurs are willing to take bigger risks than the rest of us. My limited but direct experience with them doesn't square with this. While it may seem that innovators and entrepreneurs are willing to take risks, many, in fact, spend a good deal of their waking hours taking steps to minimize or even eliminate risk. What appears on the surface to be a greater willingness to take risk is actually the different way in which innovators view and approach the future. Andy Bechtolsheim is a quiet but successful innovator who invested his own money in the formation of Sun Microsystems despite warnings from venture capitalists. When asked about it, he spoke with striking confidence of the future. "There was no risk in my mind," he said. "It was a complete no-brainer."[50]

Many years ago, I spent several days attending the annual confab of the World Futures Society—a very eclectic association populated by many who regard themselves as professional futurists. Knowing I had to write a trip report for my boss upon my return, I looked for some underlying patterns among the participants and saw three different orientations to the future.

Some tended to approach the future as something to predict. Their timeframes tended to be shorter term, and their thinking gravitated toward precision. Economists and public-policy types fell into this group. Call them "predictors." Some occupied the other end of the continuum. They viewed the future as a "blank sheet." For this type, the future is not so much something to predict as it is something to create. "The future is what you make it." You could easily imagine that folks in this camp took their parents' counsel to heart—"You can be anything you want to be, so long as you put your mind to it." The time frames for this group tended to be much longer than the first group, and their interests gravitated toward whatever could be imagined. You might call them "transformationalists."

A third group viewed the future not as something to predict, nor as a blank sheet, but as a "problem to solve" (or opportunity to address). For those who view the future in this way, the future is partly, though not completely, determined. There is still time to shape it. There seemed to be more engineers, scientists, and entrepreneurial types in this group than in the other two. Their relative time frames were more mid-term than shorter or longer term. Their focus tended to be more on needs and solutions than on anything else. Innovators are better represented in this third group. In fact, the way innovators "lean forward" is reminiscent of the way Old Testament prophets approached the future.

The Prophet's Dilemma

Many people mistakenly believe that the job of a prophet is to predict the future. The real job of the prophet—at least the Old Testament prophet—is not to predict the future, but to get people to change their habits of mind and their patterns of behavior. One way the Old Testament prophets used to change minds and hearts was to *project* the present into the future. These projections were intended to get people to wake up and think about the consequences of their present behavior. Yes, these projections could be called predictions. But the real goal of prophets was to get people to change their ways. "Repent" was the prophets' central message and purpose. Projection was what they used to drive their message home.

Unfortunately, fundamentalists hijacked the word "repentance" long ago. It actually means to change your way of thinking. *Meta-noia* is the word for repentance in the ancient Greek, which literally means to change (*meta*) your way of knowing (*noia*)). Howard Gardner's recent book *Changing Minds*[51] may help us recover that notion. Such a recovery is becoming increasingly essential to companies (and their market capitalizations). Henry Chesbrough has perceptively pointed out that part of what prevents established companies from innovating is the tyranny of their current business model.[52] Chesbrough correctly suggests most companies are looking for innovations that conform to how the company currently makes and sells it offerings and realizes its profits. Unfortunately, innovations tend not to conform, nor replicate the old. It's almost by definition that innovations will not fit the current business model. As a result, nine times out of ten it will be rejected, not because of the potential of the idea, but because of the inflexibility of the business to change its way of making a profit. The ability to change the old way of thinking is necessary to create new knowledge that fuels a company's future prospects, something Wall Street recognized in the mid-1990s.[53] This requires that the business "change its way of thinking."

Like prophets, innovators view the future as something that can be altered and influenced—a problem to solve. Unlike prophets, however, innovators are more interested in the *medium* than the message. Their role is not simply to get people to wake up and change. Innovators, by definition, have already heard the prophetic message, seen what the future could be, and have taken the plunge. They are deeply engaged in *making* changes, not simply announcing them. As such, innovators are "post-prophetic"—they have seen what the prophet is saying and have taken it to heart. Innovators understand that one cannot hear a message calling for change as anything but unwanted and unheeded criticism until and unless the hearer believes that there is an alternative to their current coping behavior. Innovators are about *showing* listeners the way so they can truly hear and respond.

Like some innovators, Old Testament prophets were somewhat ambivalent about their vocation. Ultimately, their professional reputation was based on the reliability of their projections. This was very problematic. On the one hand, if their projection turned out to be true, they could be accused of being ineffective. After all, the real goal was to get people to change (their way of thinking). On the other hand, if they did convince people to change, then their prediction turned out to be wrong. This ruined their credibility. Damned if they do, and damned if they don't. Correct but ineffective if they could not convince people to change. Unreliable but effective if their predictions didn't come true, but they convinced people to change. Perhaps this explains why "a prophet is not without honor, except in his own land among his own people."

Many innovators experience the same fate in the context of their own host companies. This irony was given voice by one of the so-called minor prophets, Zechariah, when he appealed to the defeated, exiled and dispersed descendents of the once proud nation of Israel, and called them "prisoners of hope."

> Return to your stronghold, O prisoners of hope;
> today I declare that I will restore to you double.
> —Zechariah 9.12

Look at one of the classics among biblical fables—Jonah and the whale. Most of us who had any exposure to the story at all remember little except for Jonah being swallowed by a whale and somehow living to tell about it. One of the shortest books in the Bible, Jonah is a unique character study of a recalcitrant prophet, prone to depression, partly induced by the bind he feels God has put him in. God tells Jonah to go to the people of the city of Nineveh and tell them what is going to happen if they don't change their ways. But Jonah, understandably interested in his own professional reputation, complains to God that if he is successful—that is, if he is able to convince the people of the Nineveh to repent—then his career as a prophet will be over. His predictions won't turn out to be true. No one will believe him anymore.

The book of Jonah is too long to include here, but not so long that you can't easily read it in one sitting. Read the short story for yourself. When you do, you'll see Jonah was an experienced prophet, but not particularly happy about it. He was acutely aware of the between-a-rock-and-a-hard-place liability of the profession. In fact, his attempt to escape this dilemma drove him into the belly of the beast, creating unintended collateral damage for others along the way. Finally, of course, the whale's digestive system can't what or who it swallowed and vomits him out. As grace and the story would have it, however, Jonah comes out whole and faces up to his vocational responsibilities. Jonah himself repents and does what God told him to do in the first place: he goes to Nineveh and delivers the message to the citizens. And low and behold, they hear it and respond by changing their way of thinking and altering the pattern of their behavior. They repent.

So you would think that Jonah would be pleased with his effectiveness and success. He is not. In fact, the story ends with Jonah sitting under the temporary shade of a plant that miraculously grows in the hot desert sun—depressed, whining, and full of resentment.

This quirky story provides us with a wonderful way to differentiate between authentic innovators and those who might only look like one. Many of our enterprises are full of would-be innovators. But many are iconoclasts—attackers of cherished beliefs—more than innovators. Like Jonah, they get swallowed up but never digested by the large corporation. Many ultimately get spit out, though few ever come out without a scar, as Jonah did. Prophets, on the other hand, like innovators, take great pains to effect a change of thinking and behavior for the better, even when it means risking their own professional reputations.

For a period of time, I fancied myself as a part of a prophetic tradition. However, back when I was preaching most every Sunday morning, I was chronically hampered by the letdown of Sunday afternoon. What haunted me was what haunted Jonah. The field of play for the messenger is limited. The job is done after you have called attention to the need for change. Many times you are a "voice crying in the wilderness." Even if and when someone actually hears the message and takes it to heart, there doesn't seem to be any immediate and unambiguous way to respond, at least in a local congregation. Repentance is largely left to folks to work out on their own. You can't blame churches. They are communities, not organizations. As such they are structurally ill equipped for taking on anything but the early alerts needed for societal innovation. They are hardly designed to create, much less put into practice, the solutions.

But innovators share with prophets an orientation to the future— an angle of attack—that requires changing not only their own way of thinking but also the thinking of others. In this respect, innovators and the Old Testament prophets are very much alike: the field of play for both the innovator and the prophet starts with the message. However, for the innovator it does not end there, as it does for the prophet. In fact, the innovator's approach to the future is such that the job is not finished until there is some change that is accepted and integrated, until the new becomes not so new anymore. Experienced and authentic innovators invest themselves deeply in efforts that, like prophets, are based on dissatisfaction with the present. But unlike prophets, innovators are compelled to find and bring into reality a better way. While both the prophet and the innovator are future oriented, the way the innovator relates to the future is arguably much more complex and demanding. Innovation—both process and result—is so much more than projection and prediction.

There is at least one more factor that must be accounted for in the production of lift that comes from the wings of innovators' faith muscle, the engine and fuel that power the innovator's forward movement: love.

Chapter 4

Innovators' Motivation

What motivates innovators to venture out in the face of fear and uncertainty? What keeps them striving for answers after repeated rejections, failures, and resistance of various forms and intensities?

Innovators are motivated by love—a powerful propellant well suited for attaining and sustaining the lift necessary for innovating. It's a motivation stronger than the counter forces pitted against it.

Bringing love into the subject of innovating may at first seem odd. The vast majority of what is chronicled about innovation, especially technology eneabled innovations, concentrates on hard data: economic, market, competitive, and scientific or technological know-how. Something so touchy-feely as love is rarely even whispered in connection with innovation. What dominates the vocabulary on innovation are business models, venture capitalist calculations, rates of return, and the science and technology underlying inventing or the creativity and risk taking of innovators. Love is shoved to a side street. Some would suggest it's a dead end, with no on-ramp to the realities of innovation.

But love is part of innovating, from the very beginning. Any successful innovation begins with an empathetic identification with a customer's need and the conceptual creation of a way to address that need. Sounds like love to me, though many prefer to call it "passion."

From another perspective, consider what many call "enthusiast" product development. Nike, Apple, Sony, and other companies use an "enthusiast" philosophy in their product innovation efforts, partly because it works so well. The philosophy goes like this: hire people who love the sport or product category—enthusiasts—and give them the challenge of spotting and articulating an unmet need. Then work with them to come up with a solution to that need. Enthusiasts are more likely to have an intuitive, natural feel for the real needs within their particular niche because of their love and interest in the category. They are much quicker to recognize a need than is the mercenary innovator. The enthusiast innovator has a built-in sensitivity to the customer because the enthusiast *is* one.

Experienced sponsors of innovators also know that intrinsic motivation—the "passion" of the innovator—is crucial to the outcome. They realize—perhaps from their own innovating experience—that attempting to do something out of the ordinary will be resisted, if not rejected. So, before these sponsors invest in an innovator and an innovation, they make sure the innovator has enough heart for the idea to keep plowing ahead, despite the various forms of resistance, inevitable rejections and likely set backs that will surely occur all along the way. To guage just how passionate the innovator is for the idea, a common practice among sponsors is to put up some initial resistance sponsors themselves create. Such test-case resistance can coax the innovator's intrinsic motivations out into the open. When the would-be innovator refuses take "no" for an answer, it is one indication of the intensity of the innovator's conviction and motivation. Isn't this what Samuel was told to use as his criteria in selecting David—to not look at outward appearances but to look at the heart?

Where does motivation come from? Is it a desire for fame, fortune, or career advancement? These probably are part of the motivational mix. But these extrinsic motivations seldom prove sufficient to overcome the resistance. There is another, greater and more powerful motivation that successful innovators tap into to lift them through the bad times. That motivation is found in a selfless love, empathy and understanding for the customer, an enthusiasm for the field, and a passion for the challenge. This is true love. Without some convincing signs that love is a significant part of what is motivating an innovator, wise sponsors and investors know to proceed with caution, or not at all.

In Greek (the language in which the New Testament was written and into which the Old Testament was often translated) there are three words for love: *eros*, *philos*, and *agape*. All three are engaged in the motivation that fuels innovators.

Eros is passionate aspiration and sensual longing. Might *eros* be behind the "passion" so often sought by sponsors? Might *eros* be the motivational mix underlying the so-called "enthusiast" approach to new product development? Though necessary in the fuel that propels the innovator forward, enthusiasm alone is not sufficient. It can cause one to easily confuse motion with action.

Philos denotes the kind of love demonstrated in committed affiliation. Think family, friends, familiarity. A certain degree of familiarity not only with other people but also with the knowledge domains involved in a particular innovation is necessary for success. However, subject matter expertise alone is a poor indicator of future success. Though necessary, *philos* alone is insufficient. Alone it can lead to acquiescence and premature satisfaction—the mistaken belief that all that can be invented has been invented.[54]

Agape, the third word for love in Greek, is perhaps the most challenging and interesting. *Agape* denotes the kind of love that is selfless. It shows up in purposeful acts of giving that require the sacrifice of self-interest.

All three elements of love—*eros*, *philos*, and *agape*—are blended into the fuel animating the potential energy (faith) in all of us. But for innovators, *agape* likely has a greater share of the blend. Maya Angelou's observation that we sacrifice for what we love points to this characteristic of *agape*. We sacrifice for who and what we love. This is especially true for innovators.

Innovating requires a willingness to lose one's self, even to sacrifice something near and dear for the sake of the innovation and the customer it serves. *Agape*-motivated innovation turns what would otherwise be a mere transaction into an act of faith, love, and service. That innovators have more *agape* in their mix of motivation may be one of the best-kept secrets about innovators—perhaps even a secret they keep from themselves.

Faith, hope, and love

Paul of Tarsus—the former-persecutor-turned-disciple of Jesus— placed so much emphasis on the importance of love that he assigned it priority over both faith and its vocational synonym hope. In a letter to the church at Corinth, written shortly after Jesus died, Paul wove faith and love together in an inspired and famous piece of prose. Unfortunately, many of us limit our associations of Paul's ode to love to weddings, perpetuating our culture's confinement of love to associations with marriage or intimate romantic relationships. Confining love in this way mistakenly narrows love to matters of emotions and interpersonal relationships. But love has as much relevance to the drive to learn and the drive to acquire as it does to the drive to bond and the drive to defend. *Agape* is the word Paul used for love in this passage from 1 Corinthians 13:

If I speak in the tongues of mortals and of angels, but do not have love, I am a noisy gong or a clanging cymbal. And if I have prophetic powers, and understand all mysteries and all knowledge, and if I have all faith, so as to remove mountains, but do not have love, I am nothing. If I give away all my possessions, and if I hand over my body so that I may boast,˙ but do not have love, I gain nothing.

Love is patient; love is kind; love is not envious or boastful or arrogant or rude. It does not insist on its own way; it is not irritable or resentful; it does not rejoice in wrongdoing, but rejoices in the truth. (vs. 7) It bears all things, believes all things, hopes all things, endures all things

Love never ends. But as for prophecies, they will come to an end; as for tongues, they will cease; as for knowledge, it will come to an end. For we know only in part, and we prophesy only in part; but when the complete comes, the partial will come to an end.

When I was a child, I spoke like a child, I thought like a child, I reasoned like a child; when I became an adult, I put an end to childish ways. For now we see in a mirror, dimly,˙ but then we will see face to face. Now I know only in part; then I will know fully, even as I have been fully known. And now faith, hope, and love abide, these three; and the greatest of these is love.

Notice how Paul weaves together love and faith so tightly. In verse 7, faith and love become almost indistinguishable, though Paul ends this famous passage by clearly placing *apape* in the priority position, *agape* and faith are interrelated; one cannot fully or completely operate without the other.

Innovators may have found a secret formula in this blend of love animating their faith. Love is not only a powerful motivator. It is also a powerful antidote to the viral and contagious fears that seem to mysterious appear in the atmospheres of innovating. "Perfect love casts out fear" was the way the apostle John chose to say it in his first letter (1 John 4.18). There is no fear in love—at least not in *agape*. This kind of love is powerful and efficient. *Agape* turns trust into commitment, to customers and collaborators. *Agape* catalyzes confidence into the courage to act on another's behalf. *Agape* converts hope into engaged attention and action, to lose any thought for one's self. And finally, *agape* transforms mere belief into vision of a solution that works for the intended.

The parable of the Good Samaritan illustrates this most basic and fundamental motivation of the true innovator. It also reveals some tacit but ever-present dynamics of innovating. The parable starts out with a lawyer asking Jesus *the* question: What must I do to succeed? In classic Socratic style, Jesus answers by asking a question of his own. What does the manual say? And the lawyer answers what he has learned by rote. He recites an answer that demonstrates that while he can get the answer right, he may not truly understand the underlying math. The answer is love (*agape* is the word used in the parable). It is not love as a feeling but love as a calling, a purposeful, directed act of the will, a tangible embodiment of selfless giving, the object of which is not only God but also one's neighbor. It is not simply spiritual. It is moral, social, economic, and physical. It is love that is not merely about how one feels. It is about how one orients his entire life—heart, soul, strength, and mind. The lawyer recites this answer. But it is not clear whether he truly understands what he is saying. Jesus plays along, telling him he answered correctly.

But then the twist comes. The lawyer unwittingly exposes the fact that he really doesn't understand by asking his follow-up question. Seeking to justify himself he asks, "Who is my neighbor?" The parable of the Good Samaritan provides the lesson and the obvious punchline:

> Jesus replied, "A man was going down from Jerusalem to Jericho, and fell into the hands of robbers, who stripped him, beat him, and went away, leaving him half dead. Now by chance a priest was going down that road; and when he saw him, he passed by on the other side. So likewise a Levite, when he came to the place and saw him, passed by on the other side. But a Samaritan while traveling came near him; and when he saw him, he was moved with pity. He went to him and bandaged his wounds, having poured oil and wine on them. Then he put him on his own animal, brought him to an inn, and took care of him. The next day he took out two denarii, gave them to the innkeeper, and said, "Take care of him; and when I come back, I will repay you whatever more you spend." Which of these three, do you think, was a neighbor to the man who fell into the hands of the robbers?" He said, "The one who showed him mercy." Jesus said to him, "Go and do likewise."
>
> —Luke 10.30-37

The parable is remarkably penetrating if we associate the Samaritan as the innovator. But first, let's get all the characters straight: a priest, a Levite, and a Samaritan, and the anonymous man lying helpless by the side of the road. The latter is clearly someone in need.

As a parable the story invites us to ask, Who are the priests, Levites, and Samaritans in the context of innovating today?[55] Today's priests and Levites are a part of an incumbent administrative hierarchy. Today (and yesterday) priests are those at midlevels in the hierarchy, whereas Levites are at lower levels, handling the more routine tasks and needs. In ancient Israel, priests and Levites were born into their status and identity. They are in their roles, responsibilities, and identities as a result of inheritance, not from achievement or experience. And finally, both priests and Levites are set apart from the rest so as to maintain a degree of "purity" not otherwise expected from those outside the hierarchy. This "purity" requires some effort to maintain, of course, necessitating a distancing of themselves from others and things that may defile them. "Getting their hands dirty" is something they avoid.

Samaritans, on the other hand, are identified by a place, not a bloodline. A Samaritan has no status or rank in any incumbent hierarchy. Nor does a Samaritan have any inherited privilege, or expectation (of themselves or from others) to maintain any ritual or ethnic purity. In fact, the cultural connotation of a "Samaritan" was analogous to someone who comes from the other side of the tracks.

Clearly, the example of the Samaritan is contrasted with the priest and the Levite. Unlike the priest and Levite who must maintain their purity, the Samaritan gets his hands dirty by getting involved. This "roll up your sleeves" orientation is typical of innovators. It is wonderfully captured in one of my favorite pieces of wisdom from John W. Gardner, himself an innovator, who founded Common Cause. Gardner said, "The society which scorns excellence in plumbing as a humble activity and tolerates shoddiness in philosophy because it is an exalted activity will have neither good plumbing nor good philosophy. Neither its pipes nor its theories will hold water."[56] Experienced innovators are often philosopher plumbers engaged in connecting and installing new pipes.

The example of the Samaritan points directly to what propels and compels the innovator's faith. Unlike the priest and the Levite, successful innovators are not motivated to preserve their status or position. They seldom, if ever, are born into the job of innovating. Innovators emerge.

The innovator's "roll up your sleeves" orientation is a pretty good test to differentiate the real from the false innovators.

Like the Samaritan, genuine innovators don't stay on their side of the street. This is why they can be so problematic to those who are invested in maintaining the fences surrounding the various departments of activity within an organization. Innovators cross over fences and breaks boundaries, literally, figuratively and organizationally, all the time. Innovators aren't motivated by class or rank, but by identification with a need and the answer to that need.

Innovators may not be the first to see the need. But they are typically early responders, sometimes at great personal sacrifice and professional risk to a career path. Most, like the priest and the Levite, simply walk by. It's not that they don't notice. They just don't respond.

Why does the innovator respond when others don't? It's not that the need was hidden or even that others didn't see it. It's about what's in their minds and in their hearts. The percentage of *agape* in the blend of what motivates the innovator makes all the difference. It is what enables their wings of faith to catch the lift that carries them through fear and resistance toward the solution to a need.

Agape is self*less* love. With less self to worry about, the innovator is more apt to find the lift—the passion and commitment—so necessary in innovating. The priest and Levite had too much self-interest propelling them on their way. Though they saw the man on the side of the road and recognized he needed help, they passed by on the other side. They turned away. Innovators, like the Samaritan, turn *toward* problems. Only then are needs felt and solutions conceived and put into practice.

Early on in my work with innovators, I was made aware of how often companies blind themselves to the needs of their customers. This can happen in some subtle ways. For example, when working with product developers in the disposable diaper category, I couldn't help notice how they described how the diaper performed. In lab or field tests, when the diaper got wet or soiled, developers would refer to the event as "an insult." Understandably, these fiber scientists and chemical and mechanical engineers were highly focused on how the *diaper* worked. But "insult" struck me as a bit odd. After all, isn't a diaper designed to be "insulted" by the wearer? Calling it an "insult" revealed just how central the product was in their attention, even to the point of blinding them to the need of the infant. From the mother's point of view, "insult" may make more sense. (It has long been debated by those in this product category just who the diaper is really designed for, the mother or the baby.) These engineers were beginning to sound like priests and Levites, though I suspect it was unintentional. Self-centeredness was getting in the way. In this case, it was product-centeredness.

One can hardly blame them. After all, much time, money, research, and development is invested. Such cumulative and compounded investment creates momentum that can take developers right past unmet need. It is passed by because it is not a part of the original focus. When *agape* is a significant percentage of the innovator's motivation, however, it can break away from the inertia of that momentum and free the innovator to venture over to the other side of the road, accept the situation, acknowledge the need, and begin to address it. This requires stepping out of the flow and, indeed, starting a new one. The Samaritan did not pass by on the other side. He simply went to the man. This movement of the Samaritan toward the man on the side of the road—where the need is and solutions emerge—would not be possible were Samaritan absorbed with himself. He was free to sense and respond.

Louis Pasteur was another who stepped out of the dominant flow of prevailing thinking and allowed the need he saw to trump his concern for himself. His selflessness is told by Axel Munthe's firsthand account of Pasteur's research on the rabies vaccine. In Munthe's essays *The Story of San Michele*, Pasteur, who had lost three of his five children to typhoid fever, was, "absolutely fearless. Anxious to secure a sample of saliva straight from the jaws of a rabid dog, I once saw him with the glass tube held between his lips draw a few drops of the deadly saliva from the mouth of a rabid bull-dog, held on the table by two assistants, their hands protected by leather gloves."[57] From that work, he created the first vaccine for rabies.

Marie Curie is another example of the Samaritan innovator. Curie is known not only for her work on radioactivity but also was the first person to be honored with two Nobel Prizes (in chemistry and physics) and remains the only person to have won the Nobel in more than one field of science. She selflessly pursued her research on radioactivity, deciding not to patent the radium isolation process in order to avoid encumbering the scientific community from freely pursuing related research. Albert Einstein said of Marie Curie that she was the only person who remained uncorrupted by the fame she had acquired.

Selflessness

Selflessness is an essential part of the motivational fuel for innovators. When the self is a smaller percentage of what propels the innovator, the innovator's faith can produce more lift. Distractions of self-interest are smaller and less frequent. Fears become more manageable. Selfless love gives the innovator more flight time, deepens commitment to collaborators and customers, strengthens persistence, enriches inspiration, and engenders humility. All of these enable the innovator to fly through the varied atmospheres of fear and resistance and gain more lift.

I do not intend to imply that innovators are commercial, technological, or industrial saints. Like all of us, innovators come in an infinite variety of temperaments. They are driven by a mix of motivations and a blend of incentives. However, successful ones tend to worry less about self and more about the other (end-user) they seek to serve.

One of the most persuasive motivational theories was originally put forth by Abraham Maslow in a 1943 paper entitled "A Theory of Human Motivation." Most of us know it by its nickname "Maslow's hierarchy of needs." It's worth noting that Maslow based his thought experiment regarding what motivates humans on what he called "exemplary people."[58] This was itself a bit of an innovation at that time, considering that the majority of his peers in the field of psychology were deriving their theories on work with the opposite types—mentally ill or neurotic people. Despite significant criticisms, Maslow's theory remains a popular and useful way of thinking about something as intangible and difficult to amass evidence for as human motivation.

Innovators are certainly "exemplary people," if only by the degree to which they persist against the odds and prevailing norms, thinking less of themselves and more of the need and its solution.

Our premise that *agape*, or selfless love, constitutes a greater portion of the innovator's motivation is reinforced by Maslow's research on the development of resilience, or what Maslow called "frustration tolerance." Maslow found it noteworthy that people who consciously find themselves engaged in efforts that have to do with high ideals, social standards, and values are people who are willing to sacrifice much. In Maslow's own words:

> Perhaps more important than all these exceptions are the ones that involve ideals, high social standards, high values and the like. With such values people become martyrs; they give up everything for the sake of a particular ideal, or value. These people may be understood, at least in part, by reference to one basic concept (or hypothesis) which may be called "increased frustration-tolerance through early gratification." People who have been satisfied in their basic needs throughout their lives, particularly in their earlier years, seem to develop exceptional

73

power to withstand present or future thwarting of these needs simply because they have strong, healthy character structure as a result of basic satisfaction. They are the "strong" people who can easily weather disagreement or opposition, who can swim against the stream of public opinion and who can stand up for the truth at great personal cost. It is just the ones who have loved and been well loved, and who have had many deep friendships who can hold out against hatred, rejection or persecution.

I say all this in spite of the fact that there is a certain amount of sheer habituation which is also involved in any full discussion of frustration tolerance. For instance, it is likely that those persons who have been accustomed to relative starvation for a long time, are partially enabled thereby to withstand food deprivation. What sort of balance must be made between these two tendencies, of habituation on the one hand, and of past satisfaction breeding present frustration tolerance on the other hand, remains to be worked out by further research. Meanwhile we may assume that they are both operative, side by side, since they do not contradict each other. In respect to this phenomenon of increased frustration tolerance, it seems probable that the most important gratifications come in the first two years of life. That is to say, people who have been made secure and strong in the earliest years, tend to remain secure and strong thereafter in the face of whatever threatens."[59]

Successful innovators have increased tolerance for frustration, likely born out of a sustained, untraumatized experience of love from parents when infants. Their need for self-esteem from extrinsic sources—material rewards and the recognition of others is already satisfied. In fact, it could be that their needs for self-actualization are already satisfied. As President Harry S. Truman said, "It is amazing what you can accomplish if you do not care who gets the credit." More than what is *in* the mix of love's fuel that propels and motivates the innovator, it is what's missing—the self.

Far too many failed innovations have too much "self" in them. Too many are initiated for the right-sounding but wrong-motivated reasons. For example, how many current innovation projects are under way primarily to differentiate the innovating company's product from that of the competition? Are innovators becoming more interested in the welfare of the company's profit margin than the needs of customers? Are they interested only in maintaining shareholder value in the near term instead of risking the unknown to serve customer interests in the longer term? Are they seeing only today?

The apostle Paul wrote in his famous passage on love, "Now we see as if in a mirror dimly"? (1 Corinthians 13:12). It is when innovators are able to get their own self-interest out of the way that the mirror becomes a window through which to see the real need of the customer and the undistorted view of what solution will work.

Innovators have a sense of volunteerism. In fact, innovators act as much, if not more, out of the Samaritan ideal of seeing a need and doing something about it rather than out of their identity as an employee of a company. Successful innovators are perennial amateurs—amateurs in the sense that they innovate because they want to, not because they are assigned to do so or because it is their job. This is one major reason why successful companies with large numbers of workers have difficulty innovating in any significant and sustainable fashion. The intense focus and attention innovators give to innovating has little room for self-centered concerns like job security and conformity to company incentive plans. The challenges of innovation are too demanding. Innovating is not for the faint of heart—it requires all of the heart, mind, strength, and soul.

Many believe that innovators are caught in a dilemma—the need to keep the run of success going for as long as possible, on the one hand, and pursuing the new and disruptive innovation, on the other.[60] It is selfless love, however, that breaks this dilemma and propels innovators forward to find needed lift.

Having re-examined faith, hopefully liberated it from the constraints of religion and proposed how innovators shape this "potential energy" and put it to practical use, we now turn to look more closely at the five wing settings with which innovators find the lift they need for innovating.

PART 2
Lift-Producing Faith Patterns

Innovating challenges are analogous to stages of a flight. Each stage requires lift. Innovators achieve lift with a wing setting of faith designed for each stage. Part 2 examines each of these faith patterns.

Discovering an unmet need is like take-off. Take-offs require tremendous effort to overcome the gravitation forces of the belief and mindsets of customers and of innovators themselves. Discovery of a need requires lift, and innovators find it through awe and wonder.

Inventing a new solution is like the initial ascent. To conceive of a new solution requires the innovator, at this stage an inventor, to leave the ground of what is known. Invention requires lift, and innovators create it with inspiration and appreciation.

Making the invention work for customers and all stakeholders is like midair flight. Seldom does the first iteration of the invention work for all concerned. Reducing the invention to practice happens through several tries. To make it through enough of these trials and errors requires lift. Forgiveness and persistence lead innovators to the lift they need for this stage of innovating.

Introducing the innovation to the market is like descent and landing. The smoother the landing of this new solution at the time it's introduced, the more likely customers will recognize it, accept it and find value in it. Lift keeps descents gradual and landings smooth, and submission and humility are indispensable.

Integrating the innovation into customers' routines is not only like pulling up to the gate and unloading, but also debriefing what happened during the flight. Future innovating flights are made safer by incorporating the experience of past. Acceptance and gratitude are essential to integrate these lessons.

A note about the label for each wing setting: I have used two words for each wing setting of faith because faith is both a behavior and attitude, or mode of thinking. Or, if you prefer, imagine the first word of the pair as what the innovator "receives" and the second word as what the innovator "gives" or does.

Chapter 5

Awe and Wonder

Just because a company *needs* to innovate doesn't mean it can. Just because a company *can* innovate doesn't mean it will, nor will be successful.

When innovations fail, something is lacking. That something is often an opportunity that is truly compelling. And what gives innovators ability to recognize what is compelling is a sense of awe and wonder.

Looking at Moses as an innovator gives us a close-up of just how essential awe and wonder are and how both work in discovery. His reaction to the burning bush turned out to be a mix of awe and wonder which led him directly to a compelling opportunity. Here's the story as it appears in Exodus:

> Moses was keeping the flock of his father-in-law Jethro, the priest of Midian; he led his flock beyond the wilderness, and came to Horeb, the mountain of God. There the angel of the Lord appeared to him in a flame of fire out of a bush; he looked, and the bush was blazing, yet it was not consumed. Then Moses said, 'I must turn aside and look at this great sight, and see why the bush is not burned up.' When the Lord saw that he had turned aside to see, God called to him out of the bush, 'Moses, Moses!' And he said, 'Here I am.' Then he said, 'Come no closer! Remove the sandals from your feet, for the place on which you are standing is holy ground.' He said further, 'I am the God of your father, the God of Abraham, the God of Isaac, and the God of Jacob.' And Moses hid his face, for he was afraid to look at God.

Then the Lord said, 'I have observed the misery of my people who are in Egypt; I have heard their cry on account of their taskmasters. Indeed, I know their sufferings, and I have come down to deliver them . . . [from their oppressors]. The cry of the Israelites has now come to me; I have also seen how the Egyptians oppress them. So come, I will send you to Pharaoh to bring my people out of Egypt.' But Moses said to God, 'Who am I that I should go to Pharaoh, and bring [your people] out of Egypt?' He said, 'I will be with you; and this shall be the sign for you that it is I who sent you: when you have brought the people out of Egypt, you shall worship God on this mountain.'

—Exodus 3.1-12

Like many innovators who are not innovators when they start out, Moses was occupied with other concerns. He was busy tending to his father-in-law's flock. Then something caught his eye. He got distracted, and might even have put the sheep at risk while his attention was on the burning bush. After all, the first rule for a shepherd—we call them managers now—is to stay focused. Pay attention to what's in front of you. Another perspective might suggest that Moses was simply doing his job, staying alert to any unforeseen threats to the safety and welfare of the flock. Isn't it the job of the shepherd to scan the perimeter for threats and opportunities? Perhaps this wasn't a distraction at all.

Whether Moses was on task or engaged in a divine distraction, the bush caught his eye and diverted his attention.

This happens to innovators. It can be a serendipitous distraction or an integral part of the purpose of a host company. Before looking more closely at what happens in Moses' story, it's instructive to remember *where* it happened. Location often plays a role in discovery. The story locates Moses "*beyond* the wilderness," in a place where anyone can easily get lost. Moses put himself in a place where he could get lost—"beyond the wilderness"—and there, sees something new and compelling.

This is instructive for innovators in an intellectual sense. By putting themselves in a position to become lost for a while, innovators can often find something new and compelling. Isn't this, after all, what explorers do?

For innovators, lonely, unmapped, and unoccupied spaces play a significant role. In fact innovating itself could be described as the transformation of a seemingly empty chaotic space into a meaningful and valued place. These empty spaces on the competitive landscape are often called "white spaces." By venturing into these unknown territories, innovators often discover a compelling entrepreneurial opportunity. But you first have to get lost to find them. These are spaces and places that have not as yet been explored—"frontiers" of emerging consumer or user attitudes and behavior, largely unmapped and sparsely traveled, with new links connecting previously unassociated facts. These frontiers are often mistakenly assumed to be not where the action is.

Ironically, this may be one reason why there is so much dissatisfaction with the content in innovation portfolios and pipelines. Their contents don't extend very far into the wilderness. The fear of getting lost, even appearing so, prevents many a would-be innovator from discovering what are really compelling opportunities. Moses may have had other phobias— public speaking to mention one—but the fear of getting lost was not one of them.

What Moses did when he saw this strange anomaly is revealing. The story points us to at least four elements of awe and wonder that contribute to the lift so necessary in this first stage of innovating:

- Turning aside to look.
- Seeing why.
- Hearing the call.
- Discovering the need.

Turning aside to look

Whether distracted or just doing his job, Moses' first impulse was to turn and look. Moses is very deliberate. He's emphatic about telling himself, "I must turn aside and look at this great sight."

Moses could have easily been like those working in focused and lean companies. On the job they remain focused. Any diversion, even momentary, risks wasting time, money, and effort. In this kind of pressure, turning aside to look can be difficult, even for innovators who *are* given the license to venture out and explore. At the most basic level, turning aside means breaking the routine and rhythm and opening up the relevance filters a bit from their pre-sets.

From experience, most of us have developed preconceived notions and mental models that tell us what is relevant and what is not. It's like driving with the flow of traffic and noticing something. Momentum carries us forward with the flow. "Turning aside" requires us to pull over, out of the flow, and stop, be still, check it out. We have to let go of the impulse to keep up with those ahead of us and let the traffic behind us go by. As American theologian Paul Lehman once said, "Don't just do something. Stand there."[61] This is what Moses did and this is what successful innovators do. They turn aside and look, despite the risk of getting run over from behind or the fear of being left behind.

The more experience we have, the more difficult it can be to simply turn aside and look. Our experience in a particular field reinforces the assumption that we know what is relevant and what is not. Specialization can leave innovators (who often are specialists in some domain) blind to the possibilities outside their own domain. Even within an area of specialty, innovators' conventional wisdom can prevent them from seeing that which doesn't fit. Thomas Kuhn, in his *Structure of Scientific Revolutions*, described this dilemma for experienced and recognized experts. When new evidence, which is not quite called a fact yet, emerges outside the prevailing wisdom, it often goes unrecognized or is dismissed as irrelevant.[62]

Entire companies often do something similar. Clayton Christensen pointed to how denial can affect incumbents and market-share leaders. He observed that disruptive innovations don't suddenly show up out of the blue. Rather, they appear on the competitive horizon long before they actually cause any disruption. But these weak signals are thought to be too small, too expensive, or too "niche" oriented to worry about. So they're ignored. And companies enjoying success don't notice evidence emerging that points to something new. "It's not relevant." They stay focused.

Turning aside to look is just the first step for innovators. When they do turn and look—quiet and still—innovators are able to give themselves fully to what has caught their attention, as Moses did when he looked to "see why the bush is not burned up."

Looking for the why

What Moses saw was not simply a shrub, he saw something more. He saw a mystery, something unexpected. "Evidence of things unseen."[63] The bush was burning, but it was not consumed by the fire. Moses studied the bush with a sense of awe and wonder and asked, "Why is this bush not burning up?"

Compelling opportunities are frequently overlooked in the beginning, partly because in the beginning, these opportunties don't necessarily make sense. The new is strange, and the strange is new. At first we can't accurately describe this strange new thing. Initially our description is incomplete, hesitant, often inaccurate. We have only familiar words to use, only the vocabulary that is available. What at first were called "horseless carriages" became "automobiles." "Photography" in our filmless digital age found a temporary but awkward rest stop in "digital photography" before making a transition to "imaging," which may be replaced with a new and better label. So whether the bush was actually burning and not consumed, we'll never know. What we do know is that something unexpected caught Moses' attention. His awe and wonder led him to ask "why?"

Innovators, largely because of an instinct to understand the unusual and unexpected, can't help but turn aside to look and seek some explanation for the "why." This "looking for an explanation" is not to be confused with analysis, though analytical skills do help. Taking an analytical inventory of what has captured our attention—classifying and sorting the various parts—is a useful skill but can get in the way of seeing the bigger picture. Discovery requires examing both the emerging system and the ecosystem from which it is emerging. Margaret Wheatley in her classic *Leadership and the New Science* put it this way: "Learning to observe the whole of a system is difficult. Our traditional analytic skills can't help us. Analysis narrows our field of awareness and actually prevents us from seeing the total system. We move deeper into the details and farther away from learning how to comprehend the system in its wholeness. Hans-Peter Durr, former director of the Max Planck Institute, once remarked, 'There is no analytic language to describe what we are seeing at the quantum level. I can only say that it does not help to analyze things in more detail. The more specific the information, the less relevant it is.'"[64]

Innovators encounter burning bushes and ask "why?" A sense of awe and wonder grabs them and they begin to see and understand that before them may be a compelling opportunity.

Hearing the call

What happens to Moses next is what happens to innovators when they discover a compelling opportunity.

> When the Lord saw that he had turned aside to see, God *called to him* out of the bush [emphasis added].

Three short verses into the story, and what at first appears as a possible "distraction" now becomes a calling that redirects who Moses is and what he does for the rest of his life.

Innovators not only see the unusual, they envision change and are themselves changed in the process.

Innovators are seldom if ever credentialed as innovators. Instead, like Moses, their vocation emerges out of whatever it was that captured their attention—their own burning bush. Innovating is inherently improvisational. The innovation and innovator emerge together out of the discovery of what is needed. In the nurturing and developing of the idea, the innovator must learn new patterns of thinking and acting. Moses' attention, imagination, and curiosity became fully engaged in trying to understand what was going on in the burning-but-unconsumed bush. And out of that same bush, Moses gained a new direction and purpose for his life—one that he could not have imagined. The specific calling becomes clear later in the story. "So come, I will send you to Pharaoh to bring my people out of Egypt."

This brings us to the fourth and most central element of awe and wonder.

Discovering the need

As God and Moses interact in this short narrative, God makes an observation about his people and articulates a need for a change.

> Then the Lord said, 'I have observed the misery of my people who are in Egypt; I have heard their cry on account of their taskmasters. Indeed, I know their sufferings, and I have come down to deliver them . . . . The cry of the Israelites has now come to me; I have also seen how the Egyptians oppress them.

The initial response of Moses is not unlike that of many innovators. "Who am I that I should go?" "I'm not good enough." If innovators are brutally honest with themselves, they recognize that their resumes don't stack up next to the magnitude of the need in a compelling opportunity. But the call is too strong to ignore. And faith kicks in to keep them focused on creating a solution for the compelling opportunity. Their faith gives them the lift that carries them through.

Peter Drucker called innovating primarily a *diagnostic* discipline.[65] So what makes for a good diagnostician? Stuart Brown, a recognized medical diagnostician and founder of The National Institute for Play, a nonprofit advancing the science of play, describes it this way: "A good diagnostician never leaves a solid grounding in human anatomy and human physiology. Many physicians inadvertently leave this grounding by becoming overly focused on pathology [how *this* body is working or not]. They focus on the problem so much they can lose sight of the broader context of the patient's environment and physical condition."[66] A similar temptation confronts every innovator. As excellent problem-solvers, innovators can focus so much on problems to solve, they lose sight of the broader context of the opportunity. Like good medical diagnosticians who know how the body is structured and works, innovators must be able to understand how opportunities are structured and how they work. They must be able to determine whether an opportunity is compelling and worth pursuing.

Complete *and* compelling

Innovators who see opportunity have an understanding of both the customer's need and how the need can be satisfied. They also need to be aware of the alternatives available to the customer to meet that need. Often it takes more than one innovator to see whether there is an opportunity or not. It is prudent, therefore, not to leave the task of discovery up to just one individual alone.

What are an opportunity's essential elements? For an opportunity to be complete it has to have four elements:

1. A need.
2. A value that holds some rank in the hierarchy of what is important to customers. (It's important to know where it ranks.)
3. A way to satisfy that need.
4. way to produce and deliver the satisfaction at a profit.

Any potential entrepreneurial opportunity is incomplete unless and until all four elements are present.

Figure 6. Elements of a Complete Opportunity

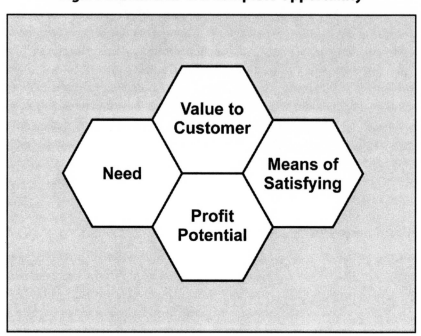

Too many innovation efforts have squandered countless hours of dedicated effort and precious resources only to discover that one or more of the four basic elements was missing. Often the profit potential just isn't there. Sometimes there is no real need. Very few use the product. Or there is no good way of satisfying the need. Cost is prohibitive.

Knowing whether an opportunity is *complete* or not takes a lot of work. Impatient sponsors, under pressure from Wall Street to show progress, often get too far down the road without actually having a complete opportunity. Thomas Edison himself had promised investors a working commercial prototype of the light bulb well before finding the filament material that would make it last long enough for commercial viability. Impatience drives development cycles to begin before the diagnosis is complete. Failed or abandoned innovation efforts are often caused as much from incomplete as from unvalidated opportunities. This ends up wasting a lot of time and resources. Better results are consistently realized when diagnostic conviction is reached *before* leaving the "front end" of the innovating process.[67]

What makes for a *compelling* opportunity is a bit more elusive but no less essential. Opportunities are all about timing and conditions. That's why the expression "window of opportunity" works so well. The "window" can be open or closed. The "ripeness" of an opportunity depends on the conditions affecting these variables. What makes an opportunity compelling has to do with whether the time is right and the conditions are favorable for a needed change (Figure 7). "The overwhelming majority of successful innovations *exploit* change," Drucker wrote. An innovation intended merely to differentiate a company's product from the competition is seldom a compelling opportunity[68] in any sustained fashion.

Figure 7. Context of a Compelling Opportunity

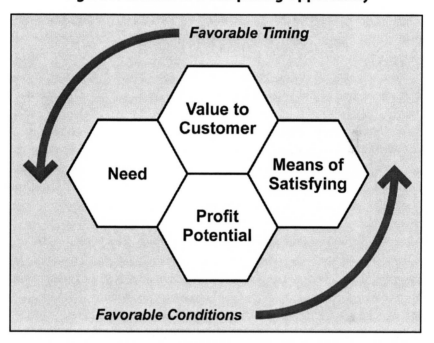

Innovators need to know what to look for and how to recognize what makes an opportunity compelling. Knowing *where* to look is just as key. Assuming that change is constant and happening all around us, how does the innovator know where to look and what to look for there? How does the innovator know what changes are significant and which ones can be ignored?

Years ago, Peter Drucker provided a healthy start on answering this question. He suggested that the origins of most successful innovations are far more mundane and commonplace than we might think. Drucker pointed to seven sources of innovation and even went on to rank them in order of predictability and reliability. Here are the three at the top:

- The first and most reliable source is the **unexpected,** whether a success or failure.

- The second most reliable source he called the **incongruity**—a difference between the way things are and the way things should be.

- Third on his list is what he called a **process need.** Customers have jobs to do and steps by which they accomplish those jobs. Needs arise within the context of the steps.[69]

Another source worth mentioning on Drucker's list are changes in industry or market structure, particularly those that catch everyone off-guard.

What is worth noting about Drucker's top three on his list, are how immediate, present, available, and accessible these sources of innovation are. The list is not about some clever counter-intuitive analysis. Nor do these sources require some super-creative brain. Instead, these sources of innovation are right under our noses, offering up signals and symptoms that present themselves to those who are observant, who stop, look, and ask why. Imagine what entrepreneurial opportunities will present themselves to meet urgent and compelling individual and social needs from climate change, rising costs of energy, relentless advances in the choreography of electrons, photons, DNA and all other forms of matter? The list goes on.

So why doesn't everyone see the potential? What's missing? No information is lacking. It's all there. Yet most don't see an opportunity. Instead they see what appears to be mundane and common. They lack awe and wonder for what might be.

One of my early experiences observing the awe and wonder of an innovator happened some twenty-five years ago. Back then anyone who was even remotely associated with Kimberly-Clark's facial tissue research and development was aware of an anomaly. The quirk had been left uninvestigated for years. What no one could explain was why. The quirk was this: when consumers looked at an unidentified sheet of facial tissue made by a Kleenex® machine and compared it to an unidentified sheet made by a Procter & Gamble (Puffs® brand) machine, they would usually say that the Kleenex® sheet *looked* softer. But when the same samples were *touched* by the same blindfolded consumers, they would usually say Puffs® was softer.

If you're in the facial tissue business, softness is a big deal. It's the number one product attribute. Yet for years, no one took the time to investigate the cause of this curiosity. The demands of other projects kept their focus elsewhere. They were curious but had more important things to worry about.

Finally, one Kimberly-Clark researcher couldn't let this anomaly go. It became her burning-but-unconsumed bush. She convinced her sponsor to give her a modest amount of time and money to figure out what was going on. Her investigation wasn't expensive. Nor did it take much time. But it resulted in a technical breakthrough that changed how facial tissue is made and measured at Kimberly-Clark.

Specifically, the results of this project changed the way technical measurements were made on the base sheet, and in making these measurement changes, the company found it much easier to impregnate lotion into a tissue, something Kimberly-Clark had been wanting and trying to do for some time.

The prophet Isaiah in about 700 BC wrote about this common tendency to neglect the wonder in the mundane.

> You shall indeed hear but never understand,
> And you shall indeed see but never perceive.
> For this people's heart has grown fat,
> And their ears are heavy of hearing,
> And their eyes have closed.
>
> —Isaiah 6.9-10

An abundance of information comes at us every day. We seem to hear, but not understand. We see, but do not perceive. Can we get better at seeing those compelling opportunities for innovating? Or have our hearts grown fat?

Several years ago, I conducted a modest experiment with a colleague at Hewlett-Packard. I asked several long-time engineers to think back over the last six to eighteen months to see if they could remember any circumstances that had piqued their wonder. I was interested in anything unexpected, surprising, curious, or unexplained they had noticed that, if given the time, they would want to explore. Each engineer had little trouble coming up with at least two or three. Few of these were pursued, given the other demands and priorities of the company. Imagine the potential, just under the surface, in the heads and hearts of innovators who are preoccupied with what may be more immediate but perhaps not as compelling.

Compelling opportunities are sitting there, waiting for us to discover them. What's missing? All it takes, at least initially, is a little time for awe and wonder to carry us through to the next step.

ℰ∩

Recent Example

Greg Blythe, Senior Technologist, Hewlett-Packard Imaging & Printing

"Why would anyone want something other than the hyper growth of the business he or she is lucky enough to be a part of?"

This was the question Greg Blythe asked himself in 2003. Greg, now a Senior Technologist at Hewlett-Packard (HP), was then one of a multitude of ink-jet printing engineers and scientists in Corvallis, Oregon, tending the flock of product and process improvement efforts in support of HP's main profit engine at the time. Earlier in that decade, Greg began to notice the speed and quality gains of ink-jet printing performance begin to level off.

Greg mused in reflection about that time when I ask him: "It wasn't obvious how I could uniquely add value to the printing leviathan I had a hand in bridling." Asked to participate in a market discovery effort, Greg found himself attracted—even he might have said at the time "distracted"—by the possibilities of shepherding a few competencies from the herd grazing in the pastures of printing applications to other greener pastures. The discovery effort explored patterns of human life and daily ritual that had little, if anything, to do with printing. This stirred his and others' hearts and minds, but the growth demands of the leviathan pulled him back into the mainstream business, printing. Tend the sheep. However, as Greg put it, "There remained a latent desire to pursue the seed kernels of that earlier market discovery work."

A year or so after that discovery effort, Greg found himself pursued by a possibility—embers of a smoldering bush? The amount of digital content was exploding, "riding the sidecar of skyrocketing Internet adoption." This explosion lit a flame, a question: "How can I manipulate my digital belongings—for example my pictures held by electrons—like I already manipulate my physical belongings?

Aware of the growing photo-printing business and the emerging entertainment business, Greg finally turned aside to look. Not sure why he was so drawn to the question or how it might be answered, Greg began looking for the "why." Scavenging the technology he might need to create a rough prototype—at least a version that would invite people to act in ways natural and familiar, without instructions—he took a business projector mounted on a rack and pointed it down at a small interactive whiteboard placed horizontally on the frame of a coffee table he took from his house (with his wife's consent, of course). "OK. So, now what? I've created a silly computer lying face up."

Jon, a college student intern, was working in a testing laboratory near where Greg had set up the prototype (of what he wasn't sure), and asked, "What are you doing?" Greg explained what he was thinking as they both sat down at the glowing "coffee table" and played with the prototype. Immediately they both saw something that neither could explain—a flat, finger-friendly "fire." The glow of the projected and reflected image on the coffee-table-whiteboard attracted not only their attention but the attention and interest of others. Pretty soon other HPers were gathering around, like campers gazing transfixed into the campfire.

Over the next couple of weeks, the novelty and possibility of this burning but unconsumed bush became the hallway scuttlebutt. Others at HP began to hear something calling to them as well, and some became as passionate and engaged as Greg, if not more passionate. Another prototype, and then another, and another emerged. More people experienced firsthand the allure of what was then dubbed "Misto." Was it the glow of information upward, the new, more natural way of interacting with pictures, maps, and even games? Or was it what Misto catalyzed between the people who gathered around it? Greg and others at HP knew there was something new here. Their interactions with the photographs and other information and with others around the coffee table took on a new dimension. Some called it "social" computing to distinguish it from "personal" computing, but that didn't quite capture all that was going on. A "solution" was definitely presenting itself and attracting many, including internal business sponsors. But the need was not yet articulated.

At about this time, what did become apparent was that Mitsubishi, Philips, Microsoft, and Samsung had apparently seen a similar bush. (Unlike Moses, it's rare that only one hears the call.) Competitive juices were flowing, accelerating the search for applications. HP decided to shift the project over to the HP-Labs (out of Greg's hands) and to show Misto at CES (the annual consumer electronics trade show) in 2006, in part to discover where the needs might surface. One came from Ford's dealer network. Representatives from Ford had seen HP's prototype at CES and expressed an interest. Ford wanted to put information between the customer and the salesman rather than having the salesman between the information and the customer. Potential commercial applications started to surface. Casino-gaming applications seemed self-evident.

But the software challenge was significant. Instead of one person interacting with the screen, the coffee table format invited many people to interact simultaneously, each facing the screen from a different angle. A year later, Microsoft introduced what it dubbed "surface computing" using infra-red sensors to capture what was placed on the surface. At the 2011 Consumer Electronics Show (CES), Samsung, in partnership with Microsoft, announced that surface computing devices, enabled by a technology called "PixelSense," would be available by the end of the year for commercial applications.

HP is keeping quiet about its interests, for now. It will likely be some time before consumer applications are cheap enough and software applications plentiful enough for this kind of social surface computing to enter the mainstream. The need is still being discovered, and more will be revealed.

But it all started from an initial sense of awe and wonder of a few "faithful" technologists, like Greg, in Corvallis, Oregon, and spread to many. It's still spreading.

Ⅎ

Awe

Awe is something all of us have experienced. Get away from the lights of the city and gaze up at the stars on a cloudless, moonless night. Witness the birth of a child. Peer into the delicate symmetry of a daisy. Gaze at the intricacies of a spider web, the grace of a fern, the crystalline structure of a snowflake.

Awe is universal. It does not take a degree from Stanford or Carnegie Mellon to enable awe. However, in matters of observation, the chance of spotting something new and significant—a proverbial bush burning without being consumed—favors the prepared mind.

When experts see something unexpected in their field and experience a sense of wonder, what they know with certainty is now in question. The prepared mind must be open to the new and willing to consider changes in the well-formed and often reinforced mental maps with which the mind navigates the domain. "Domain" itself derives from the Latin word *dominus*, meaning "lord" or "master." Experts, by definition, achieve mastery or "dominion" over their subject matter. So when experts discover something that doesn't match what they already know, they can either discount it as unimportant or try to figure out exactly what is causing the anomaly. Contempt is often associated with the discount, awe and wonder with the attempt to investigate what's going on.

Awe is an interesting combination of both faith and fear. The word *awe* comes from the Old English *ege*, which translates simply as "fear." The Oxford English Dictionary is quick to add "reverential fear" to qualify it. Awe enables us to turn aside and look instead of turn away and run. When we experience awe, there is a paradoxical mix of fear, reverence, and gratitude. The fear embedded in our first impression may simply be the fear of the unknown. We become aware that there is something we don't understand and realize that we may not have the control or mastery we thought we had. We feel a little bit smaller, just a little bit less powerful. It is the mirror reflection of what political scientist Karl Deutsch meant when he said: "Power is the ability not to have to learn anything."[70] When power is diminished, however, the invitation to learn arrives. But those in positions of power are not always able to respond. They're too caught up with self-image, with their power and mastery. They can't turn aside and see the "bush that is burning but not consumed." They miss the awe and wonder of the unexpected, the unusual, and they block the opportunity to learn something new.

Psychologist Edgar Schein made the following observation about learning: "Anxiety inhibits learning, but anxiety is also necessary if learning is going to happen at all. To understand this, we're going to have to speak about something managers don't like to discuss—the anxiety involved in motivating people to 'unlearn' what they know and learn something new."[71]

If necessity is the mother of invention, then survival is the father of learning.

Awe is the experience of being impressed.

Wonder

Like awe, wonder is not simply an emotion. It is also a process involving perception and cognition. In short, it is a pattern of faith. René Descartes described wonder as the first of all the passions. "When the first encounter with some object surprises us, and we judge it to be new, or very different from what we knew in the past or what we supposed it was going to be, this makes us wonder and be astonished at it. And since this can happen before we know in the least whether this object is suitable to us or not, it seems to me that wonder is the first of all passions. It has no opposite, because if the object present has nothing in it that surprises us, we are not in the least moved by it and regard it without passion."[72]

Centuries later, Albert Einstein chimed in, saying, "The most beautiful thing we can experience is the mysterious. It is the source of all true art and all science. He to whom this emotion is a stranger, who can no longer pause to wonder and stand rapt in awe, is as good as dead; his eyes are closed."[73]

Wonder can also be understood by its opposite—a closed mind. The temptation to closed-mindedness is particularly strong for experts whose mental models often create impenetrable barriers to recognizing and accepting realities that "don't fit." Experts do this consciously and unconsciously in the ways in which they prejudge signals coming at them from outside. In more extreme forms, this closed-mindedness builds fear-laden walls of contempt, bigotry, and parochialism to keep out realities that don't fit the mental model of the way things are, or at least, seem to be. No investigation is done. This leads to a dangerous isolation that in turn cuts the expert off from the very source through which innovations arise—those symptoms and manifestations presenting themselves as unusual, unexpected.

Closed-mindedness is born out of fear. Awe and wonder are experienced out of faith.

Robert Fuller, in his treatment of wonder, points to the work of psychologist Ernest Schactel. He focused on how what motivates us affects our perceptions of the world. Schactel suggested that our ordinary mode of perception is "autocentric." When we are so motivated, we are pre-set to assess objects and other people in our environment by their usefulness to us. In other words, that to which we attend is determined in part by the running-in-the-background questions: "Is this _____ (object, person, occurrence, etc.) good or bad for me? Does it have some usefulness to me?"

Schactel also points out, however, that we are all capable of what he called "allocentric" perception—an other-centered rather than self-centered orientation to the world. In this mode, what and who we give our attention to is not motivated by our own self-interests. Instead, it is moved to attend to "the fullness of the object rather than merely its need-meeting qualities." This kind of attention is characterized by "an inexhaustible and ineffable quality, by the profoundest interest in the object, and by the enriching, refreshing, vitalizing effect which the act of perception has on the perceiver." [74] Moses turned aside to see the bush. In doing so, his life and the lives of many others changed.

Though neuroscience is formulating hypotheses as much as it is producing answers, neuroscientists are finding experience, emotion, and cognition operationally difficult, if not impossible, to separate. According to Fuller, what fascinates neuroscientists about the experience of wonder is its "widespread and powerfully stimulating effects on the associative cortex (the frontal lobe of the brain)." Wonder appears to extend the "functional range of those intervening mental processes compelled in the creation of new, more expansive categories and new, more subtly integrated modes of understanding." [75]

Awe and wonder are often described in the reflections of scientists and researchers who have given so much of their waking lives over to the challenges of discovery—whether those discoveries are in the domain of chemistry, electrons, energy fields, or human behavior and motivation. Innovators can learn much from their reflections on their own experience of awe and wonder. Albert Einstein was one of the more prolific of these. The *New York Times* described Einstein at the time of his death as "The most thoughtful wonderer who appeared among us in three centuries." [76] Often asked to what he would attribute his mental accomplishments, Einstein said, near the end of his life, "I have no special talents. I am only passionately curious." [77] Walter Isaacson, in his biography of Einstein, wrote, "Curiosity, in Einstein's case, came not just from a desire to question the mysterious. More important, it came from a childlike sense of marvel that propelled him to question the familiar, those concepts that, as he once said, 'the ordinary adult never bothers his head about.'" [78] Einstein knew where and how to turn aside and look.

After reading Isaacson's biography of Einstein, it is difficult to miss the robust and almost continuous contributions that came through Einstein. Many of his insights were born out of intimate conversations within a vibrant, dynamic, and diverse network of very engaged scientists. While the myth of the lone hero's journey is very powerful, if we look more closely, there always seemed to be others who play supporting but essential roles. Relationships play a role in awe and wonder as well.

During the last two decades of his life, Einstein almost daily walked from his home on Mercer Street in Princeton, New Jersey, to the Institute for Advanced Study. The last decade, he picked up a walking companion, Kurt Godel. "The man may not have been recognized by many townspeople," Isaacson wrote, "but Einstein addressed him as a peer, someone who, like him, had launched a conceptual revolution. If Einstein had upended our everyday notions about the physical worlds with his theory of relativity, the younger man, Kurt Godel, had had a similarly subversive effect on our understanding of the abstract world of mathematics."[79] In fact, Einstein told people that he went to his office "just to have the privilege of walking home with Kurt Godel."

Before these two shared their walks in the little town of Princeton, Godel had struck a blow to our preconceived attributions of mathematics as being a closed, complete and consistent, if not completely logical, system. Godel's incompleteness theorems—that no logical system can capture all the truths of mathematics, and that no logical system for mathematics could, by its own devices, be shown to be free from inconsistency—have had an effect on the foundations of mathematics similar to the effect Einstein's relativity theory has had on our assumptions about the physical world. As Jim Holt put it, "Both Godel and Einstein insisted that the world is independent of our minds, yet rationally organized and open to human understanding. United by a shared sense of intellectual isolation, they found solace in their companionship."[80] They were united by a shared sense of awe and wonder.

That sense of awe and wonder enables innovators to follow and use the pattern Moses followed with the burning bush—turning aside, looking for the underlying cause, and hearing a calling in the need that reveals itself.

How awe and wonder produce the lift needed in this first stage of innovating deserves a closer look.

Inertia

The very first obstacle innovators encounter is inertia. Subtle and powerful forces of resistance are always at work to keep would-be innovators grounded. This was the case with the facial tissue anomaly in the R&D department at Kimberly-Clark. Most knew of the anomaly (that the softness of their tissue seemed different) but no one for years had the time or took the opportunity to investigate it.

The habits and practices of both customers and the companies that serve them often conspire to create an invisible but powerful force that resists change. Customers are frequently unaware of their own unmet needs. They're "satisfied" with the products they have. And the companies that sell those products are naturally invested in extending the success they've worked so hard to achieve. There appears to be more to lose than to gain from considering any change. "We've always done it that way" or "We need to stay focused" can be expressed in a variety of ways. All produce an atmosphere of inertia that keeps innovators grounded.

Overcoming inertia is difficult. There is so much that can go wrong when innovating. But when the flow of change becomes undeniable, "going with the flow" is more prudent than fighting it. The very momentum of the change the innovator intends to exploit can overcome inertia, so long as the innovator is going in the same direction of the change, not against it. The more compelling the opportunity, the easier it will be for the innovator to overcome hurdles.

Just as a pilot must calculate the air pressure before the plane can take off, innovators must read the resistance surrounding them before they launch their innovating efforts. The types and degrees of resistance can come from the mental and behavioral habits of customers, the orientation of the host company, and even from the innovator's own mindset. All three are often involved at the same time.

Customer inertia resides in habits and practices. Customers—whether a business buying services or a consumer purchasing products—have jobs they need to do. Products and services with value help customers do these jobs. In the "doing of the jobs," customers are often unaware that they even have an unmet need. As Fred Hrubecky, a sage product developer whose inventions were essential to the disposable diaper business at Kimberly-Clark, used to say, "We are all coping animals. We won't even know we have a problem unless and until we come to believe there is a better alternative to what we are doing. If and when we come to believe it, then we start complaining."

This is one of the many dilemmas innovators face. When the customer is a business, that business may be too busy attending to its own customers' needs to think differently about its own needs. If the customers are consumers, they may be so habituated with what they have available, they never give much thought to the possibility of an alternative. Customer inertia stems partly from "we have always done it this way" and partly from the often unconscious belief that there is no better alternative.

Company inertia resides in the established and success-reinforced mindsets, performance measurements, incentives, and proven production practices—sometimes years in the making. This atmosphere of inertia is reflected in the vocabulary of focus. It is saturated with operational language dominant in the speech patterns of the executives who steward the company's resources.

Focus and execution typically dominate the concerns of these executives. For example, a linguistic symptom of company inertia is the notion of *core* which has insinuated itself into the speech, thinking, and writing about innovation management for the past several years. Starting with the *Harvard Business Review* article on core competencies[81] twenty years ago, the word "core" has spread like a virus to core customers, core business, core capabilities, core technologies, etc. This notion of core leads too many of us to assume that less risky innovations can come from "adjacencies" (meaning close to the core and therefore less risky). Never mind whether these adjacent innovations are compelling or not, or whether they are more successful or profitable. These adjacent innovations might make some companies feel safer in their innovating efforts. To be fair, it does make sense to stick closer to a company's core competencies, whether in the marketing or technology realms, or both. But if "adjacent" becomes the primary limit to empathy and imagination, larger more compelling opportunities can go to the competitor.

Company inertia can be so strong that despite good intentions and considerable investments, innovation efforts never really get off the ground. Company inertia can easily cloud the perceptions current at any time in an organization, distorting the organization's formal and informal sensing mechanisms. Short runways of impatience for results won't allow for sufficient velocity to overcome the "inertial mass" of the company's previous success. Success is the enemy of innovation.

Innovator inertia may be the most subtle and powerful form of resistance. This inertia comes from innovators' own mindsets. These mindsets are derived from finely tuned mental models, baptized by years of experience within relevant domains. Innovators are often experts. As experts, their self-image and professional identity are tied up with what they know from what they have experienced. As with most, if not all, self-professed or socially acknowledged experts, well-worn neurological pathways have become embedded in their brains and thinking patterns. The clinical phrase is "long-term potentiation." These pathways—especially those reinforced by repeated experience—constitute what is known about the subject matter. When some anomaly, unexpected success, or failure surfaces during the course of observations, it is the expert who is in the best position to take notice of it first. But often it is the expert who turns out to be the one to dismiss it as a false positive.

The unlearning that authentic discovery forces upon the expert is understandably resisted. Experts have much of themselves invested in the prevailing "paradigm." What they know can block them from discovering what they don't know, especially when what they don't know is contrary to what they think we already know. Or as Mark Twain once quipped, "It ain't what you don't know that hurts you so much. It's what you know for sure that just ain't so."

This is why awe and wonder are so critical in leading innovators to the lift that accompanies the discovery of a compelling opportunity. Is it the discovery of a compelling opportunity that produces the lift? Or is it the lift that produces the discovery? Whichever answer is chosen, the key to unlock the door of discovery is the awe and wonder that enable the innovator to turn aside and look to see whether the anomaly just might be a burning bush.

In short, resistance to innovation shows up in many forms and from a variety of sources. Unseen resistance is as assured in the atmosphere of innovating as gravity is in the physical atmosphere.

Thrust (innovators' motivation)

Inertia is a given in the physical world. It is also a given and in the process of innovating. Though most of us associate inertia with a stationary state, Newton's first law of motion actually describes inertia as "an object in motion will stay in motion and an object at rest will stay at rest, unless acted upon by an external force." In the world of innovating, that last part is the key: "unless acted upon by an external force:" an external force to get their efforts off the ground.

One of the most potent "external forces" resides within the opportunity itself. This power is similar to a parent's motivation: their child. The child is a powerful "external force" that motivates personal sacrifices from parents. In principle, healthy parents will sacrifice for their child because of the love they feel. In practice, parental sacrifices arise from the immediate and specific needs observed. In the same way, innovators find their initial motivation in the opportunity itself. Similarly, a potent "external force" for lift often arises from an empathetic understanding of customer needs. Add a bit of paranoia that competitors may be looking at a similar "burning bush," and urgency to get going springs forth. Awe and wonder give innovators access to that understanding.

An example of this combination happened when Gary Erickson and Doug Gilmour got together in the early-1990s. Both men were competitive cyclists working for Avocet, a bicycle parts designer and manufacturer. While Gary was the one who felt the need for a better-tasting energy bar to eat during his endurance rides, both Gary and Doug saw the chance to preempt PowerBar™ with a better product—better tasting and better for you, especially for the endurance rider. Implied was that if the energy is easier to digest and in the proper amounts, the rider will have more of it to burn. They both realized that restoring energy on a long bike ride didn't have to be a tasteless experience, as it was then, and they believed they could bring taste to this otherwise tasteless category. Out of this empathetic understanding for endurance bicyclists, along with their own competitive instincts, Clif Bar® was created. It has been gaining market share ever since.

The trick Erickson and Gilmour were able to pull off with Clif Bar® (and subsequently with other products) was to not allow their competitiveness to override their empathetic feel for the customer need. So often when innovators are looking to discover a compelling opportunity, competitiveness can warp the diagnostic perception of whether there is a compelling opportunity there or not.

What's going on inside you can and does affect how you see what is going on around you. The truth of this saying should cause innovators to be circumspect about what drives them to innovate in the first place. Too often the need to be different distorts the perception of whether an opportunity is compelling or not. "Now I see as in a mirror dimly," the apostle Paul wrote, reminding us just how difficult it is to get out of our own way. A compelling opportunity can generate enough external force to get the effort off the ground. The need to be different alone seldom does, despite the fact that it is tried often.

Companies are often blind to customers' unmet needs because of an excessive focus on their products and their success. This blindness prevents them from seeing clearly what the need is and how important it actually is to the customer. A classic example of this was the Haloid Corporation (predecessor to Xerox). Haloid was out looking for investors in their new carbonless photocopying technology. Quite naturally, they approached some of the paper-manufacturing companies. One of those companies was embroiled at the time in an internal debate over how much to spend on a new carbon paper machine. Ironically, they had no ears to hear or eyes to see the opportunity being presented to them—an opportunity that eventually led to the obsolescence of carbon paper and the irrelevance of their internal debate.

Success and failure, particularly when they come as a surprise, can point innovators to the next compelling opportunity. But often success is met with pride and celebration alone. Emotional relief or quickness to take credit often trump an objective curiosity about the underlying causes. Likewise, failure is often met with avoidance rather than a sincere inquiry. Both successes and failures need to be examined carefully and thoroughly. Both can teach innovators much.

Hewlett-Packard had a mantra in its early days of "inventing for the next bench." Inventing for the next bench meant one engineering group observing and discovering an opportunity for innovation in the unsolved problems of another, adjacent engineering group. Many of these solutions turned into profitable businesses and proved to be a major engine for the company's early growth. This continued into the 1980s when Hewlett-Packard was actually more than two hundred different businesses. What was observed was applied. And what was applied that worked was learned. And the observations and learning didn't stop.

Hindsight is 20-20. Even the big innovation successes are more likely to have started from more humble and prosaic beginnings. In paying attention to what others often overlook. awe and wonder pay handsomely. Scanning the immediate surroundings is a common practice. If and when something is spotted that seems even slightly out of the ordinary, there is a tendency to quickly assess whether it is a threat or not, whether it is relevant or not. When the challenge is to discover something new, however, this quickness to evaluate can be the very thing that prevents us from discovering what's there underneath. Ezra Pound once said, "Glance is the enemy of wisdom." Awe and wonder suspend glance and provide time for an appreciative inquiry. Through that inquiry innovators can find not only the compelling character of an opportunity—if it is there to be found. They can also find the "external force" strong enough to produce the lift needed to get the innovating effort off the ground.

The other element necessary for the innovator to gain lift is the innovator's orientation to the future.

Angle of Attack

Getting an innovating effort launched before the sponsor runs out of patience and curtails the innovator's freedom is essential. Many a would-be innovator never makes it. They fail to recognize the difference between expectations and fundamentals.

Veteran investors in the stock market—especially value investors who follow Benjamin Graham and Warren Buffet—make the distinction between what they refer to as the "fundamentals" and "expectations." For an investor, expectations are reflected in the stock's current price. Fundamentals are understood only after a thorough analysis of the company's profitability. Opportunities to *in*vest occur when the fundamentals of a company exceed the expectations reflected in the stock price. Opportunities to *di*vest occur when the expectations carried in the company's stock price exceed the company's fundamentals.

The difference between fundamentals and expectations is relevant to innovators. This is especially pertinent in early stages of innovating where fundamentals are scarce and expectations are plentiful. Innovators may have a target in mind where they expect to find complete and compelling opportunities, but they shouldn't confuse the target with the opportunity itself. Unfortunately this happens all too often. The fundamentals of the opportunity—a need, the means of satisfying it, a relatively attractive value to the end-user, and the potential for a profit margin—must be grounded in whatever evidence can be observed.

This confusion of fundamentals with expectations happens when projections are made and values assigned *before* there is sufficient evidence to do either. The ease with which spreadsheets make it possible to do multiple "what if's" adds fuel to the fires of innovation assumptions translated into financial projections. Financial *pro formas* stand in for innovating foresight. Investments are made based on the internally generated numbers rather than externally observed evidence.

Numbers are "derivatives" of reality, and often mistaken for the reality those numbers are intended to represent. Expectations get easily mistaken for fundamentals. In one instance, a large consumer durables company even went so far as to make estimates to shareholders on the likely returns expected from innovations in their pipeline—before they were introduced. The estimates were all based on Net Present Value (NPV) analysis, as if to suggest NPV made the numbers more believable. After a couple of years of this, they became painfully aware of the error they were making, but not until they had misspent millions, believing the expectations were fundamentals. The company executives now are turning their attention to getting the "fundamentals" as clear as they can. As is often said, be careful of expectations—they can prove to be simply resentments under construction.

Innovators should *anticipate* the future, but they must *act* in and for the present. Opportunities, particularly compelling ones, are based as much on what is perceived as what can be conceived. This is one reason why awe and wonder are so useful to the innovator at this stage.

Non-innovators often view change as something going on "out there" and "in the future." The unspoken perception is that change is not "in here" or "right now." The implication is that there is time to think (or worry) about it. This is where fear (future evidence appearing real) often finds easy entrance.

Innovators, on the other hand, assume change is happening all the time. They question what changes are going on now that they can observe. Where is the change manifesting itself and what needs are revealing themselves in those manifestations? How is it showing itself? Current manifestations point innovators not only to what the future may be, but also what can be done in the present, now.

A good example of this alertness to the present tense was the speed with which Royal Dutch Shell responded to the oil crisis in the early '70s. Shell responded more quickly and deliberately than any of its rivals, thanks to a small but effective group of internal "prophets"—the scenario planning group. This group had been producing sets of future scenarios to keep senior managers at Shell alert to changes in the competitive landscape. One such scenario envisioned the oil-producing nations forming a cartel. With that scenario in the back of his mind, one of Shell's senior managers ran across an otherwise innocuous news item about a Saudi oil minister visiting his counterpart in Libya. Had the manager seen the news clipping without benefit of the cartel scenario, he might have dismissed it as "noise." But with the scenario in mind, he realized that this was perhaps a "signal," not "noise." It triggered a closer, more in-depth follow-up, which uncovered the beginnings of the cartel. This early awareness gave Shell a head start in its response. The scenario proved useful for recognizing the manifestations of change in the present—perhaps something more immediately useful than merely predicting what might happen in the future.

If there is no action to take now, there is no innovation later. Innovators who understand this typically show greater urgency in diagnosing the present. In their diagnosing, successful innovators typically have a taste for the unexpected. As diagnosticians, innovators treat the unexpected and surprises as telltales that indicate both the presence and the potential of opportunity. And because they are reading the present rather than projecting the future, they know that the hidden opportunity is likely to be a compelling one. In fact, experienced innovators know to look for compelling opportunities they can complete rather than complete opportunities that they can make compelling.

Trends—identifying and tracking them—play a useful role in the discovery phase of innovating. Trend tracking from forecasts, scenarios, inflection points, shifts, tipping points, intersections, and convergences are all useful for understanding the context of where opportunities are likely to surface. But tracking trends is only a first step. It shouldn't be confused with the work of identifying and describing whether there is a complete and compelling opportunity. In fact, this is where sponsoring executives play an essential role with innovators.

Figure 8. Locating Where Compelling Opportunities Are More Likely

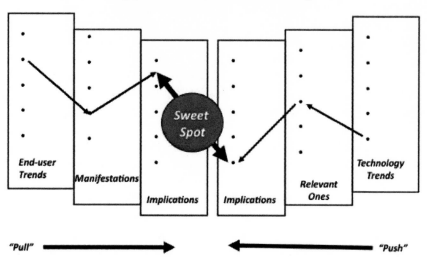

Years ago, Jane Fitzgibbons from the ad agency Ogilvy & Mather gave innovators a navigational compass to help locate target-rich territories. This aid also helps differentiate present circumstances from expectations. Forward thinking chemical engineers at Kimberly-Clark used this to discover what is now a significant and growing adult incontinence market. Kimberly-Clark's Depends® line of incontinent products remains the profitable market share leader. The approach (Figure 8) looks at both the "pull" and the "push" sides of the need discovery equation. On the "pull" side of the equation the need of an opportunity originates from the flows of societal change. On the "push" side of the equation the solution of an opportunity originates from the flows of technological change. Identifying not only societal trends (broadly or narrowly) but also their present manifestations can point the innovator to what is compelling on the need side. Identifying not just technological progress but relevant and present applications can point the innovator to what is ready on the solution side of the equation. With this information, innovators are better able to zero in on the more likely whereabouts of compelling opportunities—"sweet spots"—those with more favorable conditions and timing.

Velocity

Innovators need velocity to get their innovating efforts off the ground. Awe and wonder contribute to that velocity, both in direction and speed.

Innovators get their direction from a need, preferably a compelling one, and from identifying the means of satisfying that need. For Moses the need came first, after turning aside in awe at this "great sight." Then, from his wondering, came understanding of what was needed—relief from oppression. And in the need, he heard a distinct calling that directed the rest of his life.

With the same pattern, though perhaps less dramatically, awe drew the attention and energies of that Kimberly-Clark product developer to the unexplained anomaly between visual and tactile softness in facial tissues. Wonder enabled her to explore the underlying causes on both the consumer side and the fiber manufacturing side. And in her turning aside and looking, she discovered a compelling need that changed the way the company understood how to manipulate cellulose fibers.

Direction becomes clearer and more precise as innovators progress through the innovating process. In the early discovery phase, understanding local and present(ing) manifestations are more important than precisely predicting the final outcome. The first challenge is to get liftoff. Liftoff at this point in the innovating journey is more important than having the direction perfectly aligned with the final destination for the innovation.

Velocity for liftoff is also about speed. When flying a plane, there are three options for getting up enough speed: have a runway, make sure it's long enough, and use "larger" wings. Innovating has a similar set of three options, and awe and wonder can enable and enhance each.

It is surprising how often innovation efforts are initiated without a runway in established companies attempting to innovate. "We just want innovation, not some R&D monument to science, technology, and engineering." Attempting to get an innovation effort off the ground without some kind of runway is naïve. Runways—relatively flat, smooth, unimpeded, and protected spaces wherein momentum can build for liftoff—are as necessary for airplanes as they are for innovating efforts. Neither can take off without them. In the case of innovating, runways are sustained efforts to understanding the operating company's future external ecosystem.

This is where executive sponsors can make a big difference to innovators. Instead of being viewed as simply the "bankers" or "venture capitalists" who hold and distribute the early funding, executive sponsors can actually make a difference in making sure the runway is flat and smooth. To be able to say where and why innovations are needed requires imagination, patience, and empathetic homework to be done by the executive sponsors. By establishing and maintaining the governance, management, and resource infrastructure to sustaining innovating on an ongoing basis, executive sponsors enable both lift-offs and landings. Their contributions may not be on specific innovations themselves, but on the runways from which these efforts lift off and return. Smoothing the way by pointing to the where and the why for an innovation is a powerful tool too seldom used.

Scott Berkun cites a wonderful example of this from the precursor efforts to smart phones[82]—when we called them PDAs (personal digital assistants). Jeff Hawkins, a cofounder of Palm (now a part of Hewlett-Packard), concluded that many companies were chasing after the same need, and all the companies knew about as much as their competitors did. But it was the way Hawkins defined the challenge that made a big difference. For the Palm Pilot—arguably the first successful PDA—the runway of where and why and what was needed was this:

- Fits in a shirt pocket.
- Syncs seamlessly with a PC.
- Fast, and easy to use.
- Costs no more than $299.

Those four specifications turned out to make all the difference for the Pilot's designers and developers.

Yet even if there is a smooth runway in the form solid direction, often the runway is just too short, or gets shortened by external circumstances or internally driven budget cuts. Local conditions at the time of take-off are often considerably less than ideal. Atmospheric pressures, in effect, shorten the runway. The innovation effort will simply fail if the innovator is not allowed some time (and space) for turning aside to look and investigate the why of the need. Taking off in deteriorating conditions has become the norm for imany nnovators laboring in established companies. Deadlines get shortened. Funding gets cut. Competitors introduce something that looks better. Some new piece of information changes the perception of risk for the executive sponsor, or even of the perceived value for the end-user. Experienced innovators use awe and wonder to spread their wings for these "shortened" runways. Awe and wonder expand both creative and perceptive capability, if not capacity.

Any number of factors can keep innovators grounded at the gate or stuck on the taxiway. But if it is the discovery of a compelling need that gets innovators off the ground, then inventing a solution is what yields the altitude sufficient to keep innovators innovating. At times, the awe and wonder of innovators leads right to inspiration and appreciation—essentials for inventing needed solutions.

Chapter 6

Inspiration and Appreciation

Invention is born out of a need. Discovering a need, however, does not necessarily lead to invention, much less an innovation. What's required is finding a solution to that need. And that's where inspiration and appreciation go to work for the innovator. Inventive solutions emerge when a discovered need and a vision of what is possible come together with the material and means to make it happen.

Logic might seduce us into thinking that inventing a solution comes after discovering the need. Experience teaches us otherwise. Inventing seldom waits until discovery is finished. In practice, discovering a need and inventing a solution go hand-in-hand.

Taking a closer look at the inventing part of innovation reveals a pattern of faith that innovators use which also dispels some common misconceptions and confusion about invention itself, and the role it plays in innovation.

Many deficiencies can plague and even disable efforts to invent. Discovery efforts can end with opportunities that are neither complete nor compelling. Inventing efforts can end with solutions that are technically feasible but not commercially viable.

Both discovery and invention are essential elements in any innovation; both are necessary for innovators to understand; both require effort, skill and direct engagement from innovators; and both are the central challenges of what many call the "front end" of innovating. Each, however, is different from the other. Discovery of an opportunity focuses on the need. Invention focuses on the solution.

Figure 9: Twin Centers of Discovery and Invention

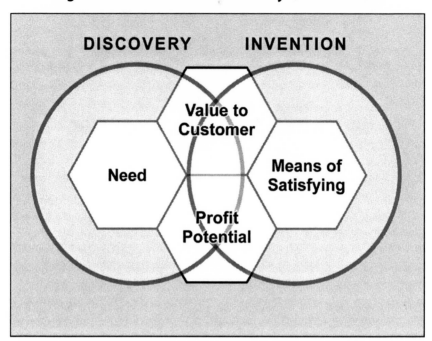

"Necessity is the mother of invention"[83] captures the experience of many inventors who find themselves in the spot where need intersects with urgency. "Genius is one percent inspiration and 99 percent perspiration" comes from Edison's experience as a lifelong inventor and innovator[84]. The wisdom is not reserved for Edison alone. Edison recognized that success for inventors requires long hours of hard work—the 99 percent perspiration—that follow the one percent inspiration gained from a sudden insight. But both sayings can be a bit deceptive.

Inventive solutions are not reserved exclusively to those in urgent need of a solution. Already successful companies house many prolific inventors. In some circles, it has become fashionable to accuse incumbent companies of sitting back and hording the profits from their current products while doing little, if anything to improve the future.

The resilience and track record of many incumbents, however, says something entirely different. Such adaptive capability, albeit at times slow, testifies to the ongoing inventive capability of these Goliaths. One stellar example of this is Intel, a company that, despite heavy capital investments in fabrication and design advances, has radically reshaped itself several times in "paranoid" alertness to changes in its business ecology.[85]

While perspiration occupies more time in the inventor's day than inspiration, this does not mean that inspiration always precedes the perspiration of hard work. Sometimes the inspiration suddenly appears, mixed in the broth of hard work, and catalyzes the work into something transformed with more purpose, more meaning, and more value.

So what is inspiration? Where does it come from? What role does it play in converting a need into an inventive solution? And what part does an innovator's appreciation play in recognizing this thing called inspiration?

Looking at one of Ezekiel's visions gives us a clear view of how inspiration and appreciation work. Whether the Old Testament prophet Ezekiel actually saw what he described or experienced it all in a dream, makes little difference. The graphic details are what remain so instructive to inventors.

His vision is not only a remarkable description of how inspiration and appreciation enable invention. It also reveals a pattern of faith familiar to serial inventors. To see this pattern, it helps to divide Ezekiel's vision (Ezekiel 37.1-10) into three parts. In the first part, God sets Ezekiel down in a valley full of dry bones and asks him, "Mortal, can these bones live?" to which Ezekiel responds uninspiringly, "I don't know." In the second part, God instructs the prophet to prophesy to the *bones*. God even tells him what to say to the bones. Ezekiel follows the instructions and observes the results. Then in the third part, God instructs the prophet to prophesy again, but this time not to the bones but to the *air*. Ezekiel follows these instructions as well and observes the results. Notice how the question that God asks in the first part—"can these bones live?"—gets answered progressively in the next two.

Here's Ezekiel's vision:

> The hand of the Lord came upon me, and he brought me out by the spirit of the Lord and set me down in the middle of a valley; it was full of bones. He led me all round them; there were very many lying in the valley, and they were very dry. He said to me, 'Mortal, can these bones live?' I answered, 'O Lord God, you know.'
>
> Then he said to me, 'Prophesy to these bones, and say to them: O dry bones, hear the word of the Lord. Thus says the Lord God to these bones: I will cause breath to enter you, and you shall live. I will lay sinews on you, and will cause flesh to come upon you, and cover you with skin, and put

breath in you, and you shall live; and you shall know that I am the Lord.' So I prophesied as I had been commanded; and as I prophesied, suddenly there was a noise, a rattling, and the bones came together, bone to its bone. I looked, and there were sinews on them, and flesh had come upon them, and skin had covered them; but there was no breath in them.

Then he said to me, 'Prophesy to the breath, prophesy, mortal, and say to the breath: Thus says the Lord God: Come from the four winds, O breath, and breathe upon these slain, that they may live.' I prophesied as he commanded me, and the breath came into them, and they lived, and stood on their feet, a vast multitude.[86]

—Ezekiel 37.1-14

There's a lot going on in these ten short verses, particularly when we read them in the context of invention. There are actually three interwoven interactions. One is between God and Ezekiel. The second is between Ezekiel and the bones, and the third is between Ezekiel and the air. The first dialogue, between God and Ezekiel, precedes and instructs the dialogue between Ezekiel and the materials he has to work with.

The pattern of inspiration and appreciation is found both in what Ezekiel is instructed to *say* to the materials and in what he observes before and after. What is so fantastic about this vision is the expectation that the inert materials will listen and respond to what Ezekiel tells them to do. The faith pattern that reveals itself is as much a sequence of mental steps to follow, as it is the set of "materials" Ezekiel is given to work with.

This pattern of inspiration and appreciation consists of four essential elements:

- *Respecting* material and memory.
- *Asking* the inventive question.
- *Making connections* as the system emerges.
- *Breathing* life into the invention.

Let's take a closer look at each one.

Material and Memory

> The hand of the Lord came upon me, and he brought me out
> by the spirit of the Lord and set me down in the middle of a
> valley; it was full of bones. He led me all round them; there
> were very many lying in the valley, and they were very dry.

What an *un*inspiring place. The valley is a desolate, lifeless, forgotten place, full of dry bones—very dry bones. This is not the normative lofty mountaintop where one might go to be inspired. It turns out this is a mass grave, and a very old one. This is the place—in the middle of a multitude of dry bones—chosen for Ezekiel to be both inspired and to inspire others.

Oddly enough, these kinds of situations turn out to be where invention actually begins. We find inventors in a "valley" surrounded by raw materials that are disjointed and disorganized, spread out in a manner quite unlike their original purpose or role. And, like Ezekiel, they notice things. They show respect for the material itself. It's not relegated to the nearest dumpster. Inventors appreciate the substance of what is there, available to them, especially if that material is there in abundance. That abundance in itself becomes important. J. B. Say, a French economist, proposed what became known as Say's Law, stating "supply creates its own demand."[87] Entire industries have evolved from recognition of, and deep appreciation for, the material itself. Sand (silica)—the most prevalent mineral in the earth's crust—is used as the base material for semiconductors.

The material the inventor uses becomes the carrier through which the inventor expresses appreciation, both for the need being addressed and the materials employed in the solution. Some materials work better than others, but an innovator must choose the material not just on the basis of what works best, but also on what is available at a reasonable cost. The more available and accessible a material is, the less it will cost and the lower the final price.

Starting with a look at what's available and finding a use for it, reveals a resourcefulness that is vital for inventing, and for innovating. Some innovators have turned this into a disciplined practice and incorporate it as a regular part of how they invent. Veteran innovator and inventor Dick Sperry who has made a full-time career out of inventing, with over 100 patents in packaging, medical applications and even 3-D printing, uses this practice formally. One of the first things he does early in a project is to create a bill-of-materials (BOM), often as he conceives of his solution. He disciplines himself to pay attention to the cost, fit, and availability of materials the innovation will require. As he builds a working prototype, Sperry's BOM goes through multiple and frequent revisions. Using a BOM early and revising it often make Sperry more efficient and effective in his inventing. The practice actually helps him develop and refine the vision inspiring him.

Deep respect for the physical material is only one way that innovators show appreciation. Innovators must practice an appreciation for the past. Bones are not merely a material. They have a past. They are memory. Just as in matters of observation where "chance favors the prepared mind," so in matters of creativity, inspiration favors an appreciation for what has gone on before. In this respect innovators must be archaeologists and historians as much as futurists. Artifacts from a previous time store memories and knowledge that otherwise might be lost. Innovators must be prepared to do a little digging. As Evan Schwartz, contributing writer to MIT's *Technology Review*, points out, "Invention is highly path-dependent. To understand an inventor's breakthroughs and contributions, you must understand what came before them . . . the knowledge that had to be abandoned as wrong or in the way."[88] Bones. Sometimes very old, very dry ones.

Unfortunately, much of the current dialogue about invention and innovation ignores the bones of what has been thought of or tried in the past, why it was tried, and even why it was tried in that way. Much organizational memory is being lost due to head-count reductions, eliminations of corporate libraries (and librarians), and from frequent job rotations. These losses reflect more managerial neglect and ignorance, perhaps, than intent.

"What's past is prologue," Shakespeare wrote in *The Tempest*. Knowing the past not only helps innovators avoid the waste and gross inefficiencies of reinventing. It is absolutely essential in assessing whether what has been conceived is actually an invention or not. Any true advance stems from an awareness of, and an appreciation for, prior art. Those who aren't aware of the past are doomed to repeat it. Repeating the past could be considered the polar opposite of innovating.

Then, Ezekiel said, "He led me round them." With very few words, Ezekiel evokes the experience of walking in a graveyard—tip-toeing with mindfulness, taking care where to take the next step. Or, perhaps like a professional golfer lining up a put. He walks gingerly on the green, taking mental snapshots from many different angles to fully appreciate the subtleties in the slope of the green, all around an imaginary line. Unlike the golfer who has a clear line of sight to where the hole is, however, Ezekiel is not even sure why he is in this valley. But even without knowing the why, Ezekiel shows great respect for the "material" that surrounds him.

When companies and innovators alike fail to keep and appreciate what they have acquired and learned, often at considerable expense, they risk wasting one of their most potent hidden assets: what experience has taught them. Appreciating prior art makes inventing possible. When companies and innovators fail to recognize this, they lose important knowledge.

The inventive question is not rhetorical

> He said to me, "Mortal, can these bones live?" I answered, "O Lord God, you know."

Ezekiel was careful to answer with a hedge. He didn't say yes. And he didn't say no, despite being surrounded by evidence clearly pointed in that direction. Ezekiel left open the possibility that these bones could live, though he obviously didn't know how. He threw it back to God. "You know (I don't)."

Asking challenging questions and expecting answers, even from themselves, is a characteristic of innovators in general and inventors in particular. Innovators ask and attempt to answer questions for which there are no obvious answers. It's part of what attracts innovators in the first place. The calculation and analysis we all use to find answers, often leads away from inspiration. To understand inspiration, look at the kinds of tough questions innovators ask, both themselves, others and the world around them. They ask these questions in the belief that more will be revealed in the search for answers, even if the question they ask is never fully answered. Ezekiel's version—"can these bones live?"—is the prototype of the "inventive" question.

The genius of an inventive question is that it places the one asking it in the middle of a conflict, dilemma, or paradox, and this is where creative tension can be found. And where there is creative tension, true invention is more likely to occur. Roger Martin refers to this as "integrative thinking." Martin, who is dean at Rotman School of Management at the University of Toronto, provided a brilliant description of the inventive question in a book aptly titled *The Opposable Mind*.[89] "The ability to face constructively the tension of opposing ideas instead of choosing one at the expense of the other. [This ability] generates creative resolutions of the tension in the form of a new idea. The new idea contains elements of the opposing ideas but is superior to each." Although he describes how to open the threshold to inspiration quite well, Martin is ultimately left with a "leap of the mind" to explain the way creative resolutions are actually generated. Did Martin mean leap of faith?

Much of what Martin says resonates with my experience facilitating hundreds of invention workshops. Prior to each workshop, I guide technical clients and business sponsors to carefully craft the proverbial "box," using "opportunity statements." These statements enable workshop participants—the inventors—to think "in and out of the box." I found that the veteran inventors of these workshops draw the borders of the "box" more sharply. Part of the sharpness of the box comes from a clear difference between what's in and what's not, and part comes from clearly understanding the opposing realities in the opportunity itself. With a well-crafted "box"—and you have to have a box—creative tension stimulates and attracts the imagination of inventors. (The work in these workshops has led to thousands of invention disclosures and hundreds of patents.) This creative tension inspires innovators, if you will, and is simply another way of asking, "Can these bones live?"

Ezekiel asks the bones themselves a similar question and expects an answer. "Then [God] said to me, "Prophesy to these bones, and say to them . . ." It's as if the bones can hear the question and respond.

Ezekiel is not only instructed to speak to these inanimate dry remains. He is also told to *prophesy* to them. Prophecy is not synonymous with predicting (page 81). Its intention is to convince the hearers—in this case the bones—to change their way of thinking about themselves. In short, Ezekiel is instructed to not only think differently about the bones but to also tell the bones to think differently about themselves.

When asked to reflect on their experiences, many experienced inventors speak about becoming a part of the very thing they are inventing. They deliberately take another point of view, one that not only gets them out of themselves, but *into* the technical problems that must be solved. This helps them take the perspective of being on the inside looking out. This technique brings a fresh energy and appreciation to the work of inventing. This is what Einstein and others referred to as a thought experiment—extended scenarios that enable the inventor to think through the possible effects, causalities, and consequences of an idea. Looking from the inside out builds deep appreciation, which can itself inspire.

While the inventive question may be phrased in a variety of ways, there is something about the way the question is asked that is worth noting. A commonly used inventive question is "What if?" But "Can these bones *live*?" feels more potent, as if the word *living* means having a purpose, a meaning, a value. Isn't this the lift innovators seek when they discover a compelling need and search for compelling solution to fill that need?

Having respect for the material and asking the inventive question can get innovators closer to inspiration. But there is more to consider in this pattern of faith, which has to do with making connections.

Making connections as the system emerges

> Then he said to me, 'Prophesy to these bones, and say to them: O dry bones, hear the word of the Lord. Thus says the Lord God to these bones: I will cause breath to enter you, and you shall live. I will lay sinews on you, and will cause flesh to come upon you, and cover you with skin, and put breath in you, and you shall live; and you shall know that I am the Lord.' So I prophesied as I had been commanded; and as I prophesied, suddenly there was a noise, a rattling, and the bones came together, bone to its bone. I looked, and there were sinews on them, and flesh had come upon them, and skin had covered them; but there was no breath in them.

Ezekiel receives the instructions, and confirms he has followed the instruction set as commanded. But the result was somewhat disappointing. "There was no breath in them."

This is not an unfamiliar experience for innovators. After putting it all together, something ends up missing. It doesn't quite work as expected. In Ezekiel's case, the bones had come together connected by the sinews or tendons; the flesh had come upon the bones and even skin covered it all. But something was missing. A current example of this is the iPad. There were plenty of tablet computers preceding the iPad. However, as of this writing, competitive alternatives to the iPad don't seem to have the "life" in them that the iPad does.

The heart of creating is the mental and even physical act of making connections—associating two or more formerly unassociated objects. The artist creates something new with strokes of a brush. The photographer superimposes one previously unrelated image on another, and by mere proximity, a novel image is created.

Inventing is a lot like that—you link two or more formerly unrelated objects. The difference for the inventor, however, is that the association must not only be novel, it must also be useful. But that is not all. The inventor has an additional consideration—the system. Inventing must either work within an existing system and its associated "infrastructure" or, in the case of a new-to-the-world system, must be a part of a new system. In the case of a new system, the invention must conform to the purpose or function of the new system—the needs that must be met. Even when inventing a whole new system, inventors are still constrained by the need. As a result, appreciation for the "innards" of the system, its boundaries, and the system's immediate environment is required. Inventors and innovators must think in the context of a system.

This is precisely what the instruction set given to Ezekiel is all about. Ezekiel's vision recognizes the importance of both making connections and seeing the entire system. His vision gives inventors a compass. It suggests not only what connections should be made first but which ones may take priority over others. Bones-to-sinews, then connections to muscles (the flesh), followed by the skin.

What does all this imply about inspiration, appreciation, lift, and innovating? Before inventors can begin to "make connections," they must have a vision of the whole system. This is why so-called mapping, modelling and simulation are so important, even if it comprised of two guys in front of a whiteboard drawing boxes and arrows.

When the U.S. Patent and Trademark Office (USPTO) got started, inventors were required to bring in not only a written description of their invention but also a working model. In part, this reflected an age dominated by mechanical inventions, which has long since been superseded by electronics and computer-aided design (CAD) and simulation. In fact, in those early days, there was a class of employees of inventors who were the model-makers. The patent office no longer requires a working model, but I can't help but feel as though we may have lost something. What might we be missing in our innovating efforts by not including model makers, and the natural dialogue that transpires between inventors and model makers? Besides, neuroscience tells us that physically involving the hands lights up more of the brain. By having electrons and software do the prototype for us, are we losing a form of appreciation and diminishing our access to inspiration?

There is one other aspect of systems that is important to mention for what it contributes to inspiration and appreciation. Feedback. Without feedback, the inventor's appreciation of the system is incomplete. This is precisely what happened to Ezekiel. He follows the instructions to the letter, then watches as "a noise, a rattling, and the bones came together, bone to its bone. I looked, and there were sinews on them, and flesh had come upon them, and skin had covered them." Innovators and inventors should never underestimate the value of direct, firsthand experience and observation.

One of my first experiences of this principle was when I was receiving clinical training as a family therapist. I had been introduced to systems theory of family therapy as a member of a "client" family going through therapy. I was "hooked" on the insight, potency of intervention, and efficiency compared to individual therapy. One of the techniques common for therapists trained in this perspective is to create a small disturbance—often with the youngest and most vulnerable family member—and watch the result. What is revealed is the implicit architecture of the family. Like a hanging mobile, delicately balanced from the ceiling, families and other systems reveal their organization in how they respond to even the slightest external stimulus.

Understanding the system through firsthand interactions lifts the confidence of inventors. In the midst of inventing, an inventor's vision of the system emerges gradually. This is the repeated experience of Dick Sperry. Sperry confesses that while he starts with a vision of the system, this vision is constantly evolving as he watches multiple feedback loops. From this feedback, Sperry gains insight into how the system speaks to itself, to its environment, and to its intended user. He appreciates what he is seeing. This watching inspires him—giving him the confidence to know what to accept, what to change, and what to do next.

Before inventors are able to articulate what they are inventing, they "see" what to them looks beautiful. I've seen it happen in the hundreds of invention workshops I have been privileged to facilitate. You see the change of facial expression and the body language of "inventors-in-heat." They see (and perhaps feel) the innovation in use before they are able to describe it in words.

This brings us to the last element we can glean from Ezekiel's vision that reveals how important inspiration and appreciation are to innovation.

Breathing life into the invention

This time Ezekiel is specifically instructed to prophesy "to the breath." This instruction is directed to the air.

> Then he said to me, "Prophesy to the breath, prophesy, mortal, and say to the breath: Thus says the Lord God: Come from the four winds, O breath, and breathe upon these slain, that they may live." I prophesied as he commanded me, and the breath came into them, and they lived, and stood on their feet, a vast multitude.

Inspiration is thought to be a one-time, isolated, out-of-nowhere kind of event, but instead is really more of an exchange—a repeated and regular interaction with the immediate environment—like breathing. And just as life requires continued breathing, so invention requires this kind of continued exchange.

How inspiration is ongoing exchange more than one-time event is illustrated by the experience of an eleven-year-old boy in eighteenth-century England. This boy just wanted to find out how long it would take spiders to die in sealed glass jars. At the time, most scientists, and eleven-year-old boys, knew spiders and small animals would die if left in a glass jar with the lid on.

The boy was Joseph Priestly, and even after leaving spiders to die in forgotten glass jars, he was still playing around with science projects at the age of thirty-seven. Priestly's early experiments with spiders progressed to plants. He fully expected to see the same thing—plants dying when they ran out of air.[90] To his surprise, the mint plant he encased in a sealed jar refused to die, but he didn't know why.

Here's how Priestly asked his inventive question in *Experiments and Observations on Different Kinds of Air*: "Once any quantity of air has been rendered noxious by animals breathing in it as long as they could, I do not know that any methods have been discovered of rendering it fit for breathing again. It is evident, however, that there must be some provision in nature for this purpose, as well as for that of rendering the air fit for sustaining flame; for without [it] the whole mass of the atmosphere would, in time, become unfit for the purpose of animal life; and yet there is no reason to think that it is, at present, at all less fit for respiration that it has ever been."[91] Priestly—both a minister and a scientist—was becoming aware of a system that involved animals and plants and the exchange of air between them. He eventually played a key role in ecosystem science. Inspiration for Priestly was both discovery *and* invention, both observation *and* inventive question, both watching a system emerge *and* identifying the invisible element in the exchange.

Inspiration is often the result of multiple interactions at multiple levels, seldom a straight-line progression. It is in this sense that innovators are neither the origin nor the final object of inspiration. Rather, they are both inspired and inspiring, a conduit through which an exchange occurs between the immediate environment and the identified need, and from which the invention (and system) emerges. This is where the faith of innovators produces lift for inventing.

That lift sometimes gets lost in the demands of business. Several years ago, the head of engineering at ArvinMeritor—an automotive subsystem manufacturer—had been bitten by the intellectual capital "bug." As a measure of engineering productivity, he expected at least one invention disclosure from every engineer every year. He initiated a program of assigning engineers to a series of invention workshops. These workshops consisted of a group of six or seven engineers specifically selected for their expertise and matched with an invention target. These engineers would be holed up in a room for a couple days and "told" to invent. While the program was well-intentioned, it carried the aura that so many company initiatives carry—involuntary servitude.

At one of these workshops the appointed engineers grudgingly showed up in a windowless conference room at a less-than-top-quality hotel in Troy, Michigan. The whole scene felt a bit depressed, including the group of inventors who had to suffer with me as their facilitator. Perhaps it was the subject matter—deliberately limited to suspensions, torsion bars, and coil springs—that seemed mundane and uninspired. From the preliminary round of introductions, which is always a chance to take the temperature of the group, I could tell this was going to be a tough slog. These engineers had obviously been told to be there. They seemed to be hardened survivors of multiple rounds of corporate "re-engineering."

After a few false starts, I broke from my script and asked the reluctant engineers to tell me about the world of automotive suspension. After all, I didn't know much of anything. Admitting my naïveté seemed to engage the older, more experienced among them. As they began explaining to me the various parts of a typical suspension subsystem, it occurred to me to ask about the history of suspension systems. How have they evolved? This seemed to engage most if not all of them. The energy level in the room started to pick up.

I asked them to collectively create a timeline marking the various eras of suspension technologies that led to where the state of the art is today. They became even more animated, debating among themselves what led to what and when whatever it was had occurred.

Once we had the roughest of timelines drawn out on a couple of paper sheets taped to the wall, I asked them to pretend they were historians writing a history of suspension systems—to look over the timeline, divide it into "chapters," and give a name to each of the eras in the timeline. This garnered even more animated debate. I wasn't quite sure where all this was headed. But at least everyone seemed engaged.

After they had reached what seemed like a natural consensus, I asked what seemed to be the next logical question: "So, if that was then, and this is now, what would you call the next era—the one we are headed for?" Without a moment's hesitation, they all agreed, quite energetically. Then I said, "Okay, that's where we need to invent."

Surprisingly, this workshop turned out to be one of the more productive of the many invention workshops I have facilitated. Inspiration may be more accessible and available than we think.

Inventing the solution

Corporate patent portfolios are often littered with the "dry bones" of unexploited inventions. Joe Danielle, who has made a study of these portfolios, estimates that a mere 5 to 10 percent of the total carry noteworthy value.[92] Global patent offices are inundated with a flood of patent applications. A disturbingly small number of inventions qualify. And even those that do carry value to users and patent owners that is often difficult to determine at the time of invention. It is often only in hindsight that the true and full value of an invention becomes clear.

Where a particular invention resides in the succession of related inventions is not always clear. John H. Lienhard, in his book *How Invention Begins*, offers a wonderful reminder of just how difficult it is to assign original authorship to one inventor. This is particularly clear in the case of the more famous inventions—the lightbulb and Edison, the airplane and the Wright brothers, the steam engine and James Watt. What is revealed is far from a singular and isolated invention or inventor. There is instead a succession—sometimes spanning multiple generations. In fact Lienhard, a mechanical engineer and historian emeritus at the University of Houston, postulates that what we call an invention is really many inventions over surprisingly long periods of time that comprise the evolution of a technology.

This succession goes through three periods: gestation, cradle, and maturation periods, each of which can span a generation (twenty-five years) or more, sometimes a lot more.[93] Despite this historical reality, society persists in its preference for picking one inventor as the representative of all who came before and after, and even for picking one invention as the archetype for all. Lienhard wrote, "I now understand how impossible it is to accurately parcel out individual credit for any invention . . . . Almost nothing has any one absolute inventor. We recite the name of this or that lively genius so often that we start believing such a person exists. Yet he is, by and large, a created hero who manifests the many builders of our present world all rolled into one person."[94]

Inventions and inventors not only come in a succession, they also come in clumps, families, or communities within the same generation. The majority of the invention workshops I have facilitated have produced not simply one-off or isolated inventions, but multiple small clusters of inventions—sometimes two or three to a cluster, sometimes more. My own experience resonates with Lienhard comparing one individual invention to an atom that combines with other atoms to form a molecule.[95] Invention is really the combination of multiple inventions and the connections between multiple inventors that congeal into what we elevate to an invention—an uber invention—when in fact from a technical and legal point of view, it is at least a family of inventions.

℘

Recent Example

Bruce Beihoff, electrical engineer, inventor,
and most recently, Sr. Principal Technologist
and Global Leader, Advanced Systems, Whirlpool

Most of us take electric power for granted. We simply flip a switch or push a button and the light, computer, or washing machine comes to life. That we are able to do this with so little thought today is a result of the art of solid-state power electronics, thanks to a generation of electrical engineering innovators who, by inspiration and appreciation, made it possible. They built on what had been discovered before.

In its natural state, electric power is wild, erratic, and extremely volatile. Think Ben Franklin's kite and lightning. Efforts to control electricity's flow have been going on for well over a hundred years.

The art of taming or converting electricity entered a new generation in 1957 with the invention of something called the "thyristor," or "silicon-controlled rectifier," which marked the beginning of the transition from electromechanical conversions to solid-state conversions. It's safe to say that solid-state power electronics has proven to be a key enabling technology of many other electronic and semiconductor-based innovations, from advances in computers and televisions to mobile phones and even hybrid vehicles.

How the succession of solid-state power electronics came about started with small but growing cadres of Ezekiels—a few diverse electrical, mechanical, and controls engineers inspired by what they saw both in the dry bones of previous attempts, and in the digital methods emerging in another domain of electronics, namely data processing. These Ezekiels asked—with no clear or obvious answer in sight—whether control techniques used in the logic of data processing might be used in power "processing." This small cadre of inventors grew in numbers and in their conviction that using digital techniques to create analog output could yield significant gains in efficiency, control, scalability, and extensibility.

This disparate network of electrical-engineering Ezekiels remained relatively small—between a hundred or two hundred. They saw in the silicon revolution going on in computers the possibility for very low cost, precise, and highly efficient means of controlling power conversion through solid-state techniques.

One of these engineers was Bruce Beihoff, laboring in the Eaton Corporation's R&D labs. Beihoff, along with others in companies like RCA, Texas Instruments, National Semiconductor, and General Electric, kept asking the inventive question: could these "bones" live? Could the logic-controls hardware in computers be used to control the conversion of power in electromechanical applications? There was no obvious answer, but Beihoff and others kept asking and kept watching the connections emerge.

Then in the late 1970s, metal oxide semiconductor (MOS) technology started to show up in integrated circuits used in computers, and this breathed life and hope into the ongoing attempts of these engineers to control power with solid-state converters. What is now known as the "variable frequency power converter" was developed in the 1980s and became widely available in various forms in the 1990s. As is the case with so many other innovations of significance, Beihoff was one of many inventors contributing many inventions for the succession of this innovation—specifically the architecture that enabled these converters to be modularized and integrated in a variety of applications. This spared others the need to redesign the converters for specific applications.

Had Beihoff and these other engineers not been wandering the valley of what to others looked like "dry bones," had they not developed a deep appreciation and respect for both the materials and the memories of what had been thought of or tried, had they not persisted in asking questions for which there were no obvious answers, and had they not kept watching the connections emerging in computer logic, they likely would have missed the breath of new life that MOS technology—integrating digital logic and embedded control—brought to their otherwise quixotic efforts.

Beihoff was but one of the Ezekiels appreciating the materials and memory in the "bones" around them, asking the inventive questions and making connections as the system emerged in data processing. This gave us an innovation that has enabled a wealth of electrical innovations.

℅

Inventions are of two types: directional or intersectional. Directional inventions arise within a dominant stream of solutions flowing largely in the same general direction. For example, Moore's Law (that oft-quoted prediction that every twelve to eighteen months the number of transistors on an integrated circuit doubles) has provided clear direction for hundreds, even thousands, of inventions in the semi-conductor industry as inventors anticipate with a relatively high degree of certainty what the next generation of product and process innovations will be need.

Intersectional inventions are those that arise at the intersection or convergence of one or more domains. For example, the digitization of content intersects with advances in data communications technology and both intersect with certain business domains, like stock-trading, or publishing, or the music distribution business. When these intersections emerge, separate streams of technology no longer run in parallel but come together in some combination to transform the entire business. Think digitial cameras replacing Polariod, and film-based photography. Frans Johansson calls these intersectional eras "the Medici Effect,"[96] named after the famous Italian banking family of the fifteenth century whose funding attracted a variety and diversity of creative types—sculptors, scientists, poets, painters, philosophers, and financiers—to Florence, which in effect became *the* intersection for what we now call the Renaissance.

Before we can understand, much less anticipate, the economics of innovation, we need to appreciate the *ecology* of invention. The best inventions are those that, like compelling opportunities, are well-timed and good fits with the ecologies in which they emerge. They breathe, have life, and stand on their own. But creating these types of inventions, much less recognizing them as such, is hardly possible without both inspiration and appreciation.

125

Inspiration (for inventing)

Inspiration may not be what we think it is. In fact, "thinking" may be partly to blame for what prevents inspiration, especially when it comes to inventing.

My early experiences with invention and the role inspiration plays in it occurred over three decades ago. While not exactly inventing, every week I had to create a sermon, a monologue that lasted fifteen to twenty minutes. The requirements were the same each week: say something meaningful that was encouraging or challenging or both. How well these weekly "inventions" fulfilled those requirements was often difficult to gauge. However, it didn't take me long to realize when I felt inspired by what I was saying, my listeners were more likely to be inspired. When I didn't, they didn't.

I had confidence that the material I was working with was subtantive. But *finding* the substance and a way to say it to my listeners in a meaningful way was the challenging part. This required getting to know both my materials—the dry bones from the biblical narrative—and my audience. The former required much study and reflection. The latter required much listening and empathy. Both required a lot of time and effort. The content of the sermon—the "solution"—seldom came easily. Most of the time I would hit the proverbial wall. On one side of the wall was the "true-to-the-text" interpretation of the biblical passage. That was usually clear. On the other side of the wall—the side I wasn't on and desperately wanted to get to—was the other half of the solution: what to say and how to say it so that the congregation would be inspired or, if not inspired, then at least satisfied that they had heard something worth hearing.

Often the wall seemed to get taller and thicker as Sunday morning approached. Many a Saturday night I found myself writing and rewriting what I had been working on all week. The fear of standing in the pulpit without anything to say started to show up as a recurring theme in my dreams, mild nightmares really.

My repeated experience with the wall became enough of a pattern that it was starting to make life a bit unmanageable. So, in an attempt to make this weekly pattern a bit more manageable, I started paying attention to what seemed to happen just prior to the times when I actually did make it over the wall. What I noticed was counterintuitive. When I encountered the wall, felt its resistance, and simply backed off—even stopped thinking entirely about the problem I was trying to solve—often a piece of the puzzle would simply fall into place or present itself. Was this inspiration?

Some psychologists and neuroscientists have stumbled on a similar pattern. They call it the "insight experience," according to Jonah Lehrer.[97] Characteristics of this pattern are reflected in the story of Archimedes shouting "Eureka" (literally, "I found it") when what he was seeing—the bath water rising as his body displaced the volume when he got in the tub—connected with the problem he was working on but couldn't solve: how to measure the volume of an irregular object, the king's crown. Characteristics of the experience, according to Lehrer include:

1. reaching an impasse where progress toward a solution stalls,

2. a sudden perception of a solution,

3. the solvers' inability to explain how the solution or insight came to them, and

4. the feeling of absolute certainty that goes along with the idea.

Neuroscientists and psychologists like Mark Jung-Beeman suggest "the sudden flash of insight occurs when solvers engage distinct neural and cognitive processes that allow them to see connections that previously eluded them."[98] Using brain-imaging technology enabled these researchers to explore the same pattern I experienced in preparing weekly sermons. First there is a "preparatory phase" wherein the brain is devoted to solving the problem. Then there is a "search phase" when the brain is looking for answers in all the relevant places. And then, assuming an answer is not found, there is what they call the "relaxation phase." "The relaxation phase is crucial," according to Jung-Beeman. "That's why so many insights happen during warm showers."[99]

In the many invention workshops I have facilitated, the "overnight effect" confirms this "relaxation phase." Inventor participants in the workshops are consistently more "creative" and "productive" in the morning of the second day. Our explanation has been simply that they have had a night to sleep on it. Lehrer expresses the neuro-research conclusions more scientifically: "One of the surprising lessons of this research is that trying to force an insight can actually prevent the insight. While it is commonly assumed that the best way to solve a difficult problem is to focus, minimize distractions, and pay attention only to the relevant details, this clenched state of mind may inhibit the sort of creative connections that lead to sudden breakthrough thoughts."[100] Concentration, it turns out, can come with the liability of diminished inventiveness. Those who are in a good mood, and even in a state of play[101], turn out to be better at solving the tougher problems.

As useful and fascinating as neuroscience is, it can only tell us part of the story—the part that happens in the brain. There is another part of the story of inspiration's involvement in inventing that happens *outside* of the brain. This other part of the story has to do with the hand—a primary instrument inventors use to explore and interact with the world around them. If an invention is to successfully provide a solution, it must do so by interoperating ("breathing") in its immediate ecosystem. Our hands—both as sophisticated instruments of manipulation and extensions through which we explore, perceive, and learn about these ecosystems— are as essential to inventing as is the brain. Frank Wilson, a neurologist who devoted much of his career to working with musicians, views the hand as essential to thinking as the brain. In fact, both brain and hands interoperate with each other and cooperate in the formation of intelligence, learning, and knowledge. Both work together at the core of the relationship between movement, perception, and learning so necessary for inventing. Wilson's reason for writing from his study of hands was "to expose the hidden physical roots of the unique human capacity for passionate and creative work."[102] Inspiration does not simply arouse cortical matter in our brains to "exalted thoughts." Inspiration motivates and encourages inventors to creative acts—to try something new. It has as much to do with stirring the heart and hands as it does arousing the mind.

Inspiration is not only about informing the inspired with a new idea to solve a problem. It also is about instilling energy into inventors. Often during the course of invention workshops, participants get overheated and tired. Energy wanes. If left to continue in this trajectory, it becomes more difficult to stay productive, much less keep participants engaged. When these inevitable lulls in energy occur—evidenced by after-lunch yawns, tired eyes, or noticeable drags in the flow of ideas—an excursion is called for. An excursion is a well-known group process technique that attempts to replicate what all of us can do, typically in the privacy of our own minds. Counter-intuitively, an excursion starts by inviting the solvers to *stop* thinking about the problem and start thinking about something else, something fun, positive, and, especially, easy for the inventors to imagine in some detail; an outside interest or passion that has nothing to do with the subject at hand. This approach is often met with initial resistance. It appears counterproductive, a waste of time. However, after only a couple of experiences with excursions, veterans of these workshops quickly see how it works. They both use and enjoy the technique with consistent results.

The results of taking excursions are twofold: For restoring energy and enthusiasm, excursions work virtually 100 percent of the time. In stimulating inventors to generate new and useful ideas that lead to inventive solutions, the technique works at least 50 percent of the time—more with experienced participants. What's going on with the excursions is that through the use of metaphor and analogy, inventors are encouraged to search for and improvise connections from a wider array of their own experiences and memories. This wider array temporarily stretches otherwise constrained thinking of what is acceptable in any solution.[103]

There is at least one other lens through which to view the role inspiration plays in inventing—the legal one. What can the law tell us about inspiration? If you were to ask this question in 1952 in the United States, the answer would have been "not much." That was the year the so-called "Flash of Genius" doctrine was struck down after a brief decade of influence.

To be patentable, an invention has to be new, useful, and not obvious to a person skilled in the art. The "Flash of Genius" test for patentability held that the inventive act had to come into the mind of an inventor in a "flash of genius" and not as the result of tinkering. For much of the 1940's at least, what we conventionally think of as inspiration was an explicit part of the way "non-obviousness" was determined. However, in 1952, the Supreme Court struck down this provision, stating "patentability shall not be negated by the manner in which the invention was made." Obviously, inspiration is a difficult thing to verify, even in court.

Since 1952, the Supreme Court came to affirm what are called the Graham Factors (*Graham, et al. vs. John Deere Co. of Kansas City, et al.* 383 U.S. 1 (1967)) as the criteria for nonobviousness. The Graham Factors are:

- the scope and content of the prior art,

- the level of ordinary skill in the art,

- the differences between the claimed invention and the prior art, and

- objective evidence of non-obviousness (e.g., commercial success, long-felt but unsolved needs, and failure of others).

Just as it is impossible to precisely pinpoint the originating source of the wind, though its effects can be seen and its source inferred, so with inventions. If the invention's origin can be determined in the prior art, then there is insufficient originality to call it an invention and, therefore, no inventor; a good problem-solver, perhaps, but not an inventor. The connection with the past is too apparent, the difference with what came before too small, for it to be regarded as an invention. Though the court struck down the *flash* of genius, it didn't completely eliminate the genius part of the criteria. With characteristic wordiness, even the legal perspective seems to suggest that inventing is about something more than deduction or calculation. Einstein put it this way: "The intellect has little to do on the road to discovery. There comes a leap in consciousness, call it intuition or what you will, and the solution comes to you and you don't know how or why."[104] The same can be said for invention. Inventors are reliant upon inspiration. The 99 percent perspiration is necessary, but not sufficient.

The Oxford English Dictionary defines inspiration as "the arousal of the mind to special or unusual activity or creativity; the prompting of the mind to exalted thoughts or to creative activity (from an undisclosed influence)." Frequently, inspiration is viewed as either present or missing. There are no "more or less" gradations of intensity. Inspiration is thought to be limited to an unusual event, a climax in one's experience.

Ezekiel's vision suggests otherwise: that inspiration for inventing may be as present and available as the air we breathe, if, of course, there is faith to receive it. And this is where its partner, appreciation, comes in.

Appreciation

In a narrow sense, appreciation has to do with understanding where the value resides and what it is—both to the end-user and the producer. Appreciation of value is essential in the search for a solution that works. As value is derived from context, innovators must appreciate the innovation's economic context and conditions, whereas inventors must appreciate the invention's surrounding physical and technical ecosystem—what some call *Sitz in Leiben* (German for "situation in life"). Ultimately, the ecology of the invention must coincide and resonate with the innovation's economy for commercial viability and success. If there is a difference between the role of innovator and inventor, the former is more oriented to business considerations, while the latter is more focused on technical ones.

Inventions seldom present themselves in a finished form. More often, an invention manifests itself partially, as when the apostle Paul when he said, "Now I know only in part." These "half-baked" solutions show up either as a problem looking for a solution or as a solution looking for a need. This is why invention workshops achieve so much success. In the flow of ideas, one workshop participant states an old problem in a new way. This triggers another to think about it differently. Or, conversely, an inventor offers a solution in need of a problem to solve. This stimulates still others to start improvising fresh connections that weren't considered before. This all happens quite rapidly. The invention can enter through the gate of an inventor stating an old problem in a new way just as it can appear in a fresh solution that finds resonance with the familiar problem. It can also arise from the inventors' recognition of the beauty of an emergent-though-partial solution.

When the beholder of that beauty is an expert in the subject matter of a particular field, that expert is quicker to recognize the beauty of a solution looking for a need. It appears in a striking, fascinating, or attractive way. Others, without such depth of expertise, lack the appreciation. This aesthetic sensitivity seems to be built right in to these experts. I've seen it as inventing is happening. Many times, in the middle of an invention workshop, I will see an expert's facial muscles flex, eyes change focus, as if gazing at some distant image nowhere in the room. When accompanied by excited scribbling on a pad of paper, I know that there is something potent going on inside the inventor's head. It is usually best to get the whole group out of whatever they are focused on and to turn aside, pause, and pay full attention to what this expert is about to share—often in the form of a crude and partial drawing. The initial descriptive words will not carry the meaning, but the picture will.

I simply step back and watch. Sometimes multiple inventors start drawing simultaneously. As other inventors begin to appreciate what their colleagues are describing, energy, ideas, and connections build. Appreciation is often simply for the beauty of an idea that attracts them. Perhaps the 99 percent Edison referred to is as much *appreciation* as it is perspiration.

Prepared minds may be more attuned to the aesthetics of a technology or domain, but appreciation does not stop at the form and elegance that appears in the inventor's mind. It reaches out to the intrinsic value of the potential solution as well. The word *appreciate* comes from the Latin "to set a price on" and means to estimate rightly. Since all value is derived from its context, this appreciation comes to those who understand the invention in its immediate ecology. Appreciation for inventing is not limited to what are called "fundamental" inventions. The fundamental invention of Edison's lightbulb—passing an electric current through a bamboo filament to produce an incandescent glow—may not have been of much value in and of itself. But the enabling invention, using a carbonized cotton filament encased in an evacuated transparent tube mounted on a screw-type fitting, paved the way for commercial use. Which was more valuable? History proved that the former would have been worthless without the latter.

While appreciation may end with a valuation of what is or is not worth keeping in any proposed solution, it begins with acknowledgement of what is.

> He set me down in the middle of a valley; it was full of
> bones. He led me all round them; there were very many lying
> in the valley, and they were very dry.

Quick criticism and snap judgments are a far cry from appreciation. Appreciation relies on an open, not a "clenched," mind. An open mind is receptive to detached but willing examination. The closed mind is more prone to contempt prior to investigation. Appreciation can be understood by looking at its opposite, rejection, whether that rejection comes from peers or from within inventors themselves.

Rejections come in at least three types: complete, partial, and conditional. A complete rejection, the most severe and usually taken personally, might be expressed this way: "I don't like anything about your idea." It's difficult to attain lift through the drag of rejections of this type. A partial rejection leaves some room for continued work on the proposed solution. A partial rejection might be expressed this way: "This part of the idea concerns me." Other parts of the idea might be acceptable. A conditional rejection is based more on how circumstances and conditions in the immediate context might cause some friction with the solution. This kind of rejection is based less on defects inherent in the proposed solution than on conditions around it. It might be expressed: "This idea doesn't account for the external conditions that exist and work against it."

Like rejection, appreciation can be complete, partial, or conditional. Partial and conditional appreciation tends to be more productive and useful because as both point inventors to the next problem to solve.

As both an emotional attitude and mental habit, appreciation is an essential skill for inventors during the process of inventing. It's especially useful to engage at the instant when a proposed solution begins to form. This moment—call it the moment of the invention's conception—is similar to what thermodynamics refers to as the "critical point." It occurs just prior to a phase or state change, for example, when water freezes into ice, or humidity (vapor) in the atmosphere condenses into drops of rain. What appears to be an instantaneous change—the "flash" so often associated with genius and inspiration—is actually preceded by a "critical point." At the "critical point," things could go either way. When an inventor first proposes a new solution, the mix of appreciation and rejection can either encourage or prevent the fullest possible expression of the idea at that time. At this "critical point," appreciation carries the transformation to the next phase.

Atmosphere

Inventing follows more closely a trajectory of a plane climbing steadily than it mimics an instantaneous flash of genius. When a plane takes off and climbs, the forces of lift and drag come into play. When inventing takes off and starts to get some momentum, an invention begins to build. But just as an airplane's wings will produce predictable vortices of drag, so also the very momentum of inventing will create resistance and rejection. Anticipating this "lift-induced drag" can make the difference between gaining enough altitude or being dragged down and stalled. Inspiration and appreciation are essential to keep the flow going and growing.

Inventing is a result of collaborative more than individual efforts. Inventing honors and appreciates the "bones" of prior art, but extends beyond it. Within its own particular context and time, every invention is a unique combination of both ideal and real, the theoretical and the practical. It is both new, in that it conceives of something that didn't exist before, and familiar, in that it uses known concepts and language to embody and describe. Inventions tend to come in multiples; seldom does one appear alone, and seldom is one ever really "finished." It lives and breathes in the ecology of what works and the economy of what is meaningful and valuable. The atmosphere in which the invention is to "live and move and have its being" is dynamic, full of the drags of rejection and the lifts of appreciation. An interesting thing about the shape of the innovator's wing of faith is that it can take what is otherwise oppositional drag and use it for lift.

The most obvious oppositional force permeating the atmosphere of inventing is rejection. Rejection comes with the territory. It's a social and political territory. When an original solution presents itself, some form and degree of rejection appears close behind. In fact there is some truth in the saying that the more original the invention, the more intense the rejection.

Rejecting new ideas is almost an instinctual reaction, especially among experts. Original ideas often threaten to redraw boundaries in their domain. As boundaries are redrawn, power shifts, giving more power to one, less to another. Rejections come quickly, often too quickly. And when rejections are crudely expressed in a categorical manner—"that's a dumb idea"—it is likely the lift-to-drag ratio will diminish, risking a stall or worse. The other two types—partial and conditional rejection—are actually more precise and useful, because they tell the inventor where to invent next.

That's why it's important to befriend critics. This was one of the first lessons my mentor, Bill Wilson, taught me. "Critics can be your best ally" was the way he put it. And then, as if this phrase turned the theater lights on in his memory, Wilson launched into a story. John Bletzinger was Wilson's own go-to critic at Kimberly-Clark during the 1960s. Wilson would bring Bletzinger a mock-up of a new product being worked on, for example a new Kleenex® dispensing package. It wouldn't take long for Bletzinger to find out what was wrong with it. Bletzinger had a knack for quickly finding the weak spots in prototypes and concepts. However, he made his critiques out of a deep respect and appreciation for both the attempt under way and the stage and state the prototype represented. He seldom, if ever, categorically rejected what was brought to him. Instead, he focused on parts and conditions. After every visit with Bletzinger, inventors were energized and directed, not deflated or dejected.

Experienced patent attorneys seem to be adept at this appreciative investigation and inquiry. Many tactfully challenge inventors to articulate and finish incomplete parts of an invention, even when the inventors think they are done. The relationship between the inventor and the patent counsel can serve as a foundation and context for appreciative criticisms. Both parties operate under the assumption of positive intent. Without this mutually shared assumption, critiques can easily be misperceived as rejections.

Those in the business of inventing should cultivate and maintain relationships with a few appreciative-but-critical allies. Every inventor needs his or her own Bletzinger.

Thrust

Appreciation contributes directly to thrust—the energy that fuels inventors to keep inventing.

Inventing is very demanding work. It requires the expenditure of much creative and emotional energy. Inventors must search and pursue many and varied hopeful avenues. Most turn out to be energy-draining dead ends. Market ecologies and organizational atmospheres are full of rejection and resistance. Additional resources, timed right, can bring a much-needed boost to inventors. But nothing provides the motivation and drive to invent quite as much as a deep appreciation for the intrinsic nature of the challenge itself. Compelling opportunities contain inherently more thrust potential than those that are less challenging.

Mihaly Csikszentmihalyi cites the challenge as the very first element of the pleasure that inventors experience in the process of inventing. "Anything that does not work as well at it could can provide a clear goal to the inventor." [105] The amount of energy stored in a well-defined target is striking. When inventors pursue it, it is released. And when these targets are defined with even a modest amount of appreciation (and a little inspiration), inventions are much more likely to survive.

Inventing is often equated with "out-of-the-box" thinking. Years ago the Center for Creative Leadership (CCL) conducted an organizational survey of R&D types—engineers and scientists—to assess their creative styles and the implications for organization and leadership. They started with the premise that everyone in R&D was creative, though each had proclivities to one of two creative styles—"adaptive" and "original." When given a technical challenge, "adaptives" tend to generate ideas inside the box, while "originals" tend to generate ideas outside the box, or even re-draw the box. The latter presents an interesting communication challenge between managers (who are typically "adaptive") and so-called "individual contributors" (who are more often "original"). However, the more important point is that no matter whether thinking is considered out of the box or inside the box, a "box" is needed. This holds true whether the context is a small group of inventors carefully selected and matched with the technical challenge—as in an invention workshop—or the clarion call from executive leaders that signals not only where inventions are needed but why.

Velocity

Inspiration and appreciation also contribute to the velocity necessary for the lift innovators seek and need when inventing.

Many mistakenly concentrate on the speed variable at this point in the innovating process. They try to minimize the time it takes for inventing and are thereby driven toward imitation. But imitation is not an option here.

A reduction in distance turns out to be where inspiration and appreciation have the largest impact. The common expression for this is "connecting the dots." When dots are connected, the distance between them is reduced or eliminated.

The late Steve Jobs, the inspired and inspiring co-founder of Apple, had this to say about connecting the dots in a 2005 commencement address at Stanford University: "You cannot connect the dots looking forward. Only back. But you must trust that you will be able to connect the dots as and when you look forward."[106] He reinforced this advice to the graduating seniors by relating the irony of his experience as a dropout at Reed College, auditing a course in calligraphy. What he learned in that course gave him sufficient appreciation and inspiration to connect the dots of what he had learned about iconography and fonts ten years later, when he applied it to the look and feel of the computer desktop—what we see on our screens. This look became standard for the industry, first on the Apple MacIntosh and then replicated by Windows.

Steve Job's example expresses this wing of innovators' faith—believing dots can be connected—the distance between them eliminated. The dots to be connected are those that build a complete opportunity, the distances shortened reside in the four elements of any opportunity:

- the discovered need,
- the means available to satisfy that need,
- what's of value to the user, and
- what's of value to the producer.

Closing distances and connecting dots require multi-lateral collaborations. The Internet may help innovators find other "dot connectors," but face-to-face dialogue prove to be a more potent creative fast track.

It is noteworthy that engineering domains—electronic, mechanical, chemical, bio-engineering—have been categorized by many patent attorneys along a continuum. On one end are the so-called "predictable arts" (mechanical and electrical engineering) and at the other end are the so-called "unpredictable arts" (chemical and bio-engineering, or life sciences). What differentiates them is a matter of confidence in connecting the dots.

Inventing within the domain of a "predictable art" allows inventors to invent more quickly. In predictable arts inventors conduct thought experiments with more confidence. In the unpredictable arts inventors have less confidence, as they are required to conduct actual lab experiments to confirm the experiments they did in their heads. Mechanical causalities are easier to predict than chemical ones. The requirements of actual rather than mental feedback loops may limit the expectations of innovators for accelerating the inventing. But in no way does it lessen the need for inspiration and appreciation. The speed of inventing is all about increasing the rate by reducing the distance between the dots of the opportunity.

Angle of Attack

As a plane makes its ascent, the angle at which the wings slice through the atmosphere matters a great deal to getting lift. Pilots are constantly fine-tuning this angle of attack during the climb. Too much and the plane will stall out, too little and the plane won't climb.

Similarly, inventors are conscious of making tradeoffs between the ideal invention as it is in their imagination and what is possible now. In fact, inventing is all about addressing the inherent tension between the ideal and the real, between what is imaginable in the future and what's possible now, between what should be and what can be. Instead of being satisfied with compromises and tradeoffs, inventors actually seek and use the tension inherent in tradeoffs to invent a solution that eliminates or transcends the tradeoff itself.

Inventors are seldom fully satisfied. They always push the envelope. Instead of looking for resolution by making a trade, they eliminate the tradeoff by means of a totally new solution. This requires a different way of looking at the tradeoff. Inventors take tradeoffs very seriously. However, they don't automatically give in to them or limit their searches for resolutions to the choices implied by the tradeoffs.

Inspiration and appreciation are the primary elements of what Roger Martin calls "stance" in *The Opposable Mind*.[107] The "stance" Martin assigns to inventors is comprised of six key beliefs—the belief that:

1. Existing and current models do not fully represent reality.
2. Conflicting models are to be used, not feared.
3. Better models are possible but not seen at the present time.
4. A better model can be brought from the ideal to concrete reality.
5. A better model is not accessible without wading into complexity.
6. Time is available to create the better model.

Martin's "stance" resonates well with our conceptual model of faith. It's synonymous with inspiration and appreciation, especially in the context of inventing. Martin observes that most of us use either deductive or inductive logic, or both. However, what we are not taught is a third kind of thinking—of which we are all capable. This kind of thinking Martin calls "abductive" logic, and this kind of thinking is useful for the "inventive construction of theories."[108]

Deductive logic needs a theory or model from which to base its reasoning. Inductive logic needs experience or observations from which to draw inferences. The abductive logic of inventing requires the ability to make up new theories by means of "leaps with your mind." And these leaps of mind are not possible without inspiration and appreciation.

Most people, Martin suggests, want to make calculations within and between tradeoffs. They want to make the trade. Inventors are not inclined to trade. Inventors want to know what the tradeoffs are so they can trump them with their inventing, but they are tilted away from compromise and toward original solutions largely because of their belief, trust, confidence, and hope that tradeoffs can be transcended. This belief makes inventors more receptive to inspiration.

The consequences of abductive logic are laden with conflicts that often become career limiting for the inventor. Inventors who are constantly pushing the envelope because they believe tradeoffs can be transcended fail to recognize some of the entrenched interests in striking a balance in the trade-off. This happened to Glen Fleischer when he insisted that Kimberly-Clark make a superior-performing product that would require a new machine for the first Pull-Ups® (the first disposable training pants). He was firmly convinced that the original solution his team had invented was ready for commercial release. However, the company saw another path and decided to make a "just good enough" product on a retrofitted diaper machine. In hindsight, the company made the right business decision at the time. The "just good enough" version of Pull-Ups® far exceeded their business expectations. Fleischer left the company over the decision, in large measure because he knew a technically superior product was possible. For Fleischer "good *was* the enemy of the best." For the company, good was good enough.

Inventors typically are oriented to invent with the best means available and are not inspired by "just good enough." However, inventors also need to see that their inventions—even the ones that are going to make it into the marketplace—are perhaps better viewed as being in a line of succession rather than the last one of the line.

Inspiration and appreciation give lift. Inspiration breathes life into dry bones. Appreciation brings the understanding necessary for innovating and inventing to occur. But to stay aloft in the innovating flight, the invention must be reduced to practice—the next challenge for the innovator. This requires another wing setting for the innovators' faith to which we now turn.

Chapter 7

Forgiveness and Persistence

An invention solves. An innovation resolves. Innovators and inventors sometimes may be one and the same, but invention and innovation are not.

While an invention solves a problem, it also creates a conflict with convention. Precisely because it solves a problem in a new way, invention disturbs the status quo. An innovation, on the other hand, must *re-solve* the inherent conflicts the invention created.

Much of what is said about innovating emphasizes the dramatic "breakthrough" characteristics of discovery and invention. Less is said about the more mundane realities of reducing an inventive new solution to practice. It's a lot of hard work—the perspiration of which Edison spoke. Innovation requires much stitching together to make the breakthrough a reality. It requires many starts, stops, and restarts, not to mention a modest accumulation of enabling and incremental inventions. While takeoffs, ascents, and landings are the more exciting moments of lift, it's the more monotonous mid-flight lift that enables the distance to be covered in a relative short period—the whole purpose of the flight to begin with.

For innovators, each stage of the innovating flight is just as critical as the next. But what is learned in resolving conflicts in mid-flight determines whether the innovation succeeds or not.

Conflicts

The conflicts innovators must resolve are both technical and political. Left unresolved, they handicap the innovation's commercial viability. The technical conflicts are specific to the context, technology, and architecture of what has been solved in principle but not yet in practice. Most technical conflicts reflect the inherent frictions between principle and practice, between concept and its embodiment, between what is new and foreign about the invention and what is familiar and known from convention. The technical challenge is to resolve as many conflicts as possible without losing either the novelty of the inventive solution or the ability to make it work.

The political conflicts are specific to the sponsoring organization and even the market for which the innovation is intended. Most of the political conflicts reflect the threats—both real and imagined—the invention poses to the conventional balance of power. What is technically feasible and commercially viable is often put on hold indefinitely because it is too menacing to the delicate balance of the company's relationships with dealers and retailers. Failure can also arise because the invention did not match the mindset of an overbearing manager. The task here is to honor and even use conventional means while simultaneously maintaining the novelty of the inventive solution in the iterative effort to make the solution work, or, to reduce it to practice.

The possibility all the conflicts will not be resolved is very real at this stage. A tactic often used to help innovators resolve multiple conflicts is to give them permission to temporarily set aside most of the conflicts so as to concentrate exclusively on one, often the toughest one first. As a thought experiment, permission can be given (not always easily received) by asking innovators to assume, at least for the moment, that all the other conflicts have been successfully resolved, except for this one. This allows them to concentrate their energy and attention on one conflict. And where attention is, energy follows.

Commercial viability can elude innovators even with an inventive solution that proves technically feasible. A technically successful embodiment may require an aesthetic look that users abhor and refuse to buy. The price-value equation may not end up making sense for the user, the producer, or both.

But failure can be purely technical as well. Available materials and methods may stubbornly resist practical adaptation to what the invention, as conceived, requires. The promised ideal may slowly fade with repeated attempts to make the solution conform to what is possible on today's terms.

In resolving conflicts, both technical and political, accommodation, avoidance, and even competition (win-lose) are possible approaches to take. But none of these resolve conflict completely. Compromise does offer some resolution. Trade-offs can be made. However, compromise can too easily sacrifice what is original in the invention. Or it can destroy timely implementation when one side in the negotiation is locked in to maintaining the purity of the "ideal." Creative and collaborative problemsolving is another way of resolving conflicts. Artful innovators combine both creative problemsolving and compromise.

At this stage, innovators must learn as much as they can as efficiently as they can through multiple development cycles. One of our clients calls this the "Slinky" for innovators, referring to the toy spring that was first introduced in Gimbels in 1945 and has held its own in Christmas stockings for kids ever since. Flexibility is enabled by attentiveness, active experimentation, and adaptation and, of course, multiple tries. Failures are to be expected, even welcomed. Failures tell innovators what to try next. The real failure is not learning anything. As a result, the pattern of faith that innovators use at this stage is forgiveness and persistence.

One of the parables of Jesus helps us understand this wing setting. It's often called the "Parable of the Prodigal Son," an unfortunate title for our purposes. This mistaken title makes us think the parable is about the younger son, that he is the innovator. After all, he is the one who left the security of his father's fields, took his father's inheritance early, and, while he didn't quite invest that inherited capital in an innovative venture, he did take a risk while his elder brother took a safer path and remained at home.

This narrow interpretation ignores the father's role—the role most instructive to innovators. Upon seeing his long-lost son return, the father rushes out to welcome him even before his son has the chance to express his well-rehearsed but humble contrition. The father spares no expense in hosting a huge celebration in recognition of his son's return.

When the older brother returns after a hard day in the field, he hears the sounds of laughter and joy from the party and asks a servant what's going on. Learning of his wayward brother's return, the elder becomes enraged. The parable ends with the father, having come out to find the recalcitrant elder, begging him to come in to join the celebration.

This parable has been used for centuries to interpret and understand the human condition. For our purposes, it defines the faith pattern of forgiveness and persistence experienced innovators demonstrate consistently, though often unconsciously. It can instruct novice innovators on how to approach the political and creative conflicts they must resolve as they reduce a conceptual invention to conventional practice. It is also instructive to companies seeking to innovate when they already have something good going. And it offers insight to the process of learning, whether the learning comes through firsthand experience, secondhand instruction, or a combination of both. Its lessons are more accessible to the innovator, however, when seen through the eyes of the father.

Here's the parable in its entirety:

> There was a man who had two sons.
>
> The younger of them said to his father, "Father, give me the share of the property that will belong to me." So he divided his property between them. A few days later the younger son gathered all he had and traveled to a distant country, and there he squandered his property in dissolute living. When he had spent everything, a severe famine took place throughout that country, and he began to be in need. So he went and hired himself out to one of the citizens of that country, who sent him to his fields to feed the pigs. He would gladly have filled himself with the pods that the pigs were eating; and no one gave him anything.
>
> But when he came to himself he said, "How many of my father's hired hands have bread enough and to spare, but here I am dying of hunger! I will get up and go to my father, and I will say to him, 'Father, I have sinned against heaven and before you; I am no longer worthy to be called your son; treat me like one of your hired hands.'"
>
> So he set off and went to his father. But while he was still far off, his father saw him and was filled with compassion; he ran and put his arms around him and kissed him. Then the son said to him, "Father, I have sinned against heaven and before you; I am no longer worthy to be called your son." But the father said to his slaves, "Quickly, bring out a robe—the best one—and put it on him; put a ring on his finger and sandals on his feet. And get the fatted calf and kill it, and let us eat and celebrate; for this son of mine was dead and is alive again; he was lost and is found!" And they began to celebrate.
>
> Now his elder son was in the field; and when he came and approached the house, he heard music and dancing. He called one of the slaves and asked what was going on. He replied, "Your brother has come, and your father has killed the fatted calf, because he has got him back safe and sound."

Then he became angry and refused to go in. His father came out and began to plead with him. But he answered his father, "Listen! For all these years I have been working like a slave for you, and I have never disobeyed your command; yet you have never given me even a young goat so that I might celebrate with my friends. But when this son of yours came back, who has devoured your property with prostitutes, you killed the fatted calf for him!"

Then the father said to him, "Son, you are always with me, and all that is mine is yours. But we had to celebrate and rejoice, because this brother of yours was dead and has come to life; he was lost and has been found."

—Luke 15.11-32

We'll never know what happened—whether the elder son joined the celebration or not. But the implication is unmistakable: both sons are included in the father's vision of the path forward. For the father, the question is not "what's next?" but "who's next?" reminiscent of the question underlying the David and Goliath narrative—perhaps the question underlying all innovating efforts.

For the father, both sons are in the answer. Each son plays an important supporting role. Each represents a different but necessary way of learning so crucial to this stage of innovating. Both new and old are essential to what happens in reducing the inventive solution to practice. In fact, the very structure of the parable itself—the conflict between the two brothers and the resolution promised through the father's forgiveness and persistence—exemplifies what innovators must do at this stage of innovating.

Just as there are three primary actors in the parable, there are three primary elements of invention-born conflicts and their resolution. The three in the parable reflect how German philosopher Friedrich Hegel described the way all progress moves. Hegel observed that progress moves through a succession where a *thesis* emerges only to be resisted by an *antithesis*. Progress move foward as conflict between the two is resolved in a *synthesis*. This synthesis then becomes a new thesis and the process starts all over again. Many call this dialectics, or the dialectical method, with roots stretching back to Socrates, Plato and the Socratic method, reminding us how essential dialogue is to innovating (and so much else).

143

Hegel's theory applies to inventions as well. A solution is conceived, but it remains an abstract ideal unless and until it can be demonstrated. Then the new concept must do battle with what is here and now. Materials and manufacturing costs, tooling, and marketing expenses all typically resist the new. The challenge for the innovator is to preserve what is new and useful about the inventive solution but make it work in real time and under actual circumstances. According to Hegel, the only way to make progress is ***through*** the antithesis—problems that must be resolved. Interestingly enough, Hegel first used the terms "immediate" for the thesis, "mediate" for the antithesis, and "concrete" for the synthesis. So, let's start with the "immediate", or in the context of the parable's narrative, the younger.

The Younger (as invention)

> The younger (son) said to his father, "Father, give me the share of the property that will belong to me." So he divided his property between them. A few days later the younger son gathered all he had and traveled to a distant country, and there he squandered his property in dissolute living. When he had spent everything, a severe famine took place throughout that country, and he began to be in need. So he went and hired himself out to one of the citizens of that country, who sent him to his fields to feed the pigs. He would gladly have filled himself with the pods that the pigs were eating; and no one gave him anything. But when he came to himself he said, "How many of my father's hired hands have bread enough and to spare, but here I am dying of hunger! I will get up and go to my father, and I will say to him, 'Father, I have sinned against heaven and before you; I am no longer worthy to be called your son; treat me like one of your hired hands.'" So he set off and went to his father.

Though we know none of the specifics that occasioned the younger son's desire to leave, it's easy to imagine why he felt compelled to get away. Family therapists call it "differentiation from your family of origin." Such differentiation is not limited to family systems. In the economic dynamics of innovation, product differentiation is a natural part of the maturation of most every product category, whether the differentiations are incremental or more radical and disruptive.

The sense of entitlement displayed by the younger son, however, may be even stronger than his desire to differentiate. Knowing his future had a protective cushion in his father's wealth, he asks to receive his share now. His self-centeredness is subtle, but undeniable. In asking to get now what is normally given later, upon the death of the giver, the younger son has committed two fundamental confusions. He confused future with present, and what is given with what is due. This is the self-centered confusion so often exhibited by those with an entitlement mentality. Had he thought about what his premature request may have implied to his father—that he would rather have his father dead—it may have caused him to reconsider. But, like those with a sense of entitlement, he wasn't thinking about anyone else.

That the younger son acted out of his sense of entitlement is not terribly surprising. What is surprising is the father's response. The father is under no compulsion to fulfill what can be considered a premature and rather presumptuous request for an early inheritance. But he did. What was the father thinking?

The father had three options: (1) keep his son against his will, which risked ill feelings from the son; (2) let him go without sufficient support and risk losing his son and absorbing some responsibility for any failure; or (3) let the younger depart, fully resourced, and risk losing both his son and the hard-earned wealth he took with him. Each represented a risk. There was no easy choice.

These are the same choices that confront companies that already have a successful business and want to do something new: (1) stay focused and discourage any departures from the established norm, or at least confine them to "adjacencies"; (2) initiate a modest effort and limit resources committed to the effort; or (3) sponsor a departure from the norm, fully aware that it could all end in failure. Unlike the father in this parable, many companies hedge their bets with one of the first two options.

The father makes the "departure from the norm" his choice, betting that what his son will learn—whether he fails or succeeds—just might prove more valuable than the inheritance itself. There was no guarantee. The father divided the property and let the son go, fully funded. That shifted the responsibility entirely to the younger. The father not only gave the younger son freedom, he gave him full responsibility for what the son would do with that freedom.

Innovators must do the same with their own inventive solutions. It's one of the more difficult choices at this stage—to give the promising new concept every opportunity to fail or succeed on its own. This degree of freedom and responsibility includes time, people, and money—an allowance, if you will—which can be lost. The risk is real.

Promising new inventive solutions are "departures" from the norm. Like the younger son, they first appear with great potential. But as many experienced innovators know, "famine" can strike and resources for innovating dry up. Time is one of these factors, as when the new solution turns out to be too far ahead of its time. The means to make it work simply don't exist, yet. Or, the innovation may be too far afield. The business assets to take the new concept to market may be lacking, or it may not fit with the host's scope, orientation, and momentum.[109] Even an emotional attitude— the desire to keep the concept on a pedestal—can plague inventors (even more than innovators), especially those who become so obsessed with the purity of their new solution they view marketing as eroding or corrupting their new concept. However, sending an innovation off to unfamiliar territories (the market) is essential despite the risk of failure. Which, of course, is what happens to the younger son in the parable. He fails.

The parable does not end there, however. The younger, having failed, "comes to himself." He learns something through his firsthand experience with failure. Had he been protected from accepting responsibility for the failure, the consequences may have been muted and the lessons muffled. Isn't this what innovators must experience in reducing a new concept to practice? Avoidance of this kind of experience is one of the reasons why it is so difficult for performance-oriented operating entities to innovate. They abhor failure. Inviting failure is against all they believe and practice. So the invitation to fail is seldom extended or accepted.

Experiencing failure is a necessary part of the process of innovating. Thomas Edison, reflecting on his own process, said, "I haven't failed. I've just found 1,000 ways that don't work." Educational theorist David Kolb at Case Western Reserve calls it "experiential learning."[110] It is comprised of four elements:

- direct, unmediated experience,
- observation of, and reflection upon, that experience,
- formation of abstract concepts from those observations and reflections, and
- using one or more of those abstract concepts in solving a problem.

The parable reflects the same four elements that Kolb describes[111].

> When he had spent everything, a severe famine took place throughout that country, and he began to be in need. [*direct experience*]
>
> So he went and hired himself out to one of the citizens of that country, who sent him to his fields to feed the pigs. He would gladly have filled himself with the pods that the pigs were eating; and no one gave him anything. [*observation and reflection*]
>
> But when he came to himself he said, "How many of my father's hired hands have bread enough and to spare, but here I am dying of hunger! [*formation of a concept*]
>
> I will get up and go to my father" [*using the concept*]

Without the experience of failure, it is unlikely the prodigal son would have come to himself. The understanding that he achieved was not the kind of understanding that can be found in books, lectures, or from observation. Rather, it was the kind of understanding that requires the tuition of direct experience.

This is the same kind of understanding acquired and tuition paid when innovators reduce a new concept to practice. As Confucius put it, "Tell me and I will forget, show me and I may remember, involve me and I will understand." Ikujiro Nonaka and Hirotaka Takeuchi refer to this kind of learning as tacit knowledge in their seminal work *The Knowledge-Creating Company*. Such knowledge comes not only from direct experience, according to Nonaka and Takeuchi, "it is a highly individual process of personal and organizational self-renewal . . . . The creation of new knowledge is as much about ideals as it is about ideas. And that fact fuels innovation. The essence of innovation is to re-create the world according to a particular ideal or vision."[112]

The rate at which experience converts to learning produces lift for innovators. Speed at this stage of innovating is the rate at which conflicts are resolved. It is the rate of learning. The speed at which innovators can progress depends on many uncontrollable variables. However, innovators can increase their rate of learning and resolution by reducing causes of delays on both the reflection and action sides of the learning loop[113] (see Figure 10).

Figure 10: Reflection and Action Modes in Iterations

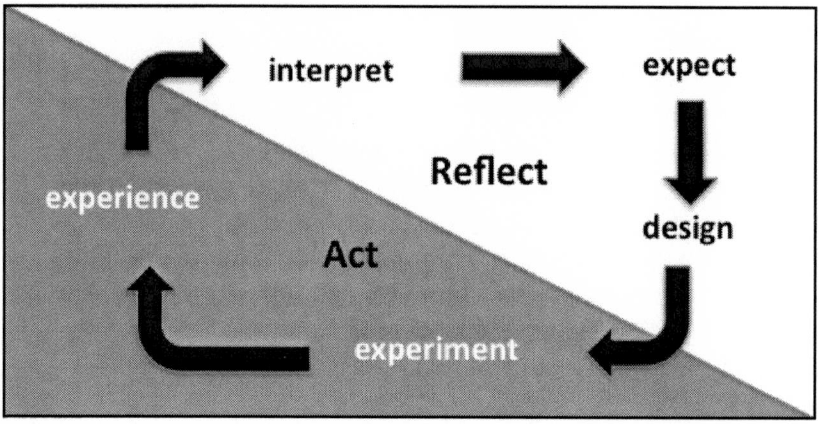

On the act side of the loop, delays are related to feedback—a direct result of how long the experiment takes to produce observable results. On the reflect side, delays are related to how quickly observations can be interpreted and transformed into a new set of hypotheses, which, in turn, are translated into an appropriate design for the next trial or experiment.

Like a well-struck shot in golf, time and effort is mostly spent in preparation, compared to the time devoted to the actual swing, much less the actual moment of contact between the club and the ball. But if the setup, alignment, posture, and balance are all done well, the ball will go where the golfer intends. So, too, with reduction-to-practice iterations or cycles. On the reflection side, collaborative "thinking out loud" among members of the innovating team can reduce delays, increase the learning rate, and maintain lift.

Increasing the number of observers and widening the opening for different, even dissenting interpretations, demands confidence from innovators in their collaborative capabilities. Innovators can easily get lost in a far country when in a dynamic cauldron of interpretations. However, when multiple interpretations are possible, "a greater *quantity* of information is less help than is a different *quality* of information," according to Karl Weick in his book *Sensemaking in Organizations*. "To resolve confusion, people need mechanisms that enable debate, clarification, and enactment more than simply be provided large amounts of data."[114]

When innovating innovators need a safe place to express dissent, especially between cycles. Asking for input more than presenting findings for feedback is preferred. Inviting others to speculate out loud about how they interpret and understand whatever it is that remains unresolved trumps direct yes or no questions. Interestingly enough, asking others what they believe to be important and what they think might be the underlying cause and why, turns out to be more productive than declaring what the consensus view is. The more permission is given for expressing uncomfortable speculations, the greater the chances for more potent experiments to be designed and run the next time. As a result, innovators end up working smarter rather than simply harder. Of course, innovators must take the responsibility of committing to the shot. At some point a selection must be made of what to do next to get out of the loop and act.

Cycle time can be reduced also by being smart with the design of the next experiment. However, the collaborative process of making sense— observing, interpreting, and reformulating hypotheses about causalities— may offer innovators the quickest gains in reducing the time between experiments, if not the time of the full learning cycle itself.

William J. J. Gordon, a researcher of creative problemsolving, was among the first to observe that when a problem-as-given becomes a problem-as-understood, a distinct shift occurs in the perspective and understanding of the problem-solvers. They have learned something new, which causes them to define the problem quite differently than they did initially. As a facilitator, I have often observed this shift. When the shift happens, there is typically a rush of ideas and energy expressed by the problem-solvers in the group. All of this requires a mental flexibility that is open to considering several competing options for a period of time.[115]

How a problem or opportunity is defined and described—framing—is important not just for the inventor when conceiving the invention. It is also important for the innovator in reducing it to practice. In both stages, re-framing will be required several times. If possible, there should be several different frames, given the fact that there are normally multiple conflicts to resolve.

This experiential learning is only one way of learning. There is another, and it's represented by the elder son.

The Older (as convention)

> Now his elder son was in the field; and when he came and approached the house, he heard music and dancing. He called one of the slaves and asked what was going on. He replied, "Your brother has come, and your father has killed the fatted calf, because he has got him back safe and sound." Then he

became angry and refused to go in. His father came out and began to plead with him. But he answered his father, "Listen! For all these years I have been working like a slave for you, and I have never disobeyed your command; yet you have never given me even a young goat so that I might celebrate with my friends. But when this son of yours came back, who has devoured your property with prostitutes, you killed the fatted calf for him!"

It is easy to understand the anger of the elder. But what he says and the way he says it reveal more about his attitude than about the actions of the younger. Resentment holds the older son in its grip. The older son labored in his father's fields out of a sense of obligation and a well-honed set of expectations. For his father to hold such an extravagant celebration for the return of his wayward brother was clearly antithetical to those expectations. In fact, it is an offense to his sense of what is right and fair. By his reaction, the older son revealed that he too had a sense of entitlement. While perhaps not as overtly narcissistic as the younger, the elder's entitlement was constructed with expectations based on merit, diligence, and loyalty. He believed he had *earned* his father's inheritance, ignoring the fact that an inheritance is something that is given, not earned. Ignorance of this generosity is the tragic fallacy of entitlement-thinking of which both sons are guilty.

The older son represents convention. As is so often the case with the oldest child,[116] he is the one who is keenly interested in order and stability. The party had already started and he, of course, was still out in the field working. Conformity and diligence to the daily demands of labor are what the elder son is all about. After all, this is where the cash is generated. While the younger son was out squandering the accumulated capital, the older son was righteously engaged daily in producing cash flow. Just as the younger son is seduced by the promises of differentiation, the older son is seduced by the promises of performance and loyalty. He never left. Conformity turned into confinement. He exhibits all the outward signs of success, following in the footsteps of his father. But those footsteps are not his own. His reliable performance has left him unsatisfied and resentful. This is due in part to the elder son's orientation to risk and failure. Unlike the younger son, who represents a complete lack of caution, the elder son represents complete risk aversion. Failure is to be avoided at all costs. He stays close to home. He never steps away from what to him is security.

The older brother represents a different way of learning. Instead of learning through firsthand experience in a distant country, he learns from conventional wisdom—knowledge gained first by others. Notice that when he returns from the field, he doesn't even find out for himself what the noisy celebration is all about. He asks a servant. His information comes to him secondhand, filtered through others. Much like the central character Tevye in *Fiddler on the Roof,* tradition is the medium through which the elder's learning occurs.

The same thing happens to companies that are succeeding but not innovating, not contributing new value to their customers, not creating the kind of new knowledge that invigorates and renews their sense of entrepreneurial vocation. Their learning is kept within the prescribed boundaries of optimizing what is already in production.

Many regard this kind of learning as less important to innovators and innovating. Innovators themselves mistakenly disparage conventional thinking and knowledge gained from others as out-of-date or old-fashioned, when in fact without due diligence to understand what has been thought of and tried before, without a thorough understanding of the prior art, any sense for what is truly new is impossible. Given the sheer volume of information and knowledge that continues to grow every day, it becomes very easy to mistakenly label something as new when in fact it has been known for some time. Unaware of it before, you become aware of it and the experience feels new. But it's not new.

Knowledge created from the elder's way of learning is described as "explicit knowledge" by Nonaka and Noburu Konno. It can be readily shared in the form of data, scientific formulae, specifications, manuals, and the like. Nonaka and Noburu Konno say that in the creation of new knowledge, both that type of explicit knowledge and the knowledge gained through firsthand experience are equal.[117] One is not more important than the other.

With the willingness to forgive both sons, and a persistence born out of his love for both, the father tries to bring the two brothers together. In this case, the father is the innovator who exemplifies the pattern of faith so necessary for reducing inventive solutions to practice.

Father (as innovator)

When we view the innovator as the father in the parable, we can understand how both sons are loved equally. The implication for innovators is to respect, seek and use all types of learning in the challenges of reducing the invention to practice.

Whereas the younger is seduced by being different, the older is seduced by being reliable. The younger is persuaded that the solution lies in a distant country; the older believes it can be found through conventional wisdom at home. The father loves them both. The father's immediate and immense relief at the younger's return reveals that things were not quite right during his absence. There was an underlying tension, perhaps a quiet grieving for unfulfilled expectations. Something was missing.

> But while he [*the younger*] was still far off, his father saw him and was filled with compassion; he ran and put his arms around him and kissed him. Then the son said to him, "Father, I have sinned against heaven and before you; I am no longer worthy to be called your son." But the father said to his slaves, "Quickly, bring out a robe—the best one—and put it on him; put a ring on his finger and sandals on his feet. And get the fatted calf and kill it, and let us eat and celebrate; for this son of mine was dead and is alive again; he was lost and is found!" And they began to celebrate . . . .
>
> His father came out and began to plead with him [*the elder*] . . . . Then the father said to him, "Son, you are always with me, and all that is mine is yours. But we had to celebrate and rejoice, because this brother of yours was dead and has come to life; he was lost and has been found."

Despite the returning son's drooping, remorseful posture, the father recognizes his son's profile anyway, even from a distance. The father's response is instantaneous. He sees what is happening and the potential it holds. There is no longer any need for the son's remaining steps to be taken alone. Well before the son has the chance to articulate his carefully rehearsed confession, the father runs out to meet him, instantly understanding the significance of what is going on and the potential it promises. The father already knows that resolution is now possible.

The father does the same thing a bit later with the elder son, who refuses to join the celebration. It's the father again who steps out toward the older son to personally urge him to come in and join the party. This father is not a proud, formal, aloof patriarch. Unlike the self-centered younger son and the self-righteous older one, the father freely acts toward both sons out of love and with a complete lack of self-consciousness. Despite the elder's voiced resentment and the younger's past disrespect, the father goes out to meet each one.

This father is operating from a different orientation. Instead of commanding the respect to which he is certainly entitled, the father's heart and mind are on something far more important. Clearly the father sees through the intramural rivalry between siblings. As an innovator, the father now sees the hope that was lost when the younger departed. What was not possible is now within reach.

This parable has no ending. We don't know whether the older brother joins the celebration or not. But at least with the return of the son, there is possibility and potential.

Not knowing is actually quite fitting for this stage of innovating. There is no guarantee innovators will resolve the conflicts between the new realities of the invention and the long-established realities of convention. If there is no resolution, there is no hope for innovation, which remains stillborn, on a pedestal of theory. Without willingness on the part of inventors to bend, alter, and morph their conceptual ideal and work with conventional means, there can be no resolution, no innovation that is attractive to customers. And without willingness by those who know the ins and outs of production to make adjustments in how things are done, there also can be no resolution, no innovation attractive to the producer. What's needed is someone to bring the two together so that a resolution can be found.

So often this is where many innovation efforts end. Conflicts are not resolved. Some deficiency in competency is often the culprit, or simply the tyrannies of the prevailing business model block progress. Too often resolutions are not even attempted because the guys in operations refuse to join in the celebration, whether from some perceived threat to a career tracks or competition for what's left of the resources. James Utterback has observed that "top management is pulled by two opposing, responsible forces: those that demand commitment to the old, and those that advocate for the future."[118]

Only when the two sides are brought together can their conflicts be resolved and hope for the innovation be restored. Both sides must participate. Both the experience-born wisdom of the younger and the convention-born knowledge of the elder must come together. "Understanding and managing this tension perceptively may well separate the ultimate winners from the losers,"[119] Utterback notes. New solutions often come from outside and from unconventional thinking. Forgiveness and persistence are surely involved. But the innovating task is hardly finished. With the hope and the energy produced from the possible, there comes lift and energy for the work ahead.

Surely the younger son returned in a different state of mind from when he left. He also returned with considerably fewer resources to show for his failed efforts. But while the son sees only defeat, failure, and the waste of resources, the father doesn't see it that way. The father sees a son who returned impoverished materially, but who also has been enriched spiritually, empowered with experience gained firsthand.

This actually happened to me. Unbeknownst to me, Bill Wilson, who became my mentor, spotted me from a distance making a career change. As he revealed to me later, what caught his initial attention and interest was that I was crossing a boundary. Which way I was headed—returning or leaving— he wasn't sure. But what he had learned in working with many innovators was that people who voluntarily and knowingly cross boundaries bring perspective and experience that is invaluable to those who don't or won't.[120]

What the father in the parable clearly demonstrates is an interest in something other than what can be measured in financial returns. The main thing is that his son is back, and he's returned in a different state—changed by the experience, knowledge, and perspective gained in the distant country.

Invention brings new experience, knowledge, and perspective from a different place, which is why inventions are initially rejected. Inventions are departures. They threaten to disorient and disrupt. These threats are easy to dismiss when the invention is only a concept. They are much more difficult to dismiss when it has been demonstrated that the invention can be done and done profitably.

The son's return is the first step in this demonstration. This is one of the reasons why the father orders the instant celebration. He recognizes the son's potential *after* his failure has been experienced and accepted, a recognition possible only with a mind and heart endowed with forgiveness and persistence.

> "Quickly, bring out a robe—the best one—and put it on him; put a ring on his finger and sandals on his feet. And get the fatted calf and kill it, and let us eat and celebrate; for this son of mine was dead and is alive again; he was lost and is found!" And they began to celebrate . . .

The father likely knew when his son left that his son would fail. Yet, when he sees his son return he sees the potential, perhaps even closer to realization then when his son left. This is like the same journey an innovator makes. The innovator initially sees in the vision of the invention something that is not without the potential of failure. However, when early attempts fail to make the inventive solution work there is much knowledge being created. Steps are often still toward turning that ideal into something concrete. And here's where the innovator can see potential where even an inventor may not.

No matter how clever the inventive solution may appear in principle, if it can't be reduced to practice and be made marketable, it will remain disconnected, in a "distant country," unable to benefit from an initial failure. This is indeed the case with what you find in the patent portfolios of so many companies. They are stuffed with patents that have never been commercialized. These ideals-in-limbo greatly outnumber those that have made their way into production.

A contemporary example of the "younger son" who hadn't made it back yet was the subject of an article by David Owen in *The New Yorker*. His name is Saul Griffith, referred to by one of his professors at MIT as "an invention engine." Griffith has won awards—including a $500,000 MacArthur Fellow "genius grant"—for his inventions and inventive promise. However, few, if any, of Griffith's inventions have become commercial successes. Inventions are one thing. Successful innovations are another.

Griffith is currently working on inventive solutions to society's energy challenges and is realizing that the real problem is not technological, but cultural. Griffith has collected statistics on energy use from around the world and located a ripe source of ideas from those countries whose residents use relatively little energy, yet still enjoy a high quality of life. "They are typically [residents of] countries like Portugal with infrastructure built before the availability of cheap coal and oil. Their houses are small and have thick walls and small windows and they heat only one or two rooms. Think about the drapes in France and England in the eighteenth and nineteenth centuries as great insulators for windows." [121]

Such low-tech ideas are crucial to forming viable environmental strategies. More complicated ones tend to consume more natural resources and produce more greenhouse gases. As a modern-day prodigal and a prolific inventor, Griffith has "returned" and is in the process of searching for resolutions, some very conventional indeed.

Another example is the team of Larry Pillote and Dick Sperry. This duo succeeded in turning Sperry's invention of Instapak® into one of Sealed Air Corporation's more profitable business units, a success these two have replicated in other packaging system innovations. They have worked together for almost three decades. After the second decade, the two invited me to reflect back on their various collaborations in an effort to see what practices could be "cloned." We found a few, but in the process we learned something none of us expected.

At first Sperry was responsible for resolving the technical conflicts and difficulties while Pillote took care of the commercial and political ones. Sperry was doing much inventing, but inventions were not his ultimate goal; a solution that works was. In the process, Pillote learned that having a revisionist orientation to contracts helped a lot. A willingness and readiness to rewrite contracts, sometime multiple times, became essential. Sperry embodied technical forgiveness while Pillote was the example of political persistence. Soon their roles intertwined. The boundaries between who was resolving technical conflicts and who was handling the political and commercial ones became more difficult to determine and less important to differentiate.

Such is the case when you have a sustained collaborative relationship as prolific and productive as theirs. The point here is that both Pillote and Sperry understood what they were trying to accomplish—how to repeatedly resolve the conflicts that were preventing them from realizing profitable new solutions, whether those conflicts were technical, commercial, or political. Early on Sperry played the younger son—brilliant but irascible and difficult to get along with, best kept at a distance from the host company, while Pillote played the role of the father. Over the course of their relatioinship, however, these two were playing and trading roles and finding faster, cheaper, and better solutions for Sealed Air Corporation to adopt whenever the time was right.

Concrete demonstration

The goal of this stage of innovating is a repeatable demonstration of how the new solution works. Patent attorneys refer to this as a "preferred embodiment," which is simply saying, a model that can be put into practice.[122] But this demonstration is still purely an expression of intent. Getting the model or prototype to work— for the customer and for the producer—is what needs to be demonstrated before there is sufficient justification to risk the next phase of innovating.

There are at least two ways of expressing the goal of this phase. Each reveals a different point of view. The first is "reduction to practice," which implies that when innovators succeed in making inventions work, they have "reduced" the concept—brought it down from the heights to the mundane reality of the concrete. The other is to "make it work now," which is a venacular way of implying that it works for the user and the producer. In the case of the user, it is valuable, valuable enough to absorb the costs of acquiring the innovation. In the case of the producer, it is profitable enough to warrant remobilizing resources devoted elsewhere. Either way, the goal is clear: Get the prototype to work. Resolve the conflicts.

Practical demonstrations for the technical resolution of conflicts are as essential as are drawings, words, and annotated explanations. But that's only the beginning of the demonstrations that the business side of things require. Actual evidence from users and production systems is crucial. If interest and investment are to be continued, some kind of trustworthy evidence must be produced. A business needs to know that the invention works economically, politically, and (increasingly) environmentally. Getting the innovation to work in the lab or even in a practice run is one thing. Experiments need to be taken out of the lab and run in the field. This is the only evidence the business decision-makers will trust. Physics, science, repeated experiments in controlled tests and simulations, as essential as they are, can't provide the credibility required by the people with real money to invest, particularly when they are seeking what they can never have—a guaranteed, risk-free return. What's needed are actual repeat sales from real customers.

Rules-of-thumb for innovators in this stage of reducing the invention to practice are ably expressed by Stefan Thomke in his book *Experimentation Matters.*[123] He tells innovators to expect failure and to be ready to repeat experiments, and each time to learn from the failure. Each experiment creates a temporary classroom for combining what was previously known with the new, where both can be experienced and observed. Conducting these experiments under actual customer conditions produces higher fidelity knowledge, as when a beta version is released to "lead customers."[124] Whether these experiments succeed or fail, what is learned in the process point innovators in the direction of what to do next.

The places where innovators conduct these experiments with prototypes may be more important than is generally thought. The Japanese have a concept called "*ba*," which, roughly translated means "space," but is not limited to physical places. This is the celebration space in our parable, the one the elder is reluctant to enter. Knowledge resides in *ba* and is intangible, in contrast to information, which resides in media and networks, or held by hard drives, flash drives, and ink on paper. Knowledge is shared and created[125] in *ba*, of which there are four basic types for innovators:

- originating places,
- interacting places,
- cyber spaces, and
- exercising spaces.

Originating places are where individuals share feelings, emotions, experiences, and mental models. Care, love, trust, and commitment are essential characteristics of originating places and normally require the physical presence of individuals. Authentic relationships are born and nurtured in places of this type.

Interacting places are more deliberately constructed than originating ones. For example, selecting people with a carefully crafted mix of specific knowledge and capabilities for a project team and bringing these people together in one place where dialogue can happen is the core characteristic of the interacting place. Metaphors and small-group techniques are valuable in promoting thought experiments. In essence, these interacting places are conceptual laboratories.

Cyber spaces are places of interaction that occur in the virtual world, using various information and connectivity technologies. Information-sharing and knowledge-sharing and some degree of collaboration can overcome, to some limited extent, the time and expense of having to get everyone in the same room at the same time.

Exercising spaces are like training rooms—physical and/or virtual—where on-the-job and hands-on learning can happen. Exercising space emphasizes learning through action, in contrast to the learning through the problemsolving that occurs in interacting places.

All of these types of places are potentially available to innovators and are not necessarily separate spaces. They tend to combine. Wherever an experiment is done, however, the goal for the innovator is always the same: resolve conflicts, but maintain most of what was promised by the inventive solution when it was conceived.

The "when" is another essential consideration in designing experiments.[126] Early and often is the rule. Conducting field experiments early turns out to have consistently higher learning-to-cost ratio than experiments run later. The more learned from the "failed" experiment, the more lift is gained to fly through the fear of failure. Well-located and well-timed experiments create new knowledge.

Occasionally experimentation is just not possible. That was the case when Weyerhaeuser Company made a bet on high-yield forestry—which at the time was a significant, unproven innovation that eventually changed the economics of the forest-products industry. Given the relatively long growing cycle of trees—at least in North American climates—someone needed to make a decision based on very little data. It would have taken too long—the time it takes for a forest to grow—to accumulate the data upon which to base a decision. George Weyerhaeuser, Sr. ended up making what turned out to be a very profitable decision without the benefit of a field experiment to tell him and his peers whether it would work or not. His decision demonstrated much faith. High-yield forestry proved successful. These kinds of "bet the company" situations without a demonstration are exceptions, not the rule.

In the fast-moving consumer-food-packaging business, companies take risks on new products subjected only to "thin" demonstrations. Risks of innovations with unresolved consumer and trade conflicts appear to be less than the risk of innovations with more technology in them. The rapid comings and goings of new products on grocery shelves can push companies to justify the risk. But even introducing an innovation in packaged food categories without a sufficiently convincing demonstration can lead to expensive and, in hindsight, unnecessary errors.

Demonstrations should test not only technical feasibility and profit potential but also whether a product is a sufficient fit with users' needs at a price that fits the customers' idea of value. Plenty of forgiveness and persistence are needed to design, conduct, and learn from these demonstrations. A more recent example of this pattern of faith is in order from an experienced innovator who works with much forgiveness and persistence.

❧

Recent Example
Paula Rosch, behaviorist, biologist, and veteran product developer

In 2002, Paula Rosch was asked by a large international consumer-products company to help reinvent one of the company's more "mature" products. Paula, a veteran of many product-innovation efforts at Kimberly-Clark for over two decades, had launched out on her own to share her experience, skills, and knowledge with a broader range of companies and product categories.

This reinvention effort focused on a well established—one might say old—product category for women. The company's product offering had been stuck in a relatively low market share position for years. As is the case with many long-standing consumer-product categories, the profits are attractive, but the conventions become entrenched, making innovating difficult. Much is known about the needs and preferences of consumers in these kinds of product categories, creating, in effect, extremely high hurdles for anything new to break through.

Given the need to break out of the bonds of conventional wisdom saturating this product category, Paula's first step with the team of innovators from her client company was to find a "far country" to go to—one that would enable a fresh flow of thinking from different but relevant perspectives. Paula has done this kind of thing many times with considerable success. She crafts what she calls a new "frame of reference"—broader, wider, and more abstract than the conventional product category without losing its relevance. This enables innovators to think along new pathways. In this particular case, the new frame of reference Paula invited her client innovators into was simply "the feminine experience."

Paula recruited and assembled what she calls "Scouts™"—intuitive thought leaders. The carefully selected individuals were a diverse set, willing and able to speak freely but knowledgeably about diverse aspects of the chosen frame of reference. The words, symbols, rituals, and routines of their new behaviors are of keen interest, so long as they relate to the frame of reference. In this particular instance, Paula created a tool to help these Scouts™ navigate and explore the context of what they associated with the feminine experience. The tool employed classic Jungian archetypes—both roles (e.g., sister, mother, wife) and characteristics (e.g., nurturing, artistic). She used this tool to guide multiple small groups of Scouts™ to consider, journal, envision, and express what they were seeing, all related to the feminine experience.

While many might view this step as too abstract and "out there," Paula's fearless improvisational confidence enables innovators to consider the relevance of areas otherwise easily dismissed. All this unconventional traveling through the "far country" ended up in a written description, from which emerged a few key proprietary insights. Both the context description and accompanying insights became invaluable grist for the mill for resolving and transcending the inevitable trade-offs between invention and convention. Interestingly, in the context of the feminine experience, aesthetic expression turned out to be a significant recurring theme.

With a rich description of the feminine experience in hand, Paula's next step was to introduce familiar materials for use by the group. She deliberately avoided the verbal medium of words and language. Instead, she recruited sculptors, weavers, jewelry designers, pastry chefs, and floral designers—people accomplished in working with three-dimensional materials, in addition to musicians and songwriters. She invited them to create a piece of art that represented something from the feminine experience. These artists jumped right in and, in short order, produced and presented to each other their works of art representing some aspect of the feminine experience.

"Then," as Paula put it, "we all had lunch." Not unlike the parable's father hosting a feast he wants both prodigal and elder sons to enjoy. After lunch Paula gave this challenge: "Reduce the works of art to both a product concept and model (in this "for women only" product category)." The energy, improvisation, and creativity were so engaging, the group worked well past their scheduled end time. By late that evening, the client had a working prototype. It quickly became commercialized and introduced in European and Australian markets, leading to market share gains in 2009 and 2010 and company plans for broader distribution in additional regions.

Undoubtedly some of what transpired can be applied to discovering needs and inventing solutions. But in this case, Paula took the role of the parable's father—with great finesse, not just technique. She brought together invention and convention and reduced their combinations into a concrete, instantly recognizable solution that worked—technically for the innovators, commercially for the company, and persuasively for the consumers. All this happened in much less time than had been anticipated, due in large measure to Paula's practical and creative techniques and a healthy dose of forgiveness and persistence among both leader and participants.

ॐ

Forgiveness

The Oxford English Dictionary tells us that "to forgive" means to give up one's resentment against someone or something that offends. This definition fits well with the parable of the prodigal son. But does it fit with innovating?

The relevance for innovators becomes a bit clearer when we remember that resentments are the result of unfulfilled expectations. Any inventive solution carries with it certain expectations. Only a few of these expectations, however, are realized. Many are not. Others change. While the task of innovators is to accomplish as many of these expectations as possible, some will need to be sacrificed because of technical feasibility, customer practicality, and profit. It's the job of the innovator to sort through which expectations can be done and which are best left undone.

However, giving up expectations—sometimes even getting in touch with what they actually are—isn't easy. This is where forgiveness comes in. Innovators must find the best resolution for any technical imperfections in the invention. The innovator must also find the best political and economic resolutions. Even customers and manufacturers are more willing to give up some of their expectations if the potential value is great enough.

Take, for example, Edison's incandescent lightbulb. Edison initially expected it would need a vacuum to surround the filament. Subsequent experimentation proved that a vacuum was unnecessary. That expectation was relatively easy to give up.

Some are more difficult, even impossible, to discard, like size expectations for early versions of portable computers. Because of their weight, early portables were more luggable than portable. It took years for the weight and bulk to progressively come down to a reasonable level. But the value of portability was too important to discard. The technical advances in miniaturization eventually combined to allow the manufacture of lightweight laptops and now pads and even smart phones.

Sometimes expectations can stymie innovating, as was the case with Kimberly-Clark's early attempts at the disposable diaper. The company's market research had left innovators with the mistaken notion that for the disposable diaper to be successful, it must cost no more than three cents and be flushable. Neither of these expectations was ever achieved. It turned out that what mothers really wanted and needed was a disposable diaper system that worked.

Expectations are part of innovating. Inventive solutions, when conceived, are full of them. In many respects, initial expectations carry the hope that motivates and inspires innovators. Just as easily, however, expectations can solidify and harden. Resentments form. This appears to be the case with the elder son who stayed home. It's also the case with those who feel compelled to defend the conventional, especially when threatened by the new in an invention. But forgiveness softens, and holds a prominent place in conflict resolutions that innovators must work through.

My own awakening to this came from a phrase an engineer used in a technical problem-solving session I was facilitating. The phrase was "graceful degradation." The session had to do with a fault-tolerant system to improve the reliability of a manufacturing system. It was not only the tension between the two words "graceful" and "degradation" that caught my attention. It was also simply the use of the word "grace" in the midst of all the technical jargon being tossed about. (Grace and forgiveness are largely synonymous, at least in theological circles.) Graceful degradation is technically an approach in fault-tolerant design that enables a system to keep operating even if one of its components or subsystems fails.

Hearing the concept of grace in this engineering context made me consider the possibility that forgiveness might be silently and anonymously at work. What these engineers were discussing was more than simply the use of a word in a different context. They were discussing failure, deviations, tolerance, and variability as interrelated principles and dynamics that play out in so much of what constitutes the basic work of design engineering. Yet these are also the basic reasons for forgiveness.

Although forgiveness *can* be given and received, it doesn't mean it *will* be. In fact, much of engineering has developed methods having to do with anticipating and minimizing the risk of failure, handling planned and unplanned variations, and understanding friction. Allowance and tolerance are two similar concepts in mechanical engineering, both of which have to do with deviations between the ideal and the actual. Allowances anticipate planned deviations. Take the example of the common 2x4. Have you ever noticed that a 2x4 is actually a 1½ by 3½? This is an established lumber industry standard that allows for anticipated changes in the wood fiber as it dries from its rough-cut stage and is smoothed with planing.

Tolerances make room for unplanned deviations between the actual and the ideal, for example when a nut and bolt are cast within a certain range of precision so that they will fit and work together, as intended. The nut and bolt are made to tolerate, within a certain range, unplanned differences in their expectations of each other. (Perhaps marriage counselors could learn something from engineers.)

Forgiveness is actually an essential part of a complex learning process innovators must go through. Without some form of forgiveness, the lessons from so-called "failed" experiments remain confined in the experience. Without some form of forgiveness, the potential of the invention will remain "lost" in idealism, unconnected to the realities of present circumstances and real time. Without some form of forgiveness, the otherwise rigid perfectionism and orthodoxies of convention—we've always done it that way—will remain locked in resistance to change. Mutations can lead to adaptation. Modifications dethrone the pedestaled ideal into the concrete vitality of a workable prototype. All of this is simply not possible without forgiveness.

Arie de Geus, who authored the Royal Dutch Shell investigation into the life expectancy of companies, had much to say about learning. Acknowledging the work of the Swiss educational theorist Jean Piaget, de Geus noted that there are generally two types of learning: assimilation and accommodation. "Learning by assimilation means taking in information for which the learner already has structures in place to recognize and give meaning to the signal. The learner can perceive, digest, and act on this information easily—in the way that a student, having looked up something in a textbook, can use it to answer a test question." This is the prevailing view of learning in our society and why teaching and learning are often equated. "The other type of learning is learning by accommodation, wherein the learner undergoes an internal structural change in beliefs, ideas, and attitudes. When we learn by assimilation, the lectures and books [representing] convention are sufficient. But learning by accommodation requires much more. It is an experiential process by which you adapt to a changing world through in-depth trials in which you participate fully, with all your intellect and heart, not knowing what the final result will be, but knowing that you will be different when you come out the other end.'" [127]

The parable of the father and his two sons leads us to believe that the younger son has learned by accommodation, while the elder has learned by assimilation. But it's the father who holds the pattern of learning for innovators. Both accommodation and assimilation are respected and honored by the father, the innovator, who with forgiveness, rebuilds the relationships.

Persistence

Experience teaches us what impatience wants us to forget. The rallying cry of the total-quality era and its more recent six sigma and lean manifestations—get it right the first time—is largely out of reach for innovators. It is highly unlikely that innovators will get it right even the second or third time. Multiple iterations, or learning loops, will be necessary to make the inventive solution work. Persistence is the quality that lifts innovators over the hurdles of unresolved conflicts created by invention.

Practice is a fitting word for the stage of innovation that turns the conceptual into something concrete that works. Persistence is necessary for practice. It is the faith pattern that keeps innovators trying and learning. Persistence is essential, whether the "no" in "don't take 'no' for an answer" comes from organizational peers and superiors or from the stubborn resistance embedded in conflicts between invention and convention. Resolution of these conflicts requires the sweaty persistence Edison spoke about.

The parable of the prodigal son presents us with two kinds of persistence: one from the elder son and the other from the father. The elder's persistence conforms to a more literal understanding: "For all these years I have been working like a slave for you, and I have never disobeyed your command." The reference to slavery speaks volumes about what the older son thinks he has been doing for all those years and why. Though the track record of compliance may be admirable, the phrase "like a slave" suggests something else. His persistence is born out of a sense of obligation. "All these years" might suggest long-suffering perseverance, but carries more than a hint of joyless drudgery and repetition. The elder son may *appear* to be experienced, but when a person tells you they've been working for twenty-five years in the same field, you really don't know whether those twenty-five years represent one year of experience repeated twenty-four times or whether it's been twenty-five years of progressive learning.

The father's persistence stands in stark contrast to that of the elder son. The father's kind of persistence did not allow anything to dampen watchfulness. The father instantly recognized the return of his son "even when he was still afar off." His persistence kept him alert to what was happening on the horizon. He was paying attention to what was happening in a broader context.

Similarly, the persistence experienced innovators demonstrate comes from holding a broader perspective. "Innovators make progress through iterative experimentation,"[128] and persistence gets them through the repetitions. Resolving an isolated conflict related to technical feasibility can make things harder to resolve on the economic side, as when the use of an exotic material to achieve technical feasibility results in a higher cost, pushing the price of the final product far beyond customers' perception of value. Or use of a relatively inexpensive component may represent an attractive profit margin for the producer, but it may not deliver what was promised in the first place. Arriving at what in hindsight looks like a "piece of cake" performance actually takes many tries and much practice. Multiple iterations are necessary, because multiple conflicts need to be resolved.

Innovators use repeat experiments to isolate certain variables to discern and differentiate what didn't work and why. Repetition serves as a baseline against which differences can be recognized more quickly. The contrast to what remains the same is instructive. There's simply no better way to know for sure than to try it out and see what happens. Simulations can help, but actual real life experiments are normally required for the degree of confidence innovators and their sponsors expect. Learning what works and what doesn't tells innovators where to focus their attention. When a conflict is resolved and does not inadvertently create another, or better yet, ends up solving another, motivation and energy get refreshed. Lift is maintained.

A dramatic example of this was the Rad Lab, established near MIT while World War II was raging in Europe. The Rad Lab was formed and initiated largely by innovator Alfred Loomis, whose story is told by Jennet Conant in *Tuxedo Park: A Wall Street Tycoon and the Secret Palace of Science That Changed the Course of World War II*. Loomis created the radar laboratory almost out of thin air. It was as if he "had simply willed the enterprise into being."[129] In a few short months, the Rad Lab not only reduced the invention of radar to a working prototype, something the British were unable to do because of incessant enemy bombing. The Rad Lab commercialized it as well. How all this was accomplished involved much faith, collaboration of deep and diverse experts, and many, rapid iterations in reducing the conceptual to practice. And though the atomic bomb may have ended the war, it was radar that won it. It is noteworthy that with all the success of the Rad Lab, Loomis could not be convinced to keep it open after the war. The "room" was shut down. Loomis considered the job was done, the tension resolved.

When the need is compelling, the invention promising, and the tension between the ideal and the real the central focus, a very powerful thrust can be created. It comes from the combustion of the right mix of resources ignited by sparks of human curiosity and inventiveness—what Lawrence and Nohira called the drive to learn. "As most detailed case studies of great innovations show, the drive that led to these breakthroughs was not so much an economic or acquiring drive but an innate drive to solve what appeared to be challenging problems."[130] In these kinds of contexts, persistence seems not to be all that heroic. More like the logical option.

Spelling out all the assumptions as early as possible, and then tracking and revising them as progress is made, may seem tedious, but is invaluable. This is the view of Rita McGrath and Ian MacMillan, who have come up with a "Discovery-Driven Planning" approach in high-uncertainty contexts.[131] In my own consulting practice, I have seen potent results when the beliefs underlying assumptions are made as clear as possible. Doing so in a collaborative process deepens the dialogue, sharpens hypotheses, and makes the next round of experimentation much more productive. When innovators know what assumptions are being held, especially by customers and producers—whether reasonable or not—innovators are in a much stronger position to resolve the conflicts. It requires persistence and some patience, to which any alternative makes little sense.

What happens *between* one iteration and the next may be as important, if not more so, as what happens within one iteration itself. Based on what was learned in the preceding iteration, innovators must reframe their expectations and develop new hypotheses not only for what is going on but for how to make it work. This is where innovators and researchers are similar, and different. Like researchers, innovators are intensely interested in the underlying cause-and-effect relationships. Understanding causal relationships goes a long way toward better hypothesis formation and more productive re-framing between iterations. But innovators also have another goal—to get the invention to work. Working together can enrich what is observed and enhance what is slated for the next iteration when both researcher and innovator perspectives are present.

This difference between innovators and researchers was of great interest to Donald Schon, a senior staff member at the industrial research firm of Arthur D. Little before holding various appointments, including director of the Institute for Applied Technology in the National Bureau of Standards and at MIT. Schon wrote a seminal work called the *The Reflective Practitioner* in which he introduced what he called "reflection-in-practice" and "reflection-on-practice," both of which innovators do during and between experiments. "The [innovator] allows himself to experience surprise, puzzlement, or confusion in a situation which he finds uncertain or unique. He reflects on the phenomenon before him, and on the prior understandings implicit in his behavior. He carries out an experiment which serves to generate both a new understanding of the phenomenon and a change in the situation."[132]

Sufficient time and space, both physical and intellectual, are also required. Due to competitive pressure, management impatience, or both, time and space for enough iterations and sufficient reframing are chronically in short supply. Lean staffing, short lead times, reactive (instead of pro-active) initiatives all contribute to the short supply. Even assigning the best, brightest, and most experienced to the innovating team does not eliminate the requirement for time and space. Innovators and their sponsors[133] must be both transparent and flexible with each other to understand and manage their own potentially conflicting expectations, including not being afraid to recalibrate when the need arises. The problem is anticipating how much will be needed when it is impossible to know for sure.

When no significant difference occurs between experiments, it may signal the goal has been reached and it's time to move on. Dick Sperry, the serial innovator we referred to earlier, calls this point a "stable innovation."

"One more loop"

The "one more loop" rule of thumb has proven useful to many. "One more loop" suggests that when innovators are near or at the place where most if not all the technical and economic conflicts have been resolved and there are no more "no's", one last experimental loop with the final version is prudent. Often innovators will do a soft launch or release to the market a beta version of the innovation as the final loop.

Too often a last experiment or loop is skipped because it seems redundant. Innovators should ask themselves if, considering the confidence gained from the "one last loop," whether skipping it is worth the risk. Many times companies skip this one last loop only to regret it later. Clayton Christensen was hinting at this when he suggested the even more general rule of thumb for innovators at this point: "Be patient for growth and impatient for profits."[134]

Michael Kennedy has suggested that instead of getting all the various subassembly engineering groups to agree on one specification up front, it is useful to work with a number of choices in the early stages. Toyota has learned to float a specification for a fixed period of time early in the process. Yes, this requires a little lead-time. But when the number and scope of alternatives considered early increases, choices made turn out to be much stronger and downstream costs of rework significantly decrease, by a factor of as much as four times according to Kennedy.[135]

Serial innovator Dick Sperry and his sponsors typically leave it up to Sperry, the innovator, to make the call as to when the innovation has reached sufficient stability to be ready for the next stage. His bias is to delay adoption until a written instruction manual for what and how the innovation can be reproduced has been completed. Sperry's bias is analogous with the rule of thumb from patent and trademark offices—that an invention is considered patentable only after it can be understood by someone *normally* schooled in the art. This readiness takes some time and space and a number of iterations, none of which is possible without forgiveness and persistence. Some think their way into a new way of acting. Others find better luck acting their way into a new way of thinking. When reducing an invention to practice, innovators must do both.

How do innovators know when they have finished in this stage? By the number of conflicts they have resolved and the degree to which those conflicts have been resolved. The incarnations may not be perfect. All the underlying cause-and-effect relationships may not be definitively understood. But if the invention works, if it brings new and valued benefits for the user and profits to the producer and can be replicated with acceptable consistency, then it is ready to be introduced.

Chapter 8

Submission and Humility

"**B**uild a better mousetrap and the world will beat a path to your door."

"If you build it, they will come."

Both sayings express a naïve faith that good work will be not only noticed but appreciated. Both have seduced many innovators. The first one came from Ralph Waldo Emerson and expresses by itself the notion that better quality—whether the result of innovation or improvement—has enough power to attract those for whom it is intended. Market victories of inferior innovations winning their respective competitions over superior ones—VHS over Betamax or Microsoft's Windows over Apple's operating system—suggest otherwise. The second saying comes from the movie *Field of Dreams* and suggests that supply creates its own demand, which has an element of truth but is incomplete. As many innovators know from hard-won experience, beaten, crowded paths don't happen overnight and seldom without effective introduction.

Every innovation must be introduced, sometimes repeatedly. The new requires introductions before it catches on, and innovators can easily underestimate both the importance and the challenges of a well-prepared introduction. After all, innovators have been preoccupied with the demands of discovering, inventing, and reducing-to-practice, and if and when they arrive at this stage, it is easy to forget that customers—new and existing— have also been preoccupied with concerns of their own. Something must interrupt prospective customers and attract their interest. Something must capture and hold their attention long enough to convince them to try and hopefully adopt this new thing. How this interruption is orchestrated consistitutes the art of introducing an innovation.

171

Introductions can just as easily irritate as attract. They require careful planning and the close collaboration of those with marketing skills. In cases where the innovation is so new and different that it requires users to make significant changes, the marketing creativity and finesse required can be as critical as what it takes to give birth to the innovation itself. Every introduction aims at what Peter Drucker calls the very purpose of a business—to create a customer.[136]

Each introduction intends to create awareness, induce trial, and encourage adoption; its main purpose is to persuade, to garner believers— whether new or renewed. An introduction cannot be neutral. It is not a mere passing of information from sender to receiver. The communication must invite and motivate potential customers to use the innovation, or at least to give it a try.

To succeed, an introduction must bridge the gap between the familiar and the foreign; between what the prospect knows and what the prospect does not yet know but is about to find out. It must arouse a person's interest, and then, with competent follow-through, fulfill that interest. In short, to be successful, the innovation's introduction must cause a willing and temporary suspension of disbelief.

The phrase, "willing and momentary suspension of disbelief," was coined in the early 1800s by Samuel Taylor Coleridge, the English poet and aesthetic philosopher. Coleridge saw it as a deliberate literary device to engage the hearts and minds of his audience. Since then it has become a standard practice of good storytellers, live theater, movies, and even video games. Artful marketers use it to overcome skepticism and suspicion, especially associated with anyone trying to sell something. The testimony of a satisfied user, especially one who is admired, is one technique. Third-party endorsements are another. The job of the pitchman—independent or not—is to get potential buyers to temporarily and willingly suspend their disbelief and to try the product. In a sense, a "conversion" is the goal of an introduction. This requires not only the convictions (belief) of the one doing the pitching. It requires some faith on the part of the prospect or customer. Trust—faith's social form—plays a pivotal role on both sides of the relationship and becomes essential to introductions.

How these "suspensions" of disbelief are accomplished is more art than science. Much can go wrong. As with any kind of communication, the message sent is frequently not the message received. Some crucial bit of information is inadvertently left out, or the content of the message sent gets overwhelmed or distorted by some outside factors over which the sender has no control. A bigger news story can happen precisely on the same day as the innovation is debuted. More often, a competitor takes deliberate aim and disrupts the introduction by running a price deal on a competing product, not only drawing attention away from the introduction but temporarily changing the value comparison. Sometimes the introduction can simply get lost in the noise of so much information and so many media channels.

Introductions experience liberal applications of Murphy's Law—if something can go wrong it will go wrong. Building in a margin for error is prudent. My mentor Bill Wilson started with the premise that introductions will be far from perfect. It is highly likely that when introducing an innovation—something that is by definition new and different—the marketing will be "screwed up," as he put it. Wilson did not intend to disparage his counterparts in the marketing department. Rather, his intent was to acknowledge the unpredictability of the communication and conversion at the heart of most introduction efforts. As a result, his preference was to take a preemptive approach by building in a healthy margin of error, assuming the introduction will miss something. He did this by making every effort to ensure that the innovation itself was on a trend. "Riding the horse in the right direction," as Bill put it, gives the innovation a better chance of breaking through into the awareness of customers. Of course, the discovery stage is the optimum time to link with a trend. But it's seldom too late to consider, even in the introduction's preparations.

Innovators and marketers often underestimate how difficult it is to communicate even the simplest and most straightforward message. At some point most of us fall victim to the assumption that what is clear to us should be clear to others. When innovators and marketers fall victim to the same assumption they can easily send the customer a message that is neither clear nor convincing.

Despite the communication challenge inherent in introducing something new, there is some good news. At the heart of every introduction is a clear and coherent value proposition—a statement of what is being proposed to the customer—the main elements of which are always the same:

- a statement of the **problem** being addressed,
- a declaration of the **promise** (or benefit) offered, and
- a statement of the **reason-to-believe** the promise.[137]

One failed introduction illustrates how all three elements of the value proposition must make sense for the adoption to occur. This was the market introduction of Avert®—Kimberly-Clark's facial tissue that killed viruses in five seconds. When it was first introduced and launched in two test markets in the 1980s, it was acknowledged as the most innovative new product that year, quickly gaining widespread awareness and earning the dubious nickname: "killer Kleenex®." But the launch failed. Despite all the positive press, the way the promise was stated—"helps prevent the spread of colds"—wasn't meaningful enough to consumers. Eventhough the technology of impregnating facial tissues with ascorbic acid worked, early two-ply versions were too scratchy for the nose. Consumers remained skeptical. The promise was weak and the tissue not soft enough. The company withdrew the product from the consumer market and shelved the patented technology, at least for a time. The promise missed and the reason-to-believe turned out to be insufficient.

Hindsight is 20/20. It's easy to second-guess the mistakes made in this introduction. I remember how devastating the withdrawal was to the inventor, Shafi Hussein. Many of us thought the innovation was worthy of a reintroduction, not in the paper products aisle, but as a wipe to eliminate viruses and germs that would be offered in the cold-remedy aisle.

That never happened. However, Kimberly-Clark successfully reintroduced an anti-virus Kleenex® in 2004. After learning how to impregnate lotion into tissue in the late '90s for added softness, the company made a three-ply version, the middle ply an adaptation of Avert®'s virucidal properties. This innovation commands a price 40 percent more than standard Kleenex® and holds a 4 percent share of the U.S. market. It also can be found in more than twenty-two countries.[138] The promise statement now states "three layers of softness with the middle layer killing 99.9 % of cold and flu virus." It took a number of years and several tries, but Kimberly-Clark innovators kept at it, and finally seem to have gotten the problem, promise, and the reason-to-believe right.

The introduction of an innovation is always a moment of truth. It reveals much that the innovator and marketer can learn. But the only way to learn is to submit to the market's judgment at the time and humbly take the consequences, good or bad, success or failure. Unreceptive prospects make for difficult and challenging introductions, but there is little else that can be done other than to humbly submit to this moment of truth.

This truth about introductions turns out to be very similar to the architecture of the faith pattern found in a famous story of faith in the book of Genesis. It's the haunting tale of God telling Abraham—often called the father of faith—to sacrifice his son Isaac.[139] Of all the narratives about Abraham's faith, this is perhaps the most revealing. While this may be reason enough to look for the pattern of faith embedded in the story, there is another reason. Just as an innovation's introduction has three progressive objectives—awareness, trial, and adoption—the story of God's test for Abraham carries the same set and progression, starting with what every relationship begins with—awareness of each other.

God calls, and Abraham replies, "Here we are." Abraham makes himself and his son, Isaac—the embodied promise (metaphorically, the innovation)—available to God.

Awareness is followed by a test, in this case a profound and horrific test, of Abraham's understanding of the requirements of God. This is the trial every introduction seeks: a test of whether innovators have understood the needs and the requirements of customers.

Just as Abraham offers Isaac as a demonstration of his submission to what God requires, so innovators offer their innovation as demonstrations of their submission to what prospective customers need.

Some context setting is necessary for a complete understanding of the story.

Before Isaac was born, God had promised Abraham that he would not only become a father but a grandfather—in fact, the great-grandfather of many descendants. God even changed his name from Abram (which means "ancestor") to Abraham (which means "ancestor of a multitude") to emphasize the point. But no son was born. In fact Abraham was getting a little impatient with God. He was getting on in years making it increasingly doubtful that he and his wife could become parents, considering their ages. So God gets more explicit with Abraham. God tells him that his wife, Sarah, despite being well past her childbearing years, will have a son. When Abraham hears this, he breaks out laughing. Whether it's the hearty laughter after a good joke or the weeping laughter of a cruel absurdity is not clear. Perhaps both.

But God's promise comes true. Sarah does become pregnant, despite her age. She has a son, and they name him Isaac, which coincidentally means in Hebrew "he laughs."[140] The promise of God and the hope of Abraham are embodied and fulfilled in the young boy Isaac through whom Abraham (and Sarah) become the ancestors of descendants more numerous than the stars. This is what every marketer and innovator might hope for from an innovation.

So it is not without serene irony and pure paradox that God tests Abraham's faith. It is one of the definitive stories of faith. Here's the story from Genesis:

> After these things God tested Abraham.
>
> He said to him, 'Abraham!' And he said, 'Here I am.' He said, 'Take your son, your only son Isaac, whom you love, and go to the land of Moriah, and offer him there as a burnt-offering on one of the mountains that I shall show you.'
>
> So Abraham rose early in the morning, saddled his donkey, and took two of his young men with him, and his son Isaac; he cut the wood for the burnt-offering, and set out and went to the place in the distance that God had shown him. On the third day Abraham looked up and saw the place far away. Then Abraham said to his young men, 'Stay here with the donkey; the boy and I will go over there; we will worship, and then we will come back to you.' Abraham took the wood of the burnt-offering and laid it on his son Isaac, and he himself carried the fire and the knife.
>
> So the two of them walked on together. Isaac said to his father Abraham, 'Father!' And he said, 'Here I am, my son.' He said, 'The fire and the wood are here, but where is the lamb for a burnt-offering?' Abraham said, 'God himself will provide the lamb for a burnt-offering, my son.' So the two of them walked on together.
>
> When they came to the place that God had shown him, Abraham built an altar there and laid the wood in order. He bound his son Isaac, and laid him on the altar, on top of the wood. Then Abraham reached out his hand and took the knife to kill his son.
>
> But the angel of the Lord called to him from heaven, and said, 'Abraham, Abraham!' And he said, 'Here I am.' He said, 'Do not lay your hand on the boy or do anything to him; for now I know that you fear God, since you have not withheld your son, your only son, from me.' And Abraham looked up and saw a ram, caught in a thicket by its horns. Abraham went and took the ram and offered it up as a burnt-offering instead of his son. So Abraham called that place 'The Lord will provide';˙ as it is said to this day, 'On the mount of the Lord it shall be provided.'˙

The angel of the Lord called to Abraham a second time from heaven, and said, 'By myself I have sworn, says the Lord: Because you have done this, and have not withheld your son, your only son, I will indeed bless you, and I will make your offspring as numerous as the stars of heaven and as the sand that is on the seashore. And your offspring shall possess the gate of their enemies, and by your offspring shall all the nations of the earth gain blessing for themselves, because you have obeyed my voice.'

—Genesis 22.1-18

Introductions are sacrificial altars upon which innovators submit their offering. Introductions are where innovators' belief in the value of what they have accomplished is put to a test.

Up to this point innovators have been the test*ers*. During the introduction, they become the test*ed*. Their offering must now speak for itself by working and providing value in the customer's world. In most cases, the test is not pass/fail, though many mistakenly think it is. A final adjustment may be accepted, if the innovator has gotten sufficiently close to understanding the prospective customer's need.

Introducing an innovation is a high-stakes test. The innovator, like a pilot landing a plane, must give complete and undivided attention to the wing settings of faith shaped for gradual descent and a smooth landing. This pattern of faith can be found in the following acts and attitude the story of God's test of Abraham (and Isaac) reveals:

- Connect and comply with the one to be served.
- Be willing to sacrifice the offer.
- Wait for the response and adapt.

Let's take a look at each one more closely.

Connect and Comply

The first part of the story starts with a verbal exchange between God and Abraham that establishes the connection. The connection is initiated by God, who calls out Abraham's name. Abraham confirms: "Here I am," and the connection is made.

This "connecting" is not a connecting between equals. This is the basic characteristic of the relationship between innovators and prospective customers. The customer is sovereign in this relationship, completely free to accept or reject what is being offered, not to mention, accept the mere connection itself. The customer establishes the terms. Innovators and marketers must submit themselves to the implications of this inequality.

Whenever innovators or marketers think they know more or better than the customer what the customer needs, this initial connection can fail. The Vice President of new products at a baking company client of mine once remarked, behind the two-way mirror of the focus-group facility, "These consumers don't know what they're talking about. They can't tell us what they really want." Many experienced innovators may have thought and felt the same, but most know from hard won experience, it's not up to consumers to articulate what they want or need in ways innovators and marketers dictate. It's just the opposite.

The second interaction—Abraham responding in silent compliance to God's instructions—points unambiguously to Abraham's act of submission and attitude of humility. In fact, what Abraham says by what he does is all but incredulous. Without a word or even an inference of protest, Abraham submits to God's request, a request that any reasonable reader of this story can't help but regard as outrageous. How could a loving God, one who promised Abraham on more than one occasion that he would be the father of many nations, who has miraculously enabled a ninety-year-old Sarah to give birth to Isaac, now require Abraham to sacrifice the very living embodiment of that promise? What kind of dark, twisted imagination could conceive of such a test?

And Abraham? What about his lack of protest? How could Abraham simply submit to this test without raising some objection? He certainly had grounds to object. This test was illogical, some called it absurd,[141] clearly and horribly unfair, not to mention a barbaric instance of human sacrifice! However, Abraham's silent but responsive compliance speaks clearly and unmistakably of his understanding of the inequality of the relationship. Abraham understood who he was talking to or, more to the point, who was talking to him. Submission and humility may not be words used in the story, but submission and humility saturate the narrative.

What does this story have to do with the introduction of an innovation and the innovator's role in it? Everything. When an innovation is introduced, it is in the context of a relationship between unequals. Where there is no relationship with a prospective customer to begin with, the innovation is the reason for a relationship to begin. Where there is an existing relationship, the innovation can affect the future fabric of that relationship. But whether new or existing, it is the relationship more than the innovation that ultimately matters and governs both the introduction and the innovating.

Sooner or later, innovators must submit themselves and their innovations—ready or not—to the ultimate test. And the test is as much about an affirmative answer to "will this innovation work for me?" as it is about "is there a relationship here that I can trust?"

Trust is always being tested in relationships. This is what an introduction is—a test. Can the customer believe in the innovator, the marketer, the innovation? Are they each telling the truth about the promise(s) they are making? Does the innovation solve the problem the customer needs to solve? Do those promoting the product have the best interests of the customer in mind? Can the customer trust what is being offered? Does the innovation work? Only the customer can answer the questions. Only through trial and testing can the customer determine whether an innovation is worth investing in.

Every relationship is built on trust. Trust often builds slowly. Innovators and marketers must demonstrate effectively that they are trustworthy and believable. They do this in the way they express the problem, the promise, and the reason-to-believe. Innovators and marketers must first connect with and then comply with the customer and the customer's world.

Be Willing to Sacrifice the Offer

Having submitted to the test, the pace of the narration slows in Abraham's story. Frame by frame Abraham prepares to make the offering required in excruciatingly slow motion.

> So the two of them walked on together. Isaac said to his father Abraham, "Father!" And he said, "Here I am, my son." [Isaac] said, "The fire and the wood are here, but where is the lamb for a burnt-offering?" Abraham said, "God himself will provide the lamb for a burnt-offering, my son." So the two of them walked on together.
>
> When they came to the place that God had shown him, Abraham built an altar there and laid the wood in order. He bound his son Isaac, and laid him on the altar, on top of the wood. Then Abraham reached out his hand and took the knife to kill his son.

This exchange is similar to the first. But this time it's *Isaac* who calls out to Abraham. Abraham responds with another "Here I am." Isaac asks the obvious, the one question we might secretly hope would not be asked by anyone, let alone by Isaac. Was Isaac starting to put two and two together, awakening to the fact that *he* was going to be the offering? "So the two of them walked on together."

Were they both hypnotically sleep walking in some joint delusion to which Abraham gives voice—"God himself will provide the lamb for a burnt-offering, my son"—all the while knowing full well what God's initial instructions were? Is this the example of Abraham's faith that we're supposed to admire? It could be just as easily an example of complete denial. Perhaps Abraham was already numb in anticipatory grief.

This is similar to the anxiety innovators encounter when their innovation is introduced. Is the innovation going to end up a "burnt offering," sacrificed on the altar of some neglected retail shelf in a failed attempt to compete for attention? Will it be summarily rejected? Or worse, ignored? Will its value or newness or both be unrecognized? Insufficient?

The innovator is a prisoner of hope. The test has been taken and turned in, but not yet graded and returned. Prospects can just as easily reject as accept. A rejection can be for anticipated, unanticipated, or even seemingly capricious reasons—or no reason at all. The turn off could be due to a simple word or phrase in the product's introduction, leaving the prospect simply with a negative feeling.

Whatever else the innovation is at this point—an invention, a new solution, a better value, a more elegant design—it is an offer, sacrificed on the altar of customers' opinions. For the innovation and the innovator, this is the moment of truth: the prospect either becomes a customer or does not. Customers hold all the cards, and some demand more than might at first seem reasonable and fair.

Let's see how this works in the real world. Experienced innovators know that the first offering may have to be sacrificed, as an "access fee," to begin the process of learning about the requirements a customer has for an acceptable solution to a need. Big customers like Volkswagen and General Motors, for example, are reluctant to adopt an innovation offered to them by a supplier without a second supplier, which takes away much of the traditional motivation for a supplier to build their own patent portfolio. The possibility of a lawsuit for patent infringement has a chilling effect on a supplier's relationship with a buyer. A supplier would think twice before filing a patent infringement suit against a customer. However, patenting an invention to tell the customer of the supplier's commitment may make sense. So, in order to build trust and obtain a potentially lucrative contract with a big and powerful customer, an innovation is offered in a manner that protects the customer from any future patent claims. The offer is a sacrifice for the innovator—in this case an automotive supplier—but holds the promise of building a long-term relationship with the customer and the possibility of selling future innovations to that customer. This is a significant sacrifice, but it can and has helped win sizable contracts in highly competitive areas.

This may be the toughest challenge—at least emotionally and spiritually—that innovators face: are they willing to sacrifice their innovation for the sake of a relationship to create a customer?

If innovators withdraw from the test too soon, they just might miss the "substance of what is hoped for, the evidence of things unseen." For as the story of Abraham unfolds, something happens right at the brink when he raises the knife—as it has for many innovators at this point. Customers provide a response that demands the innovator remain open. Humble in anticipation, more is revealed, which leads us to the third element of this pattern of faith.

Wait for the response and adapt

> But the angel of the Lord called to him from heaven, and said, "Abraham, Abraham!" And he said, "Here I am." He said, "Do not lay your hand on the boy or do anything to him; for now I know that you fear God, since you have not withheld your son, your only son, from me." And Abraham looked up and saw a ram, caught in a thicket by its horns. Abraham went and took the ram and offered it up as a burnt-offering instead of his son. So Abraham called that place "The Lord will provide"; as it is said to this day, "On the mount of the Lord it shall be provided."
>
> The angel of the Lord called to Abraham a second time from heaven, and said, "By myself I have sworn, says the Lord: Because you have done this, and have not withheld your son, your only son, I will indeed bless you, and I will make your offspring as numerous as the stars of heaven and as the sand that is on the seashore. And your offspring shall possess the gate of their enemies, and by your offspring shall all the nations of the earth gain blessing for themselves, because you have obeyed my voice."

This is the third time Abraham replies, "Here I am." It's a refrain that is more than merely an effective narrative device. Abraham hasn't left, literally or figuratively. Unfortunately, many do when they are blindly following a process, formula, or recipe. They simply check out. Up until this point, Abraham has methodically followed the test's instructions, but he has not stopped paying attention. All along he has been present, alert, and staying open to what he believed and said he believed—the hope that God would indeed provide the lamb. At the very last minute, his faith pays off. The angel intervenes (speaking on behalf of God) and declares he has passed the test—"Now I know that you fear God, since you have not withheld your son, your only son, from me." The test is over.

Innovators can glean much from Abraham's example. Abraham remained "open" to possibility even through to the very end. When a potential customer responds to an offer, the innovator must always be open to a third possibility between the "yes" and the "no"—the "maybe." With a "maybe" there is more for the innovator to learn and do. Innovators must remain open to make adjustments to the reason-to-believe.

When potential customers believe innovators have their best interests at heart, they will give them another chance, even when the innovation as introduced misses the mark. Kimberly-Clark learned this with their anti-viral Kleenex®.

Being open turns what otherwise would be a monologue into a dialogue. Too often introductions are viewed as a one-way communication, deaf to anything but a "yes" or "no" from prospective customers. There is no anticipation of any questions or comments from customers. But dialogue works, especially when done with humility, not dogmatically, in a condescending way. When innovators and marketers rigidly hold on to their particular version of the innovation's value proposition they miss "the ram caught in the thicket" and, as a result, kill the innovation.

Take the experience of an innovator and marketer at Clif Bar & Company, Tom Richardson and Michelle Ferguson. When they realized their first market introduction of Mojo® was being pulled off the shelves at Trader Joe's, they were disappointed but not defeated. They could have given up, but they both believed that Mojo®, a novel combination of sweet and salty in a snack bar at the time, was still very interesting to consumers.

So they went back to the marketing storyboards and R&D formulations to make some adjustments. In fact, their continued belief in the potential of Mojo® got them through one more miss at "getting it right." They kept making adjustments in both the product's formula and the way they talked about it until the third introduction in and through what they call a "discovery channel" gave Mojo® enough traction to take hold. It has become one of Clif Bar & Company's more sustained successes.

Both Tom and Michelle were humbly willing to submit themselves to the judgment of the marketplace. They did not give up hope or their belief in Mojo®. They just gave up their initial expectations, and they modified both their product and its presentation to better meet customer needs.

Hewlett-Packard's Imaging and Printing Group manifests a similar approach for introducing their innovations to the market. They call it "launch and learn." They anticipate the need to make adjustments to the initial offering. My mentor used to call this "make a little, sell a little," learning as much as one can from the first go-around and incorporating the lessons learned into adjustments in second and even third versions.

Anticipating adjustments will be necessary shouldn't be confused with doing a test market. The difference is that these early efforts are about learning and adapting, making offers for the sake of what can be learned in serving the customer better. A discovery channel is lower volume and slower moving, not meant to simulate the more mainstream market. It's intended to create enough time and space to learn and adjust. But that requires a willingness and readiness to make offerings and sacrifice them.

In the world of Clif Bar & Company, a discovery channel can be a collection of independent bike dealers or the camping equipment retailer REI. With what is learned, adjustments are made in the product and communications, preparing for the eventual higher-volume, faster-moving grocery and mass market. Test markets mimic the market but are limited to a geographic area or a retail channel. In contrast, discovery channels afford a place and chance to fine-tune the innovation and its value proposition.

There are in all domains modes of language and vocabulary called dogmatics and apologetics. I learned of this distinction in the study of different classifications of theology, but it applies to any domain. Dogmatics is the language experts use to communicate among themselves. For example, when experts discuss and debate the art and practice of their domain, they often use jargon and acronyms as shorthand. Shorthand can be an efficient way to help focus on the leading edge and boundary disputes of their discipline. Apologetics, on the other hand, is the language experts use, or should use, to communicate with others who are not schooled in the finer distinctions of the domain. When experts communicate with nonexperts, it cannot be assumed that the nonexpert will understand the connotations, nuances, or even denotations of the terms used. The problem of fundamentalism—whether religious, political, or otherwise—stems in part from ignoring the difference between apologetics and dogmatics. A fundamentalist basically uses dogmatic language where the situation calls for apologetics.

Apologetics is a more forgiving and a more appropriate mode of communication for an introduction, especially when introducing to a mainstream market. The challenge for innovators is to shift themselves out of dogmatics and into apologetics. Carrying dogmatic language and orientation into an introduction can make crossing the chasm between early adopters and the early majority even more difficult than it already is. Viewing the introduction as an apologetic dialogue rather than a dogmatic monologue can only increase the probably of the introduction's success. Taking this approach is just not possible without practicing submission and humility, both of which deserve a closer look. But first, a recent example.

ℰℭ

Recent Example

Doug Gilmour, artist, story/brand author, advertising at Clif Bar & Co.

In the winter of 2003, Gary Erickson—avid cyclist, endurance athlete, and founder of Clif Bar & Company—called Doug to join him in the company's R&D kitchen. Doug left his temporary workspace, a heatless corner of the warehouse attached to the company's main offices in the Berkeley industrial flats, and met Gary in the kitchen. Gary handed him a wrapperless energy bar and said, "Try this. What do you think?"

Doug Gilmour and Gary had given birth to several other energy bars— Clif Bar®, Luna®, Mojo®. Though a bit of an oversimplification, Gary typically created the eatable product while Doug authored the brand name, mark, and identity for the wrapper. Together their collaborations had proven both inspired and commercially successful, so this was not a unique encounter for the two of them. Internal responses to the prototype so far were indicating it was near ready. The question was not whether or when, but how. What story might connect all the interests and comply with the consumers' needs from which the most attractive brand, images, and text would serve the introduction of this new product in the best possible light?

Doug took a bite . . . and then another. "Pretty good. So, what gives?" That it tasted great was not surprising. Gary has a knack for making good-for-you energy bars taste like something you actually *want* to eat, not just what you should eat. This one was especially tasty—like a chocolate candy bar with a little crispy crunch. Gary understood what Doug was asking. Doug's question was intended to get at the concept he knew Gary had intended underneath the satiating chocolate and satisfying crunch. Gary replied, "Protein. Twenty grams of it."

They both knew what was about to happen, so they got right to it. Anticipating Gary's reluctance to spend much, if anything, on advertising, Doug already knew he would have precious little space to get the message across—a name, an image or two, and four or five lines of text, at most. Only what could be carried on the package—sized not much bigger than the product itself. Not much to work with. But Doug also knew that the brand would need to come from a story that both complied with Gary's intent and connected with consumers' hearts (not just their taste buds).

That initial conversation was brief. Their understanding and respect for each other was such that they didn't need to belabor possibilities. They had a product—the reason-to—believe. They just needed a story—the problem and promise—crafted in a way to create awareness, trial, and adoption. They both agreed they didn't want another medicinal protein bar story, like MegaMx™ for body builders pushing dumbbells at Gold's Gym. There were already plenty of chemical-sounding bars crowding the market. Besides, that wasn't what the company was about anyway, though at the time supplement bars were the nearest competition. Something more romantic was needed. Doug asked Gary for some of his pictures from Gary's annual biking trips in the Swiss and Italian Alps.

Understanding the concept behind the prototype—20 grams of protein and great taste—and his collaborator's intent, Doug starting looking for the missing romance to connect and comply with the reason-to-believe. The exploration and adventure in the touring Gary did every year was an obvious place to start. A tour bar emerged quickly as an initial theme for the problem and promise. Sketching out a few images and playing with related words evolved into copy and images for a tour campaign. After a week or two, Doug offered it to Gary. His response was encouraging. But something was missing for Doug. He wasn't sure what.

Then, perhaps it was the environment he was temporarily working in, perhaps it was his own intuitive genius—the idea of a blue-collar union worker "fell out of the sky" as Doug described it. The protein need of people whose work is muscular more than cranial seemed more real, authentic, and essential than the need of body builders. Developing a few sketches and some copy, he shared the idea informally with Gary, who immediately liked the point of difference, but worried out loud about the potential implications of the "union" positioning. So many of the company's target consumers were more tri-athletes than blue-collar types. However, both Gary and Doug were intrigued, and Doug returned to the drawing board.

With his characteristic penchant for finding the essence underneath— the romance—Doug found what was attracting them both. It was to honor the integrity of people who work hard with their bodies even more than simply those who work out. The name "Builder's®" surfaced in Doug's creative mind. The apostrophe in the name intended to give these hard-working souls a bar of their own. After all, their need for protein was essential for making a living. It was a story with even more value. Doug started sifting through images of workers building railroads, skyscrapers, homes—historical pictures suggesting a whole mythos—"it takes a lot protein to build a great nation."

It wasn't long before Doug had a story for the connective tissue that complied with Gary's concept. In fact, Doug prepared two—the tour campaign and the builder's campaign. With these two, Doug found himself at the familiar altar where he would make the offering—the high ritual of advertising agencies with their clients—the presentation. This time Doug was presenting not just to Gary but to the chief marketer (the CEO) and the product manager Steve Grossman, who was newly assigned to this project. Doug had been at similar altars many times before and knew full well that at least one of these campaigns would be sacrificed. In this case he wasn't sure which it would be. He presented the tour campaign first, then Builder's®. At this point, Doug could do nothing more. The offering was submitted.

Gary and the CEO conferred. The CEO was first to voice her response. "I don't know why, but I like this one (Builder's®), partly 'cause it's more risky." The romance came through. Gary agreed. The tour campaign was sacrificed, but more adjustments remained for Builder's®—painful for its creator, but necessary for the marketers to make it appealing to as many as possible. The trick was to make the adjustments without killing the romance. What happened next was what can be likened to some tough editing. Images were made more contemporary. Copy was fine-tuned. Even the descriptor was changed—"the natural protein bar" replaced "it takes a lot of protein to build a great nation"—all in an effort to optimize the chances for a successful introduction. But much to the credit of the marketers and innovators, the name, the apostrophe, and the romance were preserved. The pattern of submission and humility—connecting and complying, being willing to sacrifice the offer, and adjusting to the response—enabled Builder's® to become one of the company's core products. The only one who was not that surprised—though humbled, perhaps—was Doug.

℘

Submission and Humility

An innovation's introduction is perhaps the toughest test of faith for any innovator. In this context, submission is the only item on the menu of actions, and it is especially difficult for many to swallow. Humility is an essential companion to submission and makes it easier to digest the experience, or, to mix the metaphor, makes it a softer landing whatever the outcome.

Submission does not sit comfortably in the hearts and minds of innovators. The word shows up infrequently in normal conversation, at least in English. (The Arabic version—*islam*—shows up more often, perhaps.) The practice of submission, however, may be more frequent than many of us realize.

"Submit" has two basic meanings: to yield or give way to another, and to enter or put forward for approval or consideration. In both meanings priority is given to the other, the one to whom the submitter is yielding or making the offer. It is in this sense that the mission of innovators is sublimated, put under, if you will, the more important "mission" of the one for whom the innovation is intended.

Submission is precisely what happens to innovators when an innovation is introduced to the intended customer. As and when an innovation is offered, the prospect is ultimately and entirely free to respond as he or she sees fit. They can ignore it, accept it, reject it or "suspend their disbelief" and ask for more information. But whatever the character of the prospect's response, innovators cannot control the response. They can only submit to it.

The introduction is a powerless but not hopeless experience for innovators. The experience of powerlessness confronts innovators with the inescapable reality that despite their very best efforts, the very best of their imagination, empathy and inventiveness, the prospective customer holds all the cards. It makes little difference to the prospect how long and hard

187

the innovator has worked. If the value is not perceived to be there, what is being submitted can be simply ignored or rejected. Certainly innovators will attempt to do anything they can to achieve acceptance, stimulate trial and encourage adoption. But none of those desired outcomes are possible without first submitting to this ultimate test of faith.

To make matters worse, prospective customers are not the only ones to whom innovators must submit. Innovators must also submit to their colleagues in marketing. These partners in the design and creation of effective introductions have their own ideas and skills they bring to the introduction challenge. Like innovators, they too must submit to the perceptions and judgments of customers. And both innovators and marketers are well advised to "subject themselves to each other," as the apostle Paul admonishes his fellow followers in his letter to the Colossians 3.13-25. More will be said about this relationship between innovators and marketers, especially in the context of introducing an innovation. Suffice it to say for now that submission represents an unavoidable threshold that both innovators and markets must traverse if they are to realize the greater mission of creating and serving a customer—the very purpose of a business, not to mention, any innovation. The test of Abraham's faith is the prototype for this pattern of faith for innovators.

As difficult as it is for any of us, not just innovators, to swallow the necessities of submission, we are not left without an effective and resilient companion found in humility. The *act* of faith may be submission. Its complimentary *attitude* is found in humility.

Humility is an open-mindedness and receptivity to the truth, particularly the truth that one may not want to hear. And in whatever ways humility has been defined and described, the humble are willing to acknowledge that they don't necessarily see the complete truth; that another may see important parts of the whole the humble do not. "For we know only in part, and we prophesy only in part; now we see in a mirror, [but] dimly." (I Corinthians 13.9,12).

Humility does not come easily, particularly for overly confident innovators and marketers full of themselves or full of the enthusiasm that comes from new-found knowledge. Faith can foster its own form of over-confidence and pride. Humility is a particularly scarce and therefore precious commodity in the context of introduction strategies. These strategies are so often filled with promotional schemes oriented to "look at me" messages and communication techniques. It requires excruciating discipline—the kind Abraham demonstrated in his speechless but not hopeless compliance—for innovators to put aside their own interests, their own "mission," and even to be willing to sacrifice the very thing they have been working so hard to create, a thing that they believe will benefit the prospective customer. But despite the demanding requirements on innovators' own emotional intelligence, humility proves to be an effective companion to submission. As some describe it, humility is not thinking less of your self, but thinking of yourself, less. With fewer thoughts of your self clouding perception, the ability to perceive, understand and adapt to the response of the prospect, whatever the response, is much clearer, coherent and deliberate.

With acts of submission and attitudes of humility, innovators and marketers are in a better position to see at the very last moment the sudden and often subtle appearance of the "ram caught in the thicket."

The Collaborative Challenge

When introducing an innovation to the market, innovators and marketers submit to the collective judgment of the marketplace. They are at the mercy of the readiness, perceptions, and opinions of prospective customers. No doubt marketers will and should attempt to prepare the customer with all sorts of tactics designed to improve their readiness. But when the innovation finally arrives as promised, the customer, ready or not, is the final arbiter. The customer either adopts it or does not.

Can prospects be educated enough to establish the correct expectations of value? Can you build enough awareness of your innovation to get potential customers to pay attention? Successful introductions are the result of marketers[1] deploying their marketing acumen even more than the result of innovators exercising their innovating skills. Marketing and innovating each have their own goals. Innovators bring something new and useful into reality. Marketers make it possible for prospective customers to understand and access the value of what is being offered.

Unfortunately, confusion between marketers and innovators about their respective roles and contributions in introductions has led to a great deal of miscommunication, not only between marketers and innovators but with prospective customers as well. The close collaboration required for an effective introduction is made more difficult by the different perspectives. Innovators look at introductions more as "landings," while marketers call them "launches." These different points of view can become a source of friction, disappointment, and even failure.

---

1 "Marketer" and "innovator" are used to designate roles, not people. Though occasionally these roles are embodied in the same people, more often they are not.

A frequent remedy is to make a hand-off from innovators to marketers. But while hand-offs may clarify who is accountable at what point in the process, they contribute little to collaboration. Instead of trying to determine who is in charge, innovators and marketers might better spend their energies tuning the value proposition so that the marketers' problem and promise statements resonate with the innovators' reason-to-believe, and vice versa, and both resonate better with the customer.

Introductions are like the first publicly performed orchestral arrangement of a new melody. The basic melody remains with the innovators while the orchestral arrangement for the launch is the work of marketers. A full complement of chords joins the basic melody to bring out the richness, texture, and volume necessary to raise awareness, generate trial of the product, and ultimately increase the rate of adoption. But if the basic melody is not clearly heard within the full orchestration, value is drowned out. While marketers conduct the orchestra, innovators carry the melody.

If better, more novel mousetraps could speak for themselves, much of the confusion between marketers and innovators would vanish. Unfortunately, innovations can't speak for themselves. They must be introduced. In crafting the introduction, innovators must humbly learn to let go, but not leave. Marketers must learn to listen not only to prospective customers but to innovators as well.

To innovators, the introduction feels more like the end. The demands of discovery, invention, and reduction-to-practice can leave innovators so totally absorbed with the challenges of a particular innovation that little thought is given to its introduction. "If we build it, they will come" can unconsciously seep into innovators' thinking. After all, shouldn't the basic melody be sufficient? This attitude shouldn't surprise anyone. By the time innovators have arrived at a working prototype, the innovation is no longer new to the innovators. And to "lead customers" and early adopters, the innovation needs little introduction. These types of customers tend to be naturally inclined toward the next new thing.

Yet to the majority of customers, most innovations remain largely unknown, the consequence of being new. When innovators are left to introduce the innovation, they chronically underestimate the challenges of raising awareness and generating trials, and they overestimate the readiness of customers to adopt. Innovators are not as schooled as marketers in addressing the nuances required in picking which customers to target first for the introduction. Nor are they as adept at avoiding a word, note, tone, or image that can inadvertently send the wrong message to customers.

When marketers assume the role of innovators, however, they can easily underappreciate the delicate balance of design and engineering trade-offs embodied in the innovation's early prototypes. Even slight adjustments in form or function can amplify unintended effects—over-promising and under-delivering. This can quickly destroy credibility with would-be customers.

To marketers, introductions feel like beginnings. Insisting that introductions are launches can cause marketers to push too hard for a hand-off, sending the message that innovators no longer have a role to play. When these hand-offs do occur, innovators—who typically hold the most knowledge about the innovation—are given a back seat, if any seat at all.

Perhaps the incessant inclination to hand the innovation off to the marketing team arises from the need to avoid ambiguities regarding who is responsible for what. But the compulsion of organizations to assign clear lines of accountability may actually work against the ultimate goal of an introduction—adoption.

How can innovators collaborate more seamlessly with marketers? Submission and humility hold a significant portion of the answer. When marketers and innovators learn to let go of their mutual illusions of control and humbly work together in the broader orchestration of the basic melody, these two points of view can enhance, accelerate, and even strengthen the innovation and its introduction to the market.

The question is not "who is in control?" With submission and humility this question has been answered: the customer. The real question is "How can we attract and convert the largest number of prospects into believers?" This question has a much better chance of being answered well when the melody in the reason-to-believe can be heard clearly. But when corporate compulsion to assign responsibility to marketing trumps unfettered access to innovators' firsthand knowledge, both the innovation and the introduction can be crippled before the planning begins.[142]

Atmosphere

Atmospheric conditions surrounding an innovation's introduction still matter, perhaps even more than they did in prior innovating challenges. Here the lift-producing faith of innovators depends more on the perceptions of others than on their own, including the prospects' own readiness to believe.

When depending upon others, the fear of loss looms large. Prospects and existing customers are free to perceive what they want to perceive. They are free to choose whether to try the innovation or not, whether to adopt it or not. When innovators prepare for an introduction, the circle of those who are involved becomes much wider. It is no longer a few innovators or even a few early adopters. Now it is a much broader audience whose intensity of interest and response is much more difficult to predict and gauge.

Introducing not only brings the innovation out of a somewhat protected environment into the harsh light of public judgment, it heightens innovators' fear of losing. That fear plays out in at least two types of introduction atmospheres: entering an existing market or creating a new one.

When entering an existing market, the alternatives and values are more clearly established and more widely understood, and the relative advantage the innovation brings is easier to discern. Prospects have an easier time comparing alternatives because the parameters are known. The atmosphere is a bit clearer if not more stable than when the innovation enters or creates a new market. When entering an existing market, what innovators fear losing is prospects' recognition that the innovation has greater value than alternatives. When the innovation creates a new market, however, prospects' ability to compare the innovation's value is much more difficult. Comparisons are "apples-to-oranges." The comps are more difficult to determine. Appraisals of value are more difficult for prospects when what is being appraised is by definition new and different. Here, innovators fear losing a meaningful connection with prospects. When the innovation creates a new market, its introduction must communicate both a new content and a new (or at least reframed) *context*.

So what is an innovator to do? How do experienced innovators face these fears of loss and set their wings of faith to fly through them with hope? Hand-offs and leaving the scene aren't the answer, though they still are a common practice. Hand-offs waste the knowledge of innovators and hobble the innovation's contribution to progress. Instead, collaboration between innovators and marketers is required. And collaboration works so much better with submission and humility.

Adaptation

An introduction is not an event *in* time, but a period *of* time within which adaptations are not only likely. They are necessary. Being prepared and alert to make iterative and incremental adjustments should be a part of what is expected for this phase of innovating. But this requires time and space. The innovation cannot be adapted to match the nuances of prospects' perceptions of value without both.

As a boy I had the good fortune of having a summer job at a small rural airport in Hayward, Wisconsin, for which I was paid in flying lessons. When it came to my first solo flight, I was, to say the least, anxious. Fear was present before and during the solo. Even after the flight was complete, the adrenalin lingered. The most anxious part of the flight, however, was the descent and landing. While I had practiced many times before with an instructor by my side, the first time doing it on my own was truly a test of nerves, and confidence. Had I learned enough? Did I have the faith in myself that my instructor seemed to have?

From that experience years ago, I remember that descents, approaches, and landings are by far the most demanding, active, and adjustment-intensive part of every flight. Concentration, poise, and split-second adaptations are part of the fabric of landing. As a pilot, all my senses were tuned to receive every bit of feedback that I could absorb. I was constantly gauging where I was relative to where I wanted to land and making adjustments in the yoke, throttle, flaps, pitch, and speed; all without over correcting.

This is the challenge for innovators and their peers in marketing. Both must pay close attention to the feedback coming from prospects at every phase of the introduction. Are prospects receiving the message as intended? If not, then some adjustment needs to be made quickly but smoothly. Are prospects, when they become "believers," given every opportunity to experience the innovation for themselves? If not, what can be changed? And are they responding positively to the experience? If not, what can you adjust in the innovation or in the experience?

Everett Rogers points us to four of these "adjustables"—compatibility, complexity, trailability, and observability[143]—assuming that the relative advantage of the innovation is there.

To improve *compatibility*, innovators and marketers might ask themselves, "What can we do to make the innovation fit better with the values, norms, and experiences of prospects?" The playwright George Bernard Shaw captured this when he said, "The only man who behaved sensibly was my tailor; he took my measurement anew every time he saw me, while all the rest went on with their old measurements and expected them to fit me." His tailor demonstrated a modicum of humility that enabled him to remain open to the possibility that his assumptions and expectations about his customer may need some adjusting. Dell Computer built its original business model for making and selling personal computers on this approach.

To reduce *complexity*, innovators and marketers might ask, "How can we make the innovation simpler to understand and use, or is there a way we can divide the innovation into separate and simpler parts, each of which can provide value on its own?" For example, the essence of an effective user interface is that it hides the complexity of the system while providing the user with an easy way to interact with the product. Two examples are the touch screen of a smart phone and the LCD control panel on a washing machine. Innovators designing human-machine interfaces start with the premise of submitting to preferences people have so that machines conform to people, rather than making people conform to machines.

For *trialability*, marketers must devise easy access for prospects to experience the innovation for themselves. My mentor was fond of considering making the innovation a "play thing"—especially with respect to new technology. Putting new technology in a toy (literally or figuratively) creates safe contexts in which to explore, with little risk of harmful consequences. This play space invites and promotes discovery by potential users. The computer gaming industry has provided impetus for a whole host of performance improvements and innovations, not only in graphic processing and display, but in visualization techniques and systems modeling.

Making it easier for prospects to experience the innovation for themselves is based in part on the humble acknowledgement that every innovation requires the prospective customer to change, at least a little. And with change comes resistance. Trialability is the attempt to address this resistance.

To facilitate *observability*, marketers and innovators might ask, "In which existing community might the innovation's results and benefits be most readily seen by others?" Word of mouth works. In specific markets, communities, and special-interest domains, observability enables the contagious spread of innovations quickly and more sustainably. Understanding the community's norms is typically a wise and practical thing to do.

Thrust

Submitting to the constraints of prospects' perceptions, the market's climate, and even the concerns of peers in marketing can be deflating for innovators, often causing them to confuse "letting go" with "giving up." There's an emotional letdown. It can feel like letting the air out.

Part of this has to do with the *dis*-illusionment than can occur for innovators during an introduction. Innovators arrive at the introduction with strong emotional bonds of parentage and authorship. Like proud parents, they come with high hopes carried by their expectations, conscious and unconscious. It's only natural. When the innovation is actually introduced, however, any illusions are burned away, leaving a reality that is more trust worthy. Disillusionment, it turns out, is a good, though humbling thing. It is necessary for achieving an understanding of what makes for that elusive sustainable competitive advantage. Does the innovation have a value in use that is sufficiently greater than any other alternatives the prospect is aware of and can access? This is the final test question. It demands both the courage and creativity that make innovators the remarkable people of faith they are.

So, in the midst of an introduction, how do innovators (and marketers for that matter) maintain the presence and attention required? In the case of anti-viral Kleenex®, Kimberly-Clark stayed with the vision for two decades, aided by a proprietary position. How do innovators let go of unrealistic expectations without letting go of hope? How do they stay motivated despite an incessant whittling away of their expectations, whether by the climate of competitive alternatives, the short attention spans of prospects, or even the internal dynamics and political climate of their host organization?

What motivates people to value what they value remains the subject of much debate and inquiry. What is worth noting here is that despite the variety of theories, many in the field of motivational research differentiate between motivations that arise from within (intrinsic) and those that come from outside (extrinsic).

Intrinsic motivation is at the intersection of all the drives—the drive to bond, to defend, to acquire, and to learn. What motivates innovators at this stage is not competitive differentiation and not more money or fame. The motivation that works for innovators at this stage is simply satisfying a customer. If innovators are to remain present, engaged, and committed enough to meet the demands of the adaptations that will be required, someone else's satisfaction—the customer's—can produce the kind of thrust that keeps innovators in the game.

Competitiveness, self-interest, rewards, and recognition all play roles in what drives innovators. But the genuine desire to fulfill the requirements of the relationship with the customer is a source of great power that is tied to both economic and moral value. It is what the Old Testament and modern slang calls righteous.[144]

Velocity

Velocity—both direction and rate—also contributes to lift. And in an introduction, it's the rate of descent that is the key variable. Since rate is a function of distance and time, the time dimension plays a critical role—both for duration and how the launch date is set.

Introductions take time. Creating awareness, arranging trials, and encouraging adoption, all this happens over a period of time not only for each individual prospect but for the entire market as a whole. As such, introductions are more appropriately conceived as periods or phases than discrete events, despite the impatience of stakeholders for results. In fact, this time dimension helps innovators and marketers to keep in mind that the specific innovation they are working on is but one in a line of innovations. More are likely to follow. This is especially relevant when what is being introduced is a new technology rather than simply a new product. This is one reason why it is difficult to pinpoint with any precision the exact date or the sole inventor of major technological innovations, as John Lienhard reminds us.[145] Specific innovations are but instances in the flow of innovations. Viewing introductions as discrete, one-time events makes it harder for innovators and marketers to sacrifice the innovation for the sake of the relationship with the customer, current or future.

When does an innovation's introduction period end? Does the introduction end with the last laggard's adoption? Academics and theoreticians use the term *diffusion* to describe the spread of innovation, a strangely appropriate term when you think that the ultimate end of the introduction period is the complete diffusion of the innovation into the so-called mainstream market and culture. At one point in time, the lightbulb was considered a significant innovation. Now it is considered a necessity, a commodity, a normal part of our lives. When did it change from one to the other?

Marking the end of an innovation's introduction period may be historically intriguing but not as important to innovators as the timing of its beginning.

Timing

In an introduction, the emphasis is all about *when*. In landing an airplane, the challenge for the pilot is not to come in too fast and overshoot the runway, nor to come in too slow and fall short. Innovators face the same risks. They can come in too high and too late, giving a competitor the first-mover advantage.[146] Or they can come in too early and too low, first to market but disappointing prospects with poor quality or poor value or both.

In an ideal world, the best time to introduce an innovation is when both the market and the innovation are ready. The real world, however, rarely gets very close to the ideal. There are competitors to worry about, pressuring innovators and marketers to introduce before they are ready. A particular industry's own annual calendar, such as the new model year for automobiles, also causes pressure. Retailers also are a source of worry, at least for companies that must squeeze into limited shelf space. These pressures force introductions on a schedule that suits the readiness of others more than the readiness of the innovation. It's not unusual for these forces to enable retailers to play one supplier off another. And there is the periodic disruptive technology from an indirect competitor that can turn a market upside down.

In crowded and well-established markets, introductions are often timed to a prescribed schedule not unlike commercial flights, many of which don't even depart until a landing slot opens up. In less competitive, more "roomy" markets, innovators and marketers have more discretion in the introduction's timing. It's always preferable to be the one who chooses when instead of being forced into someone else's rhythm.

Setting the introduction date is best done on a progressive rather than a fixed basis. A progressive commitment enables the final commitment to be made at the last possible moment. Committing to the launch deadline too early robs innovators and marketers of the opportunity for final and crucial adjustments. Most practitioners and students of innovation agree: if some semblance of control over the launch date decision is to be maintained, some one (perhaps two) people need to govern that decision. I have used the following simple illustration in my consulting practice to encourage innovators and marketers to "stage" their launch date commitments in a progressive manner in three distinct phases. This resonates especially with innovators.

Figure 11: Successive Commitments to Launch Date

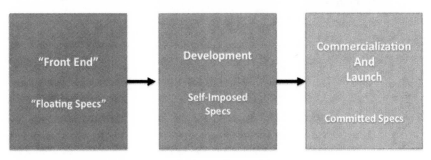

The first stage does not have any fixed specifications, no explicit targets for cost, quality, and launch timing. The specifications "float" for a period of time. Toyota follows this principle when a variety of separate disciplines are designing subsystems, all of which in the end must come together into a coherent single design. "Floating specs" point in a definite direction, but allow some room for discovery and improvisation within each individual specialty. This can't go on forever, of course. In most cases there is a point when the innovating organization (not the market) chooses to make the trade-offs in certain ways and set the launch date. Some call it a *target* launch date—a quiet reminder that they can change it if needed.

When this choice is made, the development can proceed. It is important to remember that the specifications, including the deadline for the introduction, are self-imposed. Changing them, either delaying or accelerating, is a choice that the innovators or their sponsors can make. This development stage is distinct from the final stage—commercialization and launch. What differentiates commercialization and launch from the previous stage is the explicit commitments of specifications that are made to others *outside* the company. When these external commitments are made, innovators and marketers have relinquished the ability—except at great cost—to do anything but deliver on or before the launch date. In short, successive commitments to introduction dates that have been gradually but deliberately set produce more lift and more freedom for innovators and marketers to work with the "adjustables" (i.e., compatibility, complexity, trialability, and observability).

There is one other lift-producing factor worth noting for this stage of innovating flight—innovators' prophetic orientation to the future, the angle of attack.

Angle of attack

Introducing an innovation and landing an airplane have at least one other similarity. When preparing to land an aircraft, many adjustments need to be made the closer the plane gets to the runway. A steep angle of attack at a slower airspeed aids maneuverability. When preparing to introduce an innovation, both innovators and marketers must keep in mind that the innovation itself is easier to modify than the environment into which it will be introduced.

Introducing an innovation demands close coordination between marketers and innovators—a choreography between two perspectives. The dance will not go well if one side attempts to exert too much control over the other. Innovators need to be free to tune the innovation to meet the demands of the market. So, like pilots responding to the instructions of controllers on the ground, innovators must adjust the innovation to the market's constraints, readiness, and resistance sensed by marketers. Like pilots, innovators must remain "in control" of the innovation and responsive to the feedback from prospects. Marketers, like air traffic controllers, must rely on the adaptive capability of innovators to adjust the innovation's rate of descent and speed for the most effective introduction.

Choreographing an innovation's introduction requires innovators to surrender any notions they may harbor of retaining their sole authority over the actual version introduced. For the introduction to be successful, innovators must make room for the contributions of their counterparts in marketing, with both an attitude and practice of submission and humility. This pattern of innovators' faith can be especially demanding. It's not unlike parents who have invested much time, effort, and emotion in raising a child, only to be then required to let the child go. As it "takes a village to raise a child," so also with an innovation.

Keeping innovators physically present and mentally engaged in the innovation's introduction is too often undervalued. The push and shove of resource allocation in the host organization often removes key innovators at critical junctures. Resource managers with an orientation toward "lean" staffing will pluck innovators out of this phase under the mistaken notion that introductions are mostly a task for marketing. They ignore the need to make final adjustments. Even innovators themselves can mistakenly believe that they have already made their contribution. They undervalue the intellectual capital their experience in discovery, invention, and reduction-to-practice has created. All this capital has prepared them for the fine-tuning that needs to be done in the final stages.

Why is maintaining innovators' presence and engagement in the introduction so important? First, the fidelity of feedback from prospects is at its peak. Introductions are not private simulations, but public, live reactions from prospective customers. These reactions produce a rich complex of signals that, without sufficient discernment, will go to waste, unused either in the immediate introduction or in subsequent attempts. Innovators are more prepared and better primed to read and interpret those signals than anyone else.

An example of this practice can be found in Toyota. Those familiar with Toyota's development system have noticed how innovators in that system generally abhor waste of any kind.[147] Of the many forms of waste shunned by Toyota's culture, perhaps the most serious form is "re-learning," or what some call re-invention. Far from something positive—as popular notions of "reinventing government" were thought to be a few years ago—re-invention comes from ignorance of the past, not failure. "If there is no mechanism or culture in an organization for capturing, retaining, and reusing knowledge, that organization is almost certainly engaged in constantly reinventing the wheel. Learning from experience when it involves complex, episodic experiences like introductions requires conscious reflection. Very few organizations do this well or even see the importance of doing it."[148] What is required is the alert presence of experienced innovators reading the signals from prospects.

Second, the likely deployment of the same innovators on successive innovations warrants keeping them present and engaged. This assumes, of course, that the innovation and its introduction are viewed as one instance in the larger flow of progress, not a discrete one-time event with an isolated pass-fail test.

Finally, there may indeed be something in the old adage "actions speak louder than words." The presence of innovators helps transmit to prospects the wordless reassurance that the offer, whether it is tried and adopted or not, comes from a source that can be believed. The introduction of an innovation represents the conviction that a better way is now not just possible, but practical; not just potential, but actual; not just probable, but factual; not just someday, but now.

As prisoners of hope, innovators are inherently captive to the idea of progress which itself may be more important than the specific instance represented by a particular innovation. The willingness of innovators to submit to this flow of progress—and their desire to make contributions to it—keeps them humble in the knowledge that the innovating's goal is not perfection. Though perfection is worth pursuing, it will never be attained completely or finally. As part of a succession, sacrificing the innovation itself as an offering is warranted. Excessive individualism and careerism can infect innovators and marketers alike and works against this sacrificial attitude. But whether the introduction ends up being a success or a failure, what is revealed in prospects' reactions can become an invaluable asset for subsequent iterations. This tacit knowledge is too easily squandered without the presence and engagement of the innovator in the introduction. But to be effective, this presence and engagement requires acts of submission and attitudes of humility.

Chapter 9

Acceptance and Gratitude

The innovation has been launched and evidence from the market—positive and negative—starts to come in. At this juncture, most imagine the work of innovators to be complete. Marketing and product management take over. Innovators are whisked away and redirected to the next assignment.

This is the norm, driven by the push for ever-increasing gains in work-force productivity. But it's a mistake. Experienced innovators have important contributions to make even after the initial introduction period is over.

A bit of wisdom was given to David Packard in the early years of Hewlett-Packard shortly after the company moved out its iconic garage. A retired engineer said to David Packard, "More businesses die from indigestion than starvation." The engineer had been sent to the little company by a Wells Fargo Bank executive to conduct due diligence on the bank's behalf. Of this piece of wisdom Packard wrote, "I have observed the truth of that advice many times since then."[149]

The truth of this engineer's advice became evident to me years ago when I was asked by the Keebler Company, which was engaged in what became known as the "cookie wars," to facilitate a series of new cookie product idea generation sessions. Keebler, Nabisco, and a handful of other competitors were introducing so many new cookie products that neither the companies nor the grocery stores could absorb all the innovations. Too many new products had flooded the market, with too little space on retailers' shelves. Even consumers had become confused by all the new choices. The entire market was experiencing an "indigestion problem."

That experience is a vivid reminder that an innovation, even one that is successful in the market, faces one more challenge: to be integrated in the life and routine of the consumer, the market where it's sold, and the company that produces it. Are customer expectations satisfied? Have they made the innovation part of their routine? Is it fitting into the routine of business at the parent company? If there are problems in any of these areas, the value of the innovation can be lost.

The job for innovators at this point is to examine the evidence coming in from the market and compare it to the expectations they had at the beginning. If this is not done, essential information, knowledge, and understanding are lost. When innovators are too quickly redeployed to the next opportunity, they miss the vital evidence coming in from the market. They miss seeing the unexpected. And, since the unexpected is the most reliable source of innovation, then they are missing a crucial piece of the innovation map. Innovators who are too busy chasing the next opportunity miss the unexpected evidence from the last one.

Innovations are attempts to change the world. Some succeed. Some don't. But from every attempt, evidence is produced, and this evidence is essential in giving innovators an accurate read on what needs to be corrected or improved. It also tells innovators where to innovate next.

During examinations like this, innovators need to be aware of the danger and tendency to filter out evidence that doesn't seem to fit. What psychologists call the "confirmation bias," or what many know as self-fulfilling prophecy. Unconscious filtering can distort or even blind innovators' perceptions at this important stage. An experienced market analyst, Vince Roscelli, in a moment of tongue-in-cheek candor, said to me years ago, "What I really do is round up all the evidence and torture it until it confesses."

Evidence trumps expectations. Evidence from customer reactions starts a new cycle of discovery and possibly the next innovating effort. Learning from our mistakes—accepting the evidence and revising expectations—produces the lift that carries innovators on.

To examine the evidence from the market requires innovators to do more perceiving and less doing. Innovators can learn a great deal at this stage. It's actually a diagnostic discipline, similar to the discovery stage where awe and wonder are required. Here, innovators are the ones most likely to understand the significance of the gap between the evidence and the expectations. Their understanding is enabled by acceptance and gratitude.

The parable of the landowner

One of the few economic parables of Jesus provides some principles. Most who encounter this parable can't help but be struck by the obvious lack of fairness on the part of the central character, the landowner of a modest vineyard. But as this parable unfolds, its narrative presents a startling twist having to do with the power of expectations.

A landowner goes out early to hire day laborers to work in his vineyard. He garners an agreement with those he hires first as to what he will pay. Then he sends them out to the vineyard. Act 1.

About three hours later, the landowner sees other day laborers hanging out in the marketplace. So he hires them as well, telling them, "I'll pay you whatever is right." This second batch agrees and goes out to the vineyard. At noon and at three o'clock in the afternoon the landowner again hires more workers. Finally, late in the day, the landowner sees others still "standing around." So he hires them and sends them out to the vineyard. Act 2, Scenes 1-4.

When it comes time to pay the workers—presumably at nightfall—the landowner instructs his paymaster to pay the workers in reverse order. The paymaster does as he was instructed, first paying those hired last, then those hired at three, and so on, paying those hired first, last. Here's the twist: The paymaster pays each worker the same amount, whether they worked for an hour or worked the whole day. This clearly offends those who worked the longest. Fairness has been ignored. Act 3, Scene 1.

But the parable doesn't stop there. When the first hires start complaining, the landowner reminds them of the deal they struck, a deal he honored and fulfilled. He claims it is his right to do what he chooses—including being "generous" to others. Act 3, Scene 2.

Here's the parable from the Gospel of Matthew:

> "The kingdom of heaven is like a landowner who went out early in the morning to hire laborers for his vineyard. After agreeing with the laborers for the usual daily wage, he sent them into his vineyard.
>
> "When he went out about nine o'clock, he saw others standing idle in the marketplace; and he said to them, 'You also go into the vineyard, and I will pay you whatever is right.' So they went. When he went out again about noon and about three o'clock, he did the same. And about five o'clock he went out and found others standing around; and he said

to them, 'Why are you standing here idle all day?' They said to him, 'Because no one has hired us.' He said to them, 'You also go into the vineyard.'

"When evening came, the owner of the vineyard said to his manager, 'Call the laborers and give them their pay, beginning with the last and then going to the first.' When those hired about five o'clock came, each of them received the usual daily wage.

"Now when the first came, they thought they would receive more; but each of them also received the usual daily wage. And when they received it, they grumbled against the landowner, saying, 'These last worked only one hour, and you have made them equal to us who have borne the burden of the day and the scorching heat.' But he replied to one of them, 'Friend, I am doing you no wrong; did you not agree with me for the usual daily wage? Take what belongs to you and go; I choose to give to this last the same as I give to you. Am I not allowed to do what I choose with what belongs to me? Or are you envious because I am generous?'

"So the last will be first, and the first will be last."

—Matthew 20:1:16

In and of itself, it is a disturbing parable. Effective parables always are. The parable challenges more than our conventional notions of fairness. It also speaks about the risks inherent in expectations and how expectations distort our perceptions of the evidence and reward. In the parable, there are at least four comparisons instructive for innovators. Three hold the pattern of faith I have seen in serial innovators. The fourth reflects what motivates innovators.

The first comparison concerns the gap between what was expected and what happens, and how this gap is viewed. The first hires expect everyone to be paid the same amount for each hour they work. They look for what *confirms* their expectations. The landowner has expectations also. He expects his generosity to be welcomed. But when his expectations are not confirmed, he doesn't hang on to them. He pays attention to the gap.

In the second comparison, each revises their original expectations. The first hires, upon hearing what others were paid, create a new expectation: that they will receive more money. They ignore the evidence. In contrast, the landowner evaluates *all* the evidence and revises his own expectation of being appreciated for his generosity.

The third comparison differentiates what each pays attention to. The landowner attends to what is being wasted and could serve a greater purpose. The first hires in contrast, attend to the relative status of their own situation compared to the other workers.

Embedded in these comparisons is a pattern of faith experienced innovators follow after their innovation has been introduced. These innovators take the opportunity to assess the evidence coming in from the market and:

- Investigate the gap between the evidence and expectations.

- Revise their expectations, not the evidence.

- Uncover waste and ask how it can be given a purpose.

Let's take a closer look at each.

Investigate the gap

For many, a gap between expectations and evidence points to how incorrect the initial expectations were. Gaps are to be sought for what they can teach. One company that has been particularly successful in mining these gaps is Toyota. Early on, Toyota adopted a routine practice of the Japanese culture called *Hansei.*

Hansei is roughly translated as "reflection." But it is more than merely retrospection. It is an attitude and mind-set that involves both the head and the heart. George Yamashina, who ran the Toyota Technical Center, describes *Hansei* as something akin to the American parental practice of a "time-out" after children have misbehaved. However, it is more than merely a time out. "In Japan, sometimes the mother and father say to the children, 'Please do the *Hansei.*' Some child did a bad thing. It means he or she must be sorry and improve his or her attitude. Everything is included—spirit and attitude. So once the child is told, 'Please do the *Hansei,*' he understands almost everything about what the mother and the father want him to do."[150] The objective of *Hansei* is not punishment, but correction. It requires the child to examine carefuly and dispassionately what happened and what can be done to avoid such a thing from happening in the future. The real goal is learning and improvement, not blame or punishment. When the child has completed the *Hansei*, they return to the parents and tell what they have learned and how they plan to improve. It's the child's responsibility to make this clear to the parents.

At Toyota and other companies, learning to make the product better, and the competitive advantage that derives from it, is vital. However, when Toyota installed its fabled production system in U.S.-based assembly plants, *Hansei* was consistently the most difficult part of the production system to teach to U.S. managers.

Regular and disciplined reflection for the purpose of learning and improving is not unique or confined to Toyota or to the Japanese culture. Surgeons and other medical practitioners conduct post-mortems in order to advance their knowledge. Forensic scientists and engineers conduct analyses after unexpected failures. A large portion of reliability engineering is predicated on the practice of embracing and searching the gaps between the evidence and expectations. Unfortunately, many of these practices are motivated by a fear of litigation rather than a desire to learn.

Innovators should be looking for three things when they examine the gaps between the evidence coming in and the expectations they had for the product:

- An unexpected success.
- An unexpected failure.
- Incongruities.

Unexpected success

Peter Drucker, in his book *Innovation and Entrepreneurship*, says it's difficult for management "to accept the unexpected success. It takes determination, specific policies, a willingness to look at reality, and the humility to say, 'we were wrong.' Far more often, the unexpected success is simply not seen at all. Nobody pays any attention to it. Hence, nobody exploits it."[151]

In the early '80s, the Internet was making its entre into mainstream use, as was the consumer-modem business. Paying attention to an unexpected success (or ignoring it) had dramatic consequences for two companies competing in modems. Hayes was the dominant brand, holding a 50 percent share of the U.S. market with its Smartmodem products. An upstart, U.S. Robotics—named after a fictitious company from a science fiction novel—started making faster, less-expensive models. As the incumbent, Hayes had become accustomed to a fairly stable but growing market serving the data-communication needs of businesses. Then both companies began to ride the wave of consumer demand for data communications. Unexpected successes were occurring for both. U.S. Robotics paid closer attention and responded more quickly than Hayes, although there was a time when their early success surprised them so much they couldn't keep up with the orders.

The executives at U.S. Robotics decided not to wed themselves to any fixed strategy. The market was moving too quickly, and other companies were scrambling, making and breaking alliances with each other right and left. Instead, U.S. Robotics chose to take a non-strategy they called being "strategically opportunistic." The intent was to avoid having their plan get in the way of their ability to discern what the fast-moving market was telling them. This required them to adapt quickly in the market and respond to what, in hindsight, we all now take for granted—the Internet. By the early '90s, U.S. Robotics had become the market-share leader and low-cost producer, giving them the freedom to drop the price of their modems instead of staying with fatter profit margins. That decision drove Hayes right out of the modem business and into liquidation.

Unexpected failure

The unexpected failure is a target-rich source for learning where to innovate next. According to Drucker, "Failures, unlike successes, cannot be rejected and rarely go unnoticed. But they are seldom seen as symptoms of opportunity. It is precisely because the unexpected jolts us out of our preconceived notions, our assumptions, our certainties, that it is such a fertile source of innovation."[152]

Several years ago, Ron Wilderman, an experienced innovator with years of operations and marketing experience at Weyerhaeuser, asked me to facilitate a rather delicate post-mortem of what turned out to be a very long and expensive failed effort that most in the company wanted to forget. Wilderman had just received orders to lead the development and commercialization of a promising innovation that, ironically, employed technology similar to that developed in the failed project. Wilderman wisely wanted to avoid a repeat of the same mistakes. So we agreed to conduct a formal retrospective examination, but to do so quietly, since the previous failed project had been an embarrassingly long and expensive one. We brought back the previous project's "retired" manager, reconstructed a detailed timeline of events, and brought together as many as we could find who were willing, to extract the lessons learned for the benefit of Wilderman's new project team.

Looking closely at the failure produced a solid foundation for success. Thanks in part to the detachment that time and distance afforded us, along with Wilderman's eagerness to learn, the next project avoided much relearning and saved months of time and effort. Wilderman's project quickly led to a technical success. The process improvements that came out of the project achieved commercial success that contributed to the renewal of one of Weyerhaeuser's core businesses and greater leverage in Weyerhaeuser's acquisition of McMillan-Blodel, a Canadian forest products competitor.

Incongruities

Incongruities are a third kind of gap. They are essentially discrepancies between "what is" and "what ought to be."[153] They're often symptoms of a ripe opportunity for innovation waiting to be discovered.

In October 2001, one well-read incongruous gap quickly turned into a very successful innovation—Apple's iPod and iTunes. Years before the Walkman® by Sony was the innovation that had given people the ability to listen to what they wanted to hear where they wanted to hear it. The problem that surfaced was getting music onto the Walkman. Furthermore, there was a war between music lovers—who were downloading music illegally from the Internet— versus the recording industry that was missing out on sales. The problem was well known. What was stood in direct conflict with what ought to be.

Apple seized that opportunity. It recognized that while the majority of consumers were willing to pay for music, they just couldn't download it easily from recording studios.

Apple offered a three-pronged solution: a well-designed device (the iPod), an easy-to-use download service (iTunes), and the opportunity for consumers to buy single songs rather than albums. The combination was an instant hit with music lovers despite the "just good enough" recording quality. Sony discontinued the Walkman in 2010, leaving many to wonder whether Sony failed to see the opportunity because Sony was also in the recording-studio business.

U.S. Robotics, Wilderman and Apple each investigated the gaps between expectations and the evidence. Each was rewarded handsomely as a result.

ℰↃ

Recent Example

Scott Smyers, systems architect (Apple, Sony), founding chairperson, DLNA

In 1994, Sony Electronics hired Scott Smyers away from Apple, where he had developed what later became known as FireWire. Sony wanted Scott's expertise to help Sony put FireWire into digital camcorders, thus giving users the ability to connect their digital camcorders directly to PCs and eventually to TVs. Sony also anticipated using FireWire to transfer data between a growing number of digital devices because it could very efficiently handle high bandwidth for smooth streaming of large data files, ideal for digital audio and video. Luring Smyers away from Apple was one of many things Sony was doing to make its devices more interoperable with each other.

Engineers at Sony correctly saw in Apple's FireWire—which originated as the IEEE standard known as 1394—a cost-effective data transfer bus with the ability to carry large audio and video data files in streams not vulnerable to interruptions. Avoiding interruptions is very important to audio and video data, not to mention other safety-critical kinds of applications, including avionics and industrial machine vision. Sony named the IEEE 1394 standard "i.Link."

Sony's expectations for FireWire, or i.Link, turned out to be correct at the time. In fact, Microsoft and Intel, along with IBM and Texas Instruments, among others, all saw in the IEEE 1394 standard a way to connect all sorts of digital devices to each other for data transfers at sufficient speeds and volumes. So far, so good. The engineers at Sony seemed to have had the correct expectations and made the right choice of technology at the time.

Shortly after 1394 emerged as the *de facto* standard, however, a gap appeared. With the success of 1394, more and more digital devices were being connected, requiring unimagined additional command sets and protocols that needed to be developed to accommodate each of these devices and the new uses that were anticipated. Along with others at Sony, Smyers found himself investigating these gaps and filling them by chairing a working group in the 1394 Trade Association, where Sony and many other interested companies were participants.

By 1997, another significant gap appeared. With all this content becoming digitized (and therefore easily copied) and all these devices able to transfer this content from one device to another, the movie studios in Hollywood demanded some reassurance that they were not being led down the same path that their cousins in the recording industry had experienced after the CD was introduced. Sony was particularly affected since they were (and still are) innovators of content and the devices that capture and display it and the technology through which it is distributed. Overall, the consumer electronics industry did not expect to have to do anything except provide the devices to capture, store, and play content. The initial meetings with Hollywood on this point set the positions of the two sides revealing a tremendous gap.

Working through 1997 and into 1998, Smyers played a significant role in bridging this gap by chairing a discussion group under the Copy Protection Technical Working Group. Within this discussion group, he effectively brokered a consensus among Sony, Panasonic, Hitachi, Toshiba, and Intel on a technical means for protecting content as it flowed over 1394. That consensus was known at the time as "5C" but formally named later as the Digital Transmission Copy Protection system, or DTCP. That standard represented significant revisions on many fronts to the expectations of the consumer electronics industry. Not only did this technology add cost and complexity to the devices, but under the import/export restrictions on cryptographic technology of the day, it was incredibly cumbersome to design a part in the U.S., manufacture it in Japan, then re-import it into the U.S. Smyers flew to Washington to request that these regulations be adjusted to reflect the needs of Hollywood and the logistics of designing, prototyping, manufacturing, and distributing this technology in consumer products.

During this time, two realities started to emerge, the combination of which posed an ominous cloud on the horizon of 1394 being the standard method to send audio and video content around the home. One of these realities was the growth in bandwidth and data rates. Ethernet was becoming both faster and ubiquitous, but it didn't include a facility to guarantee the timing integrity of audio/video streams as 1394 did. Nonetheless, Ethernet became so fast that problems related to synchronized streams rarely occurred, and as time went on, priority schemes were added to Ethernet, thereby essentially dissolving the problem of clock synchronization, at least for all intents and purposes. In short, fast enough was good enough. By 1999, the engineers at Sony Research re-envisioned the then not-too-distant future where there would be so much bandwidth "wasted" that audio and video would not require the special capability of FireWire /i.Link. Eventually there would be more than enough bandwidth to handle it. The other reality—advances in audio and video compression—merely put an exclamation point at the end of the sentence of more bandwidth. Both increases in bandwidth and more effective compression algorithms led to widespread recognition that all this excess bandwidth could be used as a resource for transferring streams of video data. What at first looked like waste turned out to be a resource.

Although it was difficult, Sony wisely anticipated this shift from 1394 to Ethernet and forged, along with other major consumer electronics, cable, computer, microchip, and software companies, the Digital Living Network Alliance (DLNA) in 2003. DLNA enabled the development of interoperability standards that allow various digital devices to communicate with each other using Internet Protocols, or IP. Smyers became the first president and chairman of DLNA, serving until 2010.

℘

Revise expectations, not the evidence

Experienced innovators regard evidence as the trump card. They revise their expectations accordingly.

This is not as easy as it sounds. Bias affects both perceiving and thinking. Distortions can arise due to premature evaluations and hidden expectations that are beyond innovators' awareness. Innovators, like most, are at risk of the seven deadly sins of perceiving and thinking. Cognitive researcher Massimo Piattelli-Palmarini, in his book *Inevitable Illusions: How Mistakes of Reason Rule Our Minds*, has labeled these distortions of logic and perception as:

- overconfidence
- confirmation
- predictability in hindsight
- anchoring
- ease of representation
- probability blindness, and
- seduction of a plausible narrative[154].

Experienced innovators have learned how to reduce the distortions of at least three of these biases, specifically overconfidence, confirmation, and the seduction of a plausible narrative.

The bias of over-confidence refers to the human tendency—especially of those with a certain degree of expertise in a particular field—to overestimate their ability to answer questions correctly. According to Piattelli-Palmarini, the more one knows about a subject the greater the tendency to be over-confident. Like Kuhn (*The Structure of Scientific Revolutions*), this reminds us of the tendency of acknowledged experts in a domain to discount evidence that doesn't fit their prevailing theories. Successful innovators typically have a thorough knowledge in their areas of expertise, whether technical matters or end-user behaviors or both. This over-confidence can easily influence their interpretation of the incoming evidence. Veteran innovators have enough experience of the damage from their over-confidence to be more circumspect when interpreting data. They have learned to accept the evidence as is.

The confirmation bias is the tendency to view evidence selectively for what confirms the initial hypothesis, and ignoring what contradicts it. Conforming can easily be mistaken with confirming. Imagine what must have gone through Abraham's mind when God presened him with his awful test of faith. The tendency is strong to round the facts up and "torture" them until they conform to the original expectations. To overcome this bias, innovators first see whether and how the evidence from customers contradicts any of the initial expectations. This is not being negative; it is being aggressively interested in what is true.

Unfortunately, many innovators are accused of not being team players when they take this approach. This approach toward the evidence proves irritating to those who are wed to the expectations. Evidence contrary to expectations can uncover inconvenient truths troubling to an organization, even though these expectations also reveal what might be more acceptable to the customer. Successful innovators are more interested in contrary evidence than in confirming expectations. They learn more and faster from it. It directs them more quickly to what doesn't work. They "get to the know(no)" faster. Revising expectations based on the evidence from the market contributes more to progress that attempts to justify expectations. Innovators assume that no matter how confident they are, expectations are expectations, not evidence, and always subject to revision.

The seduction of the plausible also can lead innovators astray. It's the way we think. Most of us "think it more likely that two or more things will happen together than that one . . . without regard to the other."[155] Innovators counter this bias by always favoring the evidence.

In addition to the built-in biases that distort thinking and perceiving, illusions arise from being too quick to assign a value to the evidence—"good" or "bad." The evidence becomes polarized, politicized and more difficult to accept, the lessons are more difficult to extract. Looking at evidence without evaluating it requires emotional detachment. This is not easy, especially for innovators who have been asked to demonstrate their convictions to show themselves as champions for the cause. Some innovators achieve a degree of detachment by collaborating with an objective colleague or third party in examining the evidence. Gratitude helps as well. Gratitude for even disappointing evidence can enable extraction of new insights just under the surface, leading to fresher, more relevant direction for where to go and what to do next.

Inviting varied and diverse perspectives in examing the evidence is a way to uncover what is otherwise blocked. I have facilitated many such discussions, particularly around "sensitive issues"—a polite way of saying that someone who has a lot of power is in denial of the evidence. In these discussions, a well-respected peer will express an interpretation of the evidence that is different, even a bit surprising. Heads cock sideways, jaws drop ever so slightly. And you know that a more meaningful examination of the evidence is starting to happen. As an engineer who grew up on a diary farm put it: "Like Holsteins looking at a new gate."

Disillusionment

There's also *dis*illusionment that comes from the mere presence of the evidence. Unlike the majority of us who grieve the loss of our illusions, veteran innovators regard disillusionment as a positive. No matter how methodical innovators are at documenting their original expectations, experienced innovators suspect a few expectations always persist just under the surface, outside their awareness. It is only when discrepancies (between what evidence shows and what expectations anticipated) are pursued that these hidden expectations are revealed.

The remedy is not to reduce or eliminate these expectations. They can't be eliminated entirely. Expectations are what power the innovating effort to begin with. Instead, it is the gaps between what was expected and what was experienced that need to be pursued. Closing the distance between the expectations and the evidence is what both directs and fuels innovators for what's next. These gaps are the thresholds and doorways to the secret capital of innovators—the knowledge of the causalities that are embedded in what otherwise looks at best complex, at worst, chaotic. What's of most interest to innovators is a matter of objective, causal realities—what's true or not true. That's their focus for whatever project they are working on. Experienced innovators try to keep their perceptions as free and objective as possible. With such freedom, innovators are better able to read the evidence coming in after a product launch, are better at solving problems that surface, better at seeing a new opportunity out of the unexpected.

Even if the evidence is disappointing, experienced innovators do not rate it "good" or "bad." Rather, their first move is to accept it so they can understand. Some call this "emotional intelligence." Others call it an ability to detach. It should never be confused as a sign of disinterest. Quite the opposite. It is a sign of intense interest, commitment, and discipline. Experienced innovators not only accept evidence that is disappointing, they are grateful for what they learn from it.

Innovators not only seek out the unexpected. They also look for what is going unused and wasted.

Uncover waste

What innovators have in common with entrepreneurs is that they shift resources from areas of low productivity and yield, to areas of higher productivity and yield.[156] They are able to identify and access resources being wasted. But this is possible only if one has a specific purpose or need in mind. And innovators are good at that. They frequently recognize the opportunity that turns one person's junk into another's treasure.

In the 1930s, G. H. Tomlinson invented the recovery boiler that proved to be a significant innovation in paper-making, enabling the kraft process to advance over the sulfite process and give us all less-expensive paper. What the recovery boiler does, as it is aptly named, is recover the waste chemical stream and generate steam for energy. Recovery boilers, thanks to Tomlinson's design, recover the waste, refine it, and turn what is called "black liquor" into "white liquor" to be used in segregating cellulose (what's wanted) from the lignin (what is not wanted), all the while producing enough steam-generated energy to keep the process more efficient. While the recovery boiler is far from what would be considered a green technology, it is an example of innovation derived from waste that could prove to be prototypical for future energy and recovery innovations.

A more recent example is from Gill Onions in California's Central Valley. Steve Gill grows onions and processes them at his facility in Oxnard. For years he was spending considerable effort simply disposing of the aromatic leftovers. He now has a system that turns the waste into energy by fermenting the by-product of his processing and converting it into methane. The methane in turn powers the refrigerators and lighting at his plant. Gill saves hundreds of thousands of dollars each year in disposal and energy costs. And he has reduced his carbon footprint.[157]

Rewards

Expected rewards are important in any undertaking. But how innovator-employees look at rewards differs considerably from more "normal" employees. The latter are seldom completely satisfied with their compensation—especially when compared to others. Innovators, on the other hand, often appear simply to be more interested in a new design or upgrading an old one than they are in rewards and recognition. This is not to say that rewards are insignificant to them. They are. But what is even more rewarding to innovator-employees is the lift that comes from satisfying a need other than their own. Many an innovator will leave gainful employment if they don't feel they have sufficient freedom to pursue this vocation. This makes the question of compensation for innovators sometimes a troubling one for companies.

In the thirty years that I have been a student of innovation and its parenting, the issue of how to reward innovators has surfaced repeatedly. With the success of an innovation, what does the company do for the innovators who made it all possible? Various compensation schemes have been thought of and tried. None that I am aware of—though I claim no specific expertise in the area of rewards and recognition—have ever seemed to stick. The following recent example from IBM's Emerging Business Opportunities (EBO) program is fairly typical of companies that have struggled with designing a special rewards program for innovators. Here is the conclusion of an IBM task force:

"The original EBO task force had spent considerable time debating whether a separate compensation system was needed for EBO leaders. A task force member explained why they had decided against it: 'An EBO's success comes from an integrated IBM, so teams have to work well together. The underlying premise is that the pay system should be built into the group structure because a separate system would produce haves and have-nots.'"[158]

There is something more than a paycheck, bonus, or stock options that motivates those who innovate more than once or twice. Innovators' focus is on changing a slice of the world by creating new value for customers. The freedom to pursue such a contribution is the instrinsic reward for the innovator—freedom given them to pursue making a difference.

Acceptance

Disappointment is common when an innovation seeks a home with customers. Innovations seldom fulfill all the expectations that originally fueled their pursuit. While a few projects will meet or even exceed those expectations, the gap between what was expected and what is experienced is often big enough that innovators not only are disappointed but can slide into denial.

The best defense against denial is for innovators to remain with the project and carefully examine the evidence, especially contrary evidence. This enables them to learn from what the market is saying and avoid pre-judgments.

Acceptance—at least as intended here—suggests a more detached, even clinical inventory of simply what is. It refrains from any evaluation of the evidence—positive or negative. Acceptance is simply an admission of the evidence—letting it in. This may seem like a simple thing, but it is perhaps one of the toughest things to do at this time in the innovating process. So much has been invested in the expectations—not just time, effort, and money, but the expectations of investors, peers, superiors, suppliers, trade partners, and by the innovators themselves. By this juncture, expectations have likely compounded, often in unknown ways.

The probability of some form of denial is actually quite high, fueled by multiple expectations—known and unknown, conscious or subconscious. By definition, denial hides its presence from the one who is in it. There's even an acronym for it: **D**on't **E**ven **N**otice **I A**m **L**ying.

Denial can be emotional, intellectual, and perceptual. Emotional denial can ignore the facts, minimize their relevance or seriousness, or project responsibility onto someone else. Intellectual denial is a matter of ruling out evidence that doesn't fit, in part to preserve status and position. Perceptual denial occurs amidst the noise and static of so much information flooding awareness that faint signals are missed, ignored or mistakenly identified as noise. Innovators are susceptible to any and all of these forms of denial, and experienced ones are humble enough to admit it.

A prudent starting point for innovators in overcoming denial is to assume from the beginning that to some extent they are already in denial. It's safer that way. Many innovators identify what the contrary evidence is by using a collaborative approach. They invite others in to help them know what evidence is relevant in order to break through denial, even the denial of denial. Knowledgeable and disinterested others—those who carry no political or self-interested ax-to-grind—bring fresh and diverse perspectives to the task of making sense of the evidence, especially when there is contrary evidence. When I have facilitated such discussions, the insertion of someone, often called a "naïve expert," can act as a catalyst and enable a cognitive breakthrough. Although the perspective of such an expert may prove slightly off the mark, what they notice can uncover what more knowledgeable experts won't or don't. This helps experts see behind and beyond their own blind spots.

Denial is not the only block to acceptance. Disillusionment erodes the very energy requied to investigate what part of reality went unaccounted for in the initial expectations. Though an emotional drain, disillusionment turns out to be instructive, enabling innovators to see and understand underlying causes.

In the Sermon on the Mount Jesus says, "You will be judged in the same way you judge others."[159] This applies just as well to judging evidence as it does to judging people. When innovators evaluate or judge the evidence coming in from the market without simply accepting it as it is, they risk missing out on the most reliable source of direction for the next round of innovating. Disappointmen and disillusionment can drag. Gratitude can lift, and actually make acceptance arrive a bit sooner.

Gratitude

Gratitude opens the mind to receive what the mind may not otherwise be inclined to receive. When evidence starts coming in, after a product goes to market, there may be a whisper of disappointment. The negatives of regret, resentment, and even envy can quickly infect innovators and their host organization. As an emotion, gratitude calms. As Baylor philosophy professor Robert Roberts has observed, "Gratitude makes people less susceptible to such emotions as disappointment, regret and frustration" and effectively mitigates inclinations to resentment and envy."[160]

This fits my experience of my mentor's disposition to a T. Bill Wilson earned the rarely given Mahler award for entrepreneurial excellence at Kimberly-Clark largely because of the contributions he made from this disposition. He was consistently grateful for whatever evidene he had collected, even and especially when those facts led in an apparently unfavorable direction. By being grateful for the evidence—good or bad—Wilson was able to prevent himself from any quick-to-judge stance. If Wilson didn't have evidence, he would go out and get it. And when he did have evidence, he treated it as a gift to appreciate. Wilson had a rule about "bad" news: Always assume there is something to be learned from it.

Gratitude enables this acceptance of the evidence. Gratitude is not simply a warm feeling. It is a practical and fairly reliable tool, especially when applied to contrary evidence. Most think of gratitude only in the context of positive outcomes. But experienced innovators are grateful for evidence that is unexpected and contrary. It helps them to see the bigger picture. It helps them to learn what is not generally recognized or accepted and helps break through blind spots and denial.

Expectations can easily become resentments "under construction." I have seen many a promising innovator succumb to resentment, regret, and even envy. Those who are able to escape the infection of negativity usually have a grateful disposition. Gratitude is not only a practical countermeasure to negativity. It also just might, by clearing the mind of negatives, enhance cognitive perception and processing as well.

Lift Factors

Experienced innovators know that success has a short shelf life, especially in a competitive market. Change and progress don't come to a halt with the success of one innovation. The fear of success may represent a fear of being succeeded.

In this ongoing succession of discoveries, inventions, and innovations we call progress, some innovations stick around for a while. Others, for only what seems like moments. Still others contribute to progress, though they themselves fail in the market. Experienced innovators, humbled but not defeated, know success as not only an enemy of innovation but also a fleeting seduction.

The need stream, along with the solution stream, keeps flowing. There is always opportunity for innovators to find and craft a compelling innovation. Fears of success's seductions are warranted. More money, more recognition, higher expectations from sponsors for innovators' "magic" applied to the next opportunity—each of these residuals of success can erode the innovators' freedom to fly unnoticed the next time, a freedom to pursue and contribute, which innovators likely value more than any of the extrinsic and monetary rewards they may receive and enjoy.

Innovators are more likely to fly through this fear of success with companies that have a respect for the knowledge they created. This innovator-created knowledge proves to be the intellectual capital that enables companies to sustain their relevance. In this kind of organizational atmosphere, innovators have more freedom, more autonomy, and more recognition.

Those who have the wings of faith to fly through the fear of success have learned there are always more needs to discover, understand and to invent solutions for. Knowing and experiencing this provides lift-producing *thrust* for innovators. This thrust keeps innovators alert, interested, and engaged.

Finding what others are not seeing is so much a part of innovating. I learned this in the form of an unusual question I heard asked early in my career. LeRoy Peterson, a Senior Vice President, asked it at Kimberly Clark in the 1980s. It's as relevant today as it was then. We had just finished a presentation, complete with visuals, on where innovators find their next opportunity using the now canonical S-curve theory introduced by Richard Foster in his book *Innovation: The Attacker's Advantage*.[161] Peterson leaned forward and pointed to an empty space to the immediate left of the S-curve and asked, "What about the opportunities that we are not seeing here?"

It didn't matter that "here" was no where. What mattered were the words: "What about the opportunities we are not seeing?" Peterson had put his finger on a gap ignored by many who become so enamored with their own success that it blinds them to the deeper lessons and opportunities that are right there in front of them—unseen.

Years later, Bruce Beihoff, a veteran innovator with Eaton, Rockwell International, Whirlpool, and others, gave me another bit of practical wisdom. It comes from a systems engineering perspective. Beihoff is convinced that the gap between the evidence coming in—particularly contrary evidence—and the original expectations, merely reflects our partial and incomplete understanding of the system, whatever the system. In the early steps of innovating, the innovator may not even know what to ask. It's only after information begins coming in, especially evidence of the unexpected, that gives us a start in understanding more about the web of cause, effect, and interdependence that so affects the innovating.

Viewing the gaps between expectations and evidence as invitations from the underlying system enables innovators to investigate and indeed discover additional needs and new opportunities to pursue.

Innovating speed has received much attention lately. The caffeinated pace of innovation in many sectors has been a consistent theme for the past several years: reducing the time-to-market, time-to-break-even, time-to-positive cash flow, cycle time. Some studies suggest that innovating faster can lead to more successful and more profitable results.[162] Faster development may make resource managers feel better about their own stewardship for the limited time, talent, and money in their charge. But to go faster, good brakes come in handy. Speed is not just a function of time. It's also a function of distance, and distance has been the one factor that is often ignored.

Distance in this context can be thought of as detachment. Distance, understood as "dissociation from the immediate," provides innovators a sense of perspective that otherwise goes missing as they examine the evidence coming back from the market. Perspective plays a central role in innovators' acquisition of wisdom and understanding. And this stage represents a prime time for such wisom and understanding to develop.

Innovators can easily find themselves so caught up in the innovating that it becomes difficult to see what, if anything, they are learning that is transferrable and applicable to future innovating efforts. Just as a painter or sculptor steps away from the work in progress to see the whole, the innovator must to step back to restore and refresh a sense of proportion and thereby gain insight and wisdom. Slowing down may actually be a way of speeding up.

The lift produced at this stage comes from what innovators actually learn from the experience that carries the potential for them to create new and substantive value and lasting contributions in the future. This lift has to do with picking both *what* is next and *who* is next. In a sense, the lift that can come to innovators at this stage is, at the very least, manifested in gratitude for having the opportunity to contribute to the ongoing succession of innovations called progress, and in the wisdom of accepting things that cannot be changed. With that lift comes courage to change the things that need to be changed.

The following bit of wisdom comes from Irish playwright, Nobel laureate, and founder of the London School of Economics, George Bernard Shaw:

"The reasonable man adapts himself to the world; the unreasonable one persists in trying to adapt the world to himself. Therefore all progress depends on the unreasonable man."

I'd like to think Shaw was talking about innovators, those "unreasonable" but faith-full men and women—engineers, scientists, artists, and such—who see what others fail to see, create something new and bring it into reality. Innovators are clearly men and women of hope, both prisoners and free.

Postscript: The Next Generation

Innovators, like parents, play many roles. The roles, and the individuals who fill them, are defined and shaped by the developmental needs of their progeny. Innovators who get the chance to innovate more than once understand that each innovation they develop has an individual personality all its own. Not surprisingly, this is also true for innovators themselves. The types of needs they discover, the technologies they use in their solutions, and the market ecologies of which they are a part, all work together to shape the innovators they become, and are becoming. I suspect this evolving caldron will keep the practice of innovation, like parenting, more art than science, less a repeatable process and more an adaptive capability.

The fact that each innovation and innovator is different prevents established companies—prone to seek repeatable formulas—from finding a completely repeatable formula for innovating. Despite the variety of innovators and the variability between one innovation and the next, there are predictable challenges for every innovator. For each of these challenges innovators must take on another role and learn to master another pattern of faith. To discover a need, innovators become explorers wherein awe and wonder serve them well. To invent solutions, innovators become creators where inspiration and appreciation are essential. To make the inventive solution work for all concerned, they must become practitioners enabled by forgiveness and persistence. For the challenge of introduction, innovators must become resolvers who reduce the conflicts created by the newness of the invention itself. Submission and humility prove indispensable here. And finally, throughout all the challenges innovators face, they must remain the agile learners they are. Here, gratitude and acceptance are essential tools.

Like parents, the roles innovators play over the course of "raising" the innovation enable the innovation to stand on its own. The more roles an innovator can handle, the fewer the hand-offs, the better it can be for the innovation and the innovating. In reality, these roles are more complementary and concurrent than consecutive, often requiring innovators to simultaneously play multiple roles and use more than one pattern of faith at the same time, each one enabling productive improvisations on the next.

Innovators who can handle all of the roles and patterns of faith required are few and far between. Companies that persist in their quixotic search for such lone heroes are at best naïve. Innovators who believe they have all these capabilities themselves are simply arrogant. Innovating is neither a solo, nor *a capella*. But it would also be a mistake to assume that simply getting experienced people at the right time focused on the right thing is sufficient for success. Collective experience is helpful, indeed necessary, but not sufficient. *In*experience is always present when innovating, even when the innovators are all seasoned veterans. An inescapable truth about innovation is that "we've never done this before," to a greater or lesser extent. If it has been done before then it is not innovating. It is either adopting or imitating.

When innovation is attempted by inexperienced or novice innovators, however, what is already difficult can easily be made even more difficult. Countless companies often take experienced innovators and move them into other organizational responsibilities, thereby robbing themselves—and their next generation of innovations—of experienced "parents." Several years ago, Hank Marcy and I were discussing how companies treat their innovators. Hank is a very articulate, thoughtful and experienced manager of innovation efforts from his experience at several companies, including Rockwell Scientific, Whirlpool Corporation and now BISSELL. Hank rarely complains (at least out loud), which was one reason his lament caught my attention. Here's the gist of what he said: "As soon as they get a little experience under their belt, what do we do? We move them to responsibilities far away from anything that looks like innovation, and we end up losing their knowledge and experience. No wonder our track record is so difficult to improve. We are not building any foundation of experience or knowledge in managing innovation."

Most parents would agree; experience with the first child helps them manage the parenting challenges with the next. So also with innovators and their innovations. This is why venture capitalists favor an experienced entrepreneur with a so-so idea over an inexperienced entrepreneur with a breakthrough idea. These investors know that the odds favor experience.

But it may not be the particular content of the experience that matters so much as it is the faith (confidence, belief, trust and vision) that the experienced bring to the innovating task.

While this reflects what is known to venture capitalists, it is often trumped in established companies by the organization's formal and informal human resource, promotion and career development policies, not to mention the career aspirations of individuals themselves. Often a tour of duty on the innovation "front" ends for the first time innovator with a quick reassignment of duties—shuffling him or her off to a different staff or operating role, frequently because it would be too damaging to their career to risk any more relationship capital than has already been spent. This is all very understandable from the point of view of the individual's reputation inside an organization. However, it makes little sense in developing, building and transferring innovating experience in the enterprise. *How* this building and transferring is done between generations, not to mention within the same generation, is certainly worth thinking through. *That* it should be done seems obvious.

What of the next generation of innovations and innovators? Most want to distance themselves from the infamous comment mistakenly attributed to Charles Duell, the commissioner of patents in 1899—"what can be invented already has been invented." It is a more prudent bet that more will be discovered and invented.

A more interesting and relevant question, perhaps, is to what extent the next generation of innovations and innovators will carry the genes of the previous generation? Will the next generation simply improvise on what is known by the previous one, or will the next ignore what the previous generation knows in an attempt to be truly original? To what extent is that even possible? Will the next generation of innovators and their host companies choose safer, seemingly less risky, more reasonable opportunities to pursue, or will they take on the more compelling ones that require Shaw's unreasonable men and women?

Whatever the answers to these questions it behooves this generation of innovators to be as clear, concise and explicit about what we do know about innovating and make it available to the next generation, leaving it to them to decide whether they will choose to learn from the past or repeat it. However much content from the previous generation shows up in the next, the next generation will be defined not simply by what comes next, but by who comes next.

Suffice it to say that nothing shapes the innovator more than the developmental process of innovating. A parent *becomes* a parent by having (by birth or adoption) and raising a child. Similarly, innovators become innovators through the direct, firsthand experience of innovating. Innovators are not made by being assigned or named innovators, no matter how clever or creative they happen to be. Nor can they be taught in the classroom how to innovate. They emerge and develop along with their innovations, successful or not. Experience is essential.

But experience alone is not sufficient. Experience is limited and can be limiting. Experience with failure can deflate and drag. It can also teach. Experience of success can satisfy enough to satiate the innovator and turn him or her into an incumbent. Experience can just as easily turn into dogma and doctrine as it can inform, suggest and instruct. David eventually became like Saul, afraid of what might he might lose in the succession of progress.

Though experience is the tuition necessary for innovators to become innovators, there is something as, if not more, important. Samuel Johnson described it as that which "triumphs over experience." That something is hope.

Hope is a precious form of faith that captivates, empowers and lifts innovators to become and remain relevant to the next generation, of innovations and innovators. It may be found in purer forms on the side streets and intersections between faith and innovation. It is certainly carried in the hearts and minds of innovators and incarnated in their innovations. It may be the *sine qua non* of innovating.

In *The Irony of American History*[163], the Protestant and American theologian Reinhold Niebuhr expressed his view of what this hope is—this lift—in the way hope captivates those who, despite their experience of failure or success, keep innovating:

> Nothing that is worth doing can be achieved in our lifetime; therefore we must be saved by hope.
> Nothing which is true or beautiful or good makes complete sense in any immediate context of history; therefore we must be saved by faith.
> Nothing we do, however, virtuous, can be accomplished alone; therefore we are saved by love.
> No virtuous act is quite as virtuous from the standpoint of our friend or foe as it is from our own standpoint. Therefore we must be saved by forgiveness.

Acknowledgements

Gratitude has been called a gateway emotion. This fits with my experience with this project. The feeling ushers me into a state of mind and heart wherein I am surrounded by this book's "communion of saints." Each made offerings, in some cases, sacrifices, which catalyzed and shaped what I have written and how I wrote it. The generosity of these contributors leaves me in a grateful state, hoping I have honored as much as I appreciate their offerings.

Some say writing is not a team sport. However, this endeavor has been far from an individual effort. Many contributed, often unwittingly. It is difficult to assign a proportion to what each gave in the formation and composition of this book. However, I can and want to mention a few, in addition to those mentioned in the book, who generously have given me and this project time, attention, care, consideration and encouragement, without which I would still be sketching. These include:

- Doug Gilmour, a piercing-but-gentle thought partner, designer of the cover, author of the foreword, and the example in Chapter 8.

- Bruce Beihoff, Greg Blythe, Paula Rosch, Scott Smyers, who, along with Doug, were willing examples of faith patterns described in Part II, so generous with their own experience. Each subjected themselves to my pesky speculations of what is essentially *their* experience and my characterization of it. Thank you.

- Bill Wilson, my late mentor, who, at Kimberly-Clark, along with many other engineers—chemical, mechanical and electrical, and scientists—paper chemists and biologists—first caught my attention with the exercise of his faith.

- Many veteran, technology-savvy innovators in client companies with whom I have had the privilege of working—many of them prolific inventors—who were not only willing to tolerate me in a facilitating role, but who were also generous enough to reflect outloud with me about what they perceive they do, how they do it, and most importantly, why. In addition to those I have already mentioned in the book, John Raley, Lloyd Hughes, Jim Tanner, Jim O'Shaughnessy, Mikio Ishmaru, Sujeet Chand, John Miller, Nihat Cur, Ron Vogleweede, Adriano Scaburri, Beat Stocker, Steve Kuehl, George Weyerhaeuser, Jr., Ron Wilderman, Gib Comstock, Norm Johnson, George Kychakoff, Del Raymond, Amar Neogi, Eric Wood, Mark Hehnen, Denny Hunter, John Watkins, Christine Dean, Peter Farnum, Stan Floyd, Mike Millman, Tom Ruhe, Stuart Asakawa, John Greeven, Rich Phelan, Steve Wright, Ross Allen, Ron Gompertz, David Wetchler, Larry Plotkin, Paul Speer, Rich Duncombe, Ed Rinker, Randy Erickson, Yana Kushner, Shelley Martin, Kevin Cleary, and Michael Dillane, are important to thank specifically. Hank Marcy, though mentioned in the epilogue, has been a special example to me of an innovator in a leadership role, exhibiting a relentless faith in challenging organizational atmospheres; he's never even appeared to lose hope.

- Members of the Innovation Practitioner's Network and the Mavericks Roundtables, many of whom gave me critical but encouraging feedback on early versions of the ideas and themes of the book, including Dave Lundgren, Andy Zander, Waguih Ishak, Curt Schauer, Alec Glover and Andy Proehl.

- My teachers in biblical and theological studies, including Harry and Teddy Vincent (my late parents), Brevard Childs (Yale Divinity School), Max "the ax" Polley (Old Testament at Davidson College), David Kaylor (New Testament at Davidson College) and Leander Keck (New Testament at Yale Divinity School), and Sandy McKelway (theology at Davidson College). By example each taught me what is written in the collection of wisdom called the Bible can be *the* practical key that unlocks a redemptive understanding of present circumstances—mine and others—whether good or bad, sad or joyous.

- Members of the St. John's of Ross Episcopal Church lectionary study group (2007-2010) who suffered through some early versions of the basic definitions of faith.

Thank you, all.

Jane Haradine's editing and coaching was invaluable in cutting out the extraneous fat and coaching me out of some habits of expression that get in the way. The bad habits that may remain are certainly not a result of her expert advice and counsel, but simply the imperfections of the writer. Thank you, Jane.

And lastly, I want to acknowledge Jane Gannon, my associate for almost two decades, who put up with many "thinking out loud" lunches, and my, at times, manic writing, all the while keeping a busy consulting and facilitating practice afloat when I would rather be writing. Jane's steady nature was like an anchor to windard in stormy seas. Thank you, Jane.

End Notes

Introduction

1. "faith," in Lesley Brown, The New Shorter Oxford English Dictionary, vol. 1 (Oxford: Clarendon, 1993), 908.

2. Where possible, the collection of stories comes from more familiar stories from the Old and New Testaments (NRSV), recognizing that these collections themselves have some relevance not simply to Christians but to Muslims and Jews as well. However, my particular religious upbringing happened to be of the so-called mainline liberal Protestant flavor, specifically Presbyterian. It was as a Presbyterian that I was ordained as a "teaching elder" and served as a pastor to churches in North Carolina and Wisconsin for a little over five years in the late '70s and early '80s.

Chapter 1

3. Clayton M. Christensen and Michael E. Raynor, *The Innovator's Solution: Creating and Sustaining Successful Growth* (Boston: Harvard Business School Press, 2003).

4. Peter Chernin, then COO of Fox Corporation, said this in a meeting I was facilitating for *Gemstar-TV Guide* in 2005.

5. Peter F. Drucker, *Innovation and Entrepreneurship: Practice and Principles* (New York: Harper & Row, 1985), 35.

6. David Welch and Ian Rowley, "Toyota's All-Out Drive to Stay Toyota," *BusinessWeek* (December 3, 2007) and subsequent interview in BusinessWeek with the chairman of Toyota.

7. Jim Collins, *How the Mighty Fall and Why Some Companies Never Give In* (New York: HarperCollins, 2009).

8. Louis Pasteur, Inaugural Address as Professor of Chemistry and Dean of Faculty of Science, Lillie, France (December 7, 1854. In Hugh Chisholm, The Encyclopedia Britannica Dictionary of Arts, Sciences, Literature and General Information (1911), Vol. 20, 893.

9. Geoffrey A. Moore, *Dealing with Darwin: How Great Companies Innovate at Every Phase of Their Evolution* (New York: Penguin, 2005).

10. Richard N. Bolles, *What Color Is Your Parachute? A Practical Manual for Job-Hunters & Career Changers* (Berkeley: Ten Speed, 1982), 106-7.

11. Chris Argyris, "Teaching Smart People How to Learn," *Harvard Business Review*, vol. 63, no. 9 (May-June 1991), 100.

12. Stefan H. Thomke, *Experimentation Matters: Unlocking the Potential of New Technologies for Innovation* (Boston: Harvard Business School Press, 2003), 2.

13. Thomas J. Peters and Robert H. Waterman, *In Search of Excellence: Lessons from America's Best-Run Companies* (New York: Harper & Row, 1982), 134-35.

14. Stuart Brown, M.D., *Play: How It Shapes the Brain, Opens the Imagination, and Invigorates the Soul* (New York: Penguin, 2009), 181.

15. David Packard, *The HP Way: How Bill Hewlett and I Built Our Company* (New York: HarperCollins, 1995), 108.

16. Paul R. Lawrence and Nitin Nohria, *Driven: How Human Nature Shapes Our Choices* (San Francisco: Jossey-Bass, 2002).

17. Maya Angelou interview, "Reflects on a Glorious Life," National Public Radio (April 6, 2008).

18. Jim Collins, *Good to Great: Why Some Companies Make the Leap . . . and Others Don't* (New York: Harper Business, 2001), 41ff.

19. Edward de Bono, *Lateral Thinking: Creativity Step by Step* (New York: Harper & Row, 1970).

20. Clayton M. Christensen, *The Innovator's Dilemma: When New Technologies Cause Great Firms to Fail* (Boston: Harvard Business School Press, 1997).

21. Lanny Vincent, "Innovation Midwives: Sustaining Innovation Streams in Established Companies," in *Research-Technology Management*, vol. 48, no. 1, Industrial Research Institute (January-February, 2005).

22. Frank J. Sulloway, *Born to Rebel: Birth Order, Family Dynamics, and Creative Lives* New York: Pantheon, 1996).

Chapter 2

23. Ahlston Chase, *In a Dark Wood: The Fight over Forests and the Myths of Nature* (New Brunswick, N.J.: Transaction, 2001). Chase points to biocentrism as an emergent religion of radical and fundamentalist ecologists.

24. "faith," Lesley Brown, *The New Shorter Oxford English Dictionary*, vol. 1 (Oxford: Clarendon, 1993), 908.

25. Saint Anselm, "The Theistic Proofs" (2.1), "Faith Seeks Understanding," *Stanford Encyclopedia of Philosophy* (City: Publisher, 2007).

26. Al Ward, quoted in, Ikujiro Nonaka and Hirotaka Takeuchi, *The Knowledge-Creating Company: How Japanese Companies Created the Dynamics of Innovation* (New York: Oxford University Press, 1995), and Michael N. Kennedy, *Product Development for the Lean Enterprise: Why Toyota's System is Four Times More Productive and How you Can Implement It*. The Oaklea Press, Richmond. 2003. Page 11 (in the Foreword by Dr. Allen Ward).

27. "potential energy," *www.wikipedia.com.*

28. William James, *The Varieties of Religious Experience: A Study in Human Nature* (New York: Random House, 2002), 549-50.

29. Paul R. Lawrence and Nitin Nohria, *Driven: How Human Nature Shapes Our Choices* (San Francisco: Jossey-Bass, 2002).

30. Robert C. Solomon and Fernando Flores, *Building Trust in Business, Politics, Relationships, and Life* (New York: Oxford University Press, 2001).

31. C. S. Lewis, *The Four Loves,* (Orlando: Harcourt Brace, 1960).

Chapter 3

32. Richard C. Cheverton with Lanny Vincent and Bill Wilson, *The Maverick Way: Profiting from the Power of the Corporate Misfit* (La Palma, Calif.: Maverickway.com, 2000), 107.

33. David Packard, *The HP Way: How Bill Hewlett and I Built Our Company* (New York: HarperCollins, 1995), 108.

34. W. Edwards Deming, *Out of Crisis* (Cambridge, Mass.: MIT Press, 2000). Deming, after being largely rejected in the United States, took his statistics-based observations to a more receptive Japanese corps of managers, who eventually led their companies to trounce and then teach American management.

35. Ron Turner and Linda Turner, a paper on the work of W. Edwards Deming, 1998, *www.endsoftheearth.com/Deming14pts.html.*

36. Ibid.

37. Clayton M. Christensen and Michael E. Raynor, *The Innovator's Solution: Creating and Sustaining Successful Growth* (Boston: Harvard Business School Press, 2003); Clayton M. Christensen, *The Innovator's Dilemma: When New Technologies Cause Great Firms to Fail* (Boston: Harvard Business School Press, 1997); Henry William Chesbrough, *Open Innovation: The New Imperative for Creating and Profiting from Technology* (Boston: Harvard Business School Publishing, 2006).

38. It has become a common practice among practitioners of innovation management to insulate rather than isolate innovating from the more "adult-rated" established performance metrics common to operating environments.

39. From conversations with Leo J. Shapiro at the Maverick's Roundtable in Tucson, Arizona, 2003.

40. Edgar H. Schein, "Anxiety of Learning: An Interview with Edgar H. Schein," *Harvard Business Review* (March 1, 2002).

41. Stefan H. Thomke, *Experimentation Matters: Unlocking the Potential of New Technologies for Innovation* (Boston: Harvard Business School Press, 2003).

42. "talent," George Arthur Buttrick, ed., *The Interpreter's Dictionary of the Bible*, vol. 4 (Nashville: Abingdon, 1962), 510.

43. Peter F. Drucker, *Management: Tasks, Responsibilities, Practices* (New York: Harper & Row, 1973), 274.

44. Stephan H. Haeckel, *Adaptive Enterprise: Creating and Leading Sense-and-Respond Organizations* (Cambridge: President and Fellows of Harvard, 1999).

45. Ikujiro Nonaka and Hirotaka Takeuchi, *The Knowledge-Creating Company: How Japanese Companies Create the Dynamics of Innovation* (New York: Oxford University Press, 1995).

46. Richard C. Cheverton with Lanny Vincent and Bill Wilson, *The Maverick Way: Profiting from the Power of the Corporate Misfit*, (La Palma, Calif.: Maverickway.com, 2000), 10.

47. Stephan H. Thomke, *Experimentation Matters: Unlocking the Potential of New Technologies for Innovation* (Boston: Harvard Business School Press, 2003), 99-107.

48. In the early 2000s, Paul Lienberger (then senior vice president of Roper-Starch/NOP) made the observation that one reason the long prophesied convergence between the worlds of television and computers hadn't happened was not a function of the lack of technological innovation. Rather, it was that when consumers watch TV, they lean back. When they are at their computers, they generally tend to lean forward. Different postures were blocking the convergence. (Pad computers may be changing this.)

49. David Packard and Bill Hewlett, *The HP Way: How Bill Hewlett and I Built Our Company* (New York: HarperCollins Publishers, 1995), 96.

50. Don Clark, "In Silicon Valley, A Tech Legend Lays Big Plans," *Wall Street Journal* (February 3, 2005).

51. Howard Gardner, *Changing Minds: The Art and Science of Changing Our Own and Other People's Minds* (Boston: Harvard Business School Press, 2004).

52. Henry William Chesbrough, *Open Innovation: The New Imperative for Creating and Profiting from Technology* (Boston: Harvard Business School Press, 2006).

53. Margaret Blair, "The Brookings Institute Task Force on Intangibles," Brookings Institute (1996).

Chapter 4

54. The apocryphal story is often told of one of the first U.S. patent and trademark commissioners making this statement. Though the truth of this story is suspect, the persistence of its telling is revealing.

55. There is still some controversy among biblical scholars regarding the precise nature of the differences between priests and Levites, at least at the time this parable was first told. George Arthur Buttrick. Editor. The Interpreter's Dictionary of the Bible. Volume 3. Abingdon Press, Nashville. 1962.

56. John W. Gardner, like many other innovators, found himself in a variety of contexts, serving as the secretary of Health, Education and Welfare in the Johnson administration and later becoming the president of the Carnegie

Corporation. John W. Gardner. Excellence: Can We Be Equal and Excellent Too? (New York: W.W. Norton, 1961).

57. Alex Munthe, *The Story of San Michele* (New York: Avalon, 2002).

58. Abraham Maslow, "A Theory of Human Motivation," originally published in *Psychological Review* (1943), 50, 370-96.

59. Ibid., point 7.

60. Clayton M. Christensen. *The Innovator's Dilemma: When New Technologies Cause Great Firms to Fail.* Harvard Business School Press. Boston. 1997.

Chapter 5

61. Thomas Kuhn, *The Structure of Scientific Revolutions* (Chicago: University of Chicago Press, 1962).

62. Clayton M. Christensen. *The Innovator's Dilemma: When New Technologies Cause Great Firms to Fail.* Harvard Business School Press. Boston. 1997.

63. Hebrews 11.1.

64. Hans-Peter Durr, quoted in Margaret Wheatley, *Leadership and the New Science: Discover Order in a Chaotic World*, 3rd ed. (San Francisco: Berrett-Koehler, 2006), 140.

65. Peter F. Drucker, *Innovation and Entrepreneurship: Practice and Principles* (New York: Harper & Row, 1985), 35.

66. Conversations with Dr. Stuart Brown, M.D.

67. Michael N. Kennedy, Product Development for the Lean Enterprise: Why Toyota's System Is Four Times More Productive and How You Can Implement It (Richmond, Va.: Oaklea, 2003).

68. Peter F. Drucker, *Innovation and Entrepreneurship: Practice and Principles* (New York: Harper & Row, 1985), 35.

69. Ibid.

70. Karl Deutsch, quoted by Edgar H. Schein, "Organizational and Managerial Culture as a Facilitator or Inhibitor of Organizational Transformation," Working Paper 3831 (July 1995), presented to the Inaugural Assembly of Chief Executive and Employers in Singapore, June 29, 1995. (http://dspace.mit.edu/bitstream/handle/1721.1/2581/SWP-3831-33296477.pdf?sequence=1)

71. Edgar H. Schein, "Organizational and Managerial Culture as a Facilitator or Inhibitor of Organizational Transformation," Working Paper 3831 (July 1995), 17. presented to the Inaugural Assembly of Chief Executive and Employers in Singapore, June 29, 1995. (http://dspace.mit.edu/bitstream/handle/1721.1/2581/SWP-3831-33296477.pdf?sequence=1)

72. René Descartes, *The Passions of the Soul* (1649), Stephen H. Voss, trans. (Indianapolis: Hackett, 1989), article 53.

73. Albert Einstein, Speech to the German League of Human Rights, Berlin (Autumn 1932; as published in Einstien: A Life in Scinece (1994) by Michael While and John Gribbin. Cited by wikiquote.

74. Ernest Schactel, in Robert C. Fuller, *Wonder: From Emotion to Spirituality* (Chapel Hill, N.C.: University of North Carolina Press, 2006), 99.

75. Ibid.

76. Walter Isaacson, *Einstein: His Life and Universe* (New York: Simon & Schuster, 2007), 545.

77. Ibid. 548.

78. Ibid.

79. Jim Holt, "Time Bandits." *The New Yorker Magazine*. February 28, 2005.

80. Ibid., 41.

81. C. K. Prahalad and Gary Hamel, "The Core Competence of the Corporation," *Harvard Business Review*, vol. 90, no. 3 (May-June 1990)

82. Scott Berkun, *The Myths of Innovation* (Sebastopol, Calif.: O'Reilly, 2010), 129-30.

Chapter 6

83. Dire situations inspire ingenious solutions. If worse comes to worst, people will apply all their imagination and skill to deal with the problem. In Latin: *'Mater artium necessitas.'* The adage has been traced back to 'Vulgaria' (1519). In 1658, Richard Franck wrote in his 'Northern Memoirs': 'Art imitates Nature, and Necessity is the Mother of Invention.' The proverb was first attested in the United States in 'William Fitzhugh and His Chesapeake World' (1681)." From "Random House Dictionary of Popular Proverbs and Sayings" (1996) by Gregory Y. Titelman (Random House, New York, 1996).

84. "Inventor" and "Innovators" are primarily role identities more than identities of individuals. Sometimes innovators are also inventors, and vice versa. Sometimes not. Most often inventors are not single, lone individuals but a part of communities of practice. Likewise for innovators. One way to understand the difference between the two is to acknowledge that inventors are more engaged in making the conceptual invention technically feasible, whereas innovators are more engaged in making the invention economically viable.

85. Andy Grove. Only The Paranoid Survive: How to Explooit the Crisis Points That Challenge Every Company. (New York: Random House, 1996).

86. Ezekiel 37.1-10. Verses 11-14 offer the vision's original interpretation—a message of hope to the otherwise despondent exiles who had been separated from their promised land for years. I could be accused of taking this vision of Ezekiel out of its original historical context. However, what Ezekiel's vision reveals about inspiration and appreciation, especially in the context of invention brings a fresh perspective to the innovator and inventor alike. While the historical objectives of verses 11-14 may not be immediately pertinent to our reader, the message of hope and instructiveness of the pattern of faith, I believe, is faithful to the original vision (verses 1-10).

87. Peter F. Drucker *Innovation and Entrepreneurship: Practice and Principles.* Harper & Row Publishers. New York. 1985. Page 46ff.

88. Evan I. Schwartz, *Juice: The Creative Fuel That Drives World-Class Inventors* (Boston: Harvard Business School Press, 2004), 9.

89. Roger Martin, *The Opposable Mind: How Successful Leaders Win through Integrative Thinking* (Boston: Harvard Business School Press, 2007).

90. Steven Johnson. *The Invention of Air: A Story of Science, Faith, Revolution and the Birth of America.* New York: Penguin. Page 59.

91. Ibid. 83.

92. John Tao and Joeseph Daniele, et. al. "Developing an Effective Intellectual Asset Management Strategy" 2004; study.http://www.strategicalliance.com/articles/Managing_Intellectual_Ass.htm

93. Roger Lenhard, *Where Invention Begins: Echoes of Old Voices in the Rise of New Machines* (New York: Oxford University Press, 2006), 160-161.

94. Ibid, 238.

95. Ibid., 241.

96. Frans Johansson, *The Medici Effect: Breakthrough Insights at the Intersection of Ideas, Concepts & Cultures* (Boston: Harvard Business School Press, 2004).

97. Jonah Lehrer, "The Eureka Hunt," *The New Yorker* (July 28, 2008).

98. Mark Jung-Beeman, et al., "Neural Activity When People Solve Verbal Problems with Insight" (2004) PLoS Biol 2(4): e97. doi: 101371/journal.pbio.0020097.

99. Ibid.

100. Jonah Lehrer, "The Eureka Hunt," *The New Yorker* (July 28, 2008), 43.

101. Stuart Brown, M.D. *Play: How It Shapes the Brain, Opens the Imagination, and Invigorates the Soul.* Avery (Penguin Group, USA). New York. 2009.

102. Frank Wilson, *The Hand: How Its Use Shapes the Brain, Language, and Human Culture* (New York: Random House, 1998), 307. The important contribution prototyping plays to the invention process (as described at length in Schrage, Michael. *Serious Play: How the Worlds's Best Companies Simulate to Innovate.* Havard Business School Press, Boston. 2000) and the hand-brain co-evolution (discussed at length in Wilson's *The Hand*) won't let inventors think only. They must sculpt, or model, and think their way to an invention that works.

103. George Prince and W. J. J. Gordon formalized this approach and taught it to thousands of people under the Innovative Teamwork Program (Synectics), early sponsors (late '50s and early '60s) of which were Exxon Chemical Company, Kimberly-Clark, and Westinghouse.

104. Walter Isaacson, *Einstein: His Life and Universe* (New York: Simon & Schuster, 2007)

105. Mihaly Csikszentmihalyi, *Creativity: Flow and the Psychology of Discovery and Invention* (New York: HarperCollins, 1996), 114.

106. Steve Jobs. Citation: www.ted.com/talks/steve_jobs_how_to_live_before_you_die.html

107. Roger Martin, *The Opposable Mind: How Successful Leaders Win through Integrative Thinking* (Boston: Harvard Business School Press, 2007), 111ff.

108. Ibid.

Chapter 7

109. This "fit" issue is rampant with NIH (not-invented-here), NMH (not-made-here) and NSH (not-sold-here) anti-bodies that reflect the inflexibility of the host's mental model of its business. But in some instances, the ability to find a fit does become an irresolvable issue. Ikujiro Nonaka and Hirotaka Takeuchi, *The Knowledge-Creating Company: How Japanese Companies Create the Dynamics of Innovation* (New York: Oxford University Press, 1995), 10-11.

110. David Kolb. *Experiential Learning: Experience as the source of learning and development.* Prentice Hall, Engelwood Cliffs, N.J. 1984

111. Ibid.

112. Ikujiro Nonaka and Hirotaka Takeuchi*The Knowledge Creating Company: How Japanese Companies Create the Dynamics of Innovation*. Oxford. 1995. The kind of learning that the reduction to practice challenge requires is not limited to the learning of something that someone else knows and the innovator only recently learns from a book, a web-search or a course in school, and the like. It also requires the kind of learning that creates new knowledge. Coming from a Japanese perspective, Nonaka and Takeuchi have much to say about the various ways in which new knowledge is created, though they do not explicitly mention forgiveness, it seems built right into their SECI model.

113. Donald A.Schon, *The Reflective Practitioner: How Professionals Think in Action* (New York: Harper, 1983), 68.

114. 114Karl E.Weick. *Sensemaking in Organizations.* (Thousand Oaks: Sage Publications, Inc. 1995). 99 (quoting Daft, R.L., & Lengel, R.H. Organizational information requirements, media richness, and structural design. *Management Science*, 32, 1986) 554-571)

115. W.J.J. Gordon and George Prince formalize this approach and taught thoughsands of people undert the Innovative Teamwork Program (Synectics). Early sponsors (late 50s and early 60s) include Exxon Chemical Company of America, Kimberly-Clark Corporation, Xerox, and Westinghouse.

116. Frank J. Sulloway. Born to Rebel: Birth Order, Family Dynamics, and Creative Lisves (New York: Pantheon, 1995.)

117. Ikujiro Nonaka and Noboru Konno. "The concept of "Ba": Building a foundation of knowledge creation." *California Management Review.* Vol. 40. No. 3 spring 1998. Pg 42.

118. James M. Utterback, *Mastering the Dynamics of Innovation: How Companies Can Seize Opportunities in the Face of Technological Change* (Boston: Harvard Business School Press, 1994), 216.

119. Ibid. 145.

120. Richard C. Cheverton with Lanny Vincent and Bill Wilson, *The Maverick Way: Profiting from the Power of the Corporate Misfit* (La Palma, Calif.: maverickway.com, 2000).

121. David Owen, "The Inventor's Dilemma," *The New Yorker* (May 17, 2010), 42.

122. "preferred embodiment," wikipedia.

123. Stefan H. Thomke, *Experimentation Matters: Unlocking the Potential of New Technologies for Innovation* (Boston: Harvard Business School Press, 2003).

124. Eric von Hippel. *Democratizing Innovation.* (Cambridge: MIT Press, Cambridge, 2005).

125. Ikujiro Nonaka and Noboru Konno. "The Concept of "Ba": Building a foundation for knowledge creation." *California Management Review.* Vol. 40. No. 3. Spring 1998

126. Michael N. Kennedy. *Product Development for the Lean Enterprise: Why Toyota's System is Four Times More Productive and How you Can Implement It.* (Richmond: The Oaklea Press, 2003); and Stefan H. Thomke. *Experimentation Matters: Unlocking the Potential of New Technologies for Innovation.* Cambridge: Harvard Business School Press, 2003).

127. Arie de Geus, *The Living Company: Habits for Survival in a Turbulent Business Environment* (Boston: Harvard Business School Press, 1997), 59ff.

128. Stefan H. Thomke. *Experimentation Matters: Unlocking the Potential of New Technologies for Innovation.* Cambridge: Harvard Business School Press, 2003).

129. Jennet Conant, *Tuxedo Park: A Wall Street Tycoon and the Secret Palace of Science That Changed the Course of World War II* (New York: Simon & Schuster, 2002), 212.

130. Paul R. Lawrence and Nitin Nohria, *Driven: How Human Nature Shapes Our Choices* (San Francisco: Jossey-Bass, 2002), 124.

131. Rita McGrath and Ian MacMillan, "Discovery Driven Planning," *Harvard Business Review* (July-August, 1995).

132. Donald A.Schon, *The Reflective Practitioner: How Professionals Think in Action* (New York: Harper, 1983), 68.

133. Lanny Vincent. "Innovation Midwives: Sustaining Innovation Streams in Established Companies." *Research•Technology Mangement.* Volume 48 No. 1. Industrial Research Institute, Inc., Arlington. January-February, 2005.

134. Clayton M. Christensen and Michael E. Raynor, *The Innovator's Solution: Creating and Sustaining Successful Growth* (Boston: Harvard Business School Press, 2003), 236.

135. Michael N. Kennedy. *Product Development for the Lean Enterprise: Why Toyota's System is Four Times More Productive and How you Can Implement It.* (Richmond: The Oaklea Press, 2003); and Stefan H. Thomke. *Experimentation Matters: Unlocking the Potential of New Technologies for Innovation.* Cambridge: Harvard Business School Press, 2003).

Chapter 8

136. Peter Drucker, *Management: Tasks, Responsibilities, Practices* (New York: Harper & Row, 1954, 1973), 61.

137. Some kind of call to action (or what next step can be taken, e.g., a number to call) could arguably be regarded as a fourth part that should show up in every concept.

138. Ellen Byron, "Can Re-Engineered Kleenex Cure Brand's Sniffles?" *Wall Street Journal* (January 22, 2007).

139. Abraham is considered the first "believer" in Judiasm, Christianity, and Islam, as all three have as a part of their respective scriptures the stories of Abraham's faith.

140. "Isaac," George Arthur Buttrick, ed., *The Interpreter's Dictionary of the Bible*, vol. 2 (Nashville: Abingdon, 1962), 728.

141. Soren Kierkegaard, *Fear and Trembling and Sickness Unto Death*, Introduction and Notes by Walter Lowrie, trans., (Princeton: N.J.: Princeton University Press, 1954).

142. Both innovators and marketers must submit to customers' perception of value. The more they do this collaboratively, the better off the introduction. Marketers are typically better suited to the crafting of the problem statement and the declaration of the promise. Innovators are better at providing the reason-to-believe. Marketers may be in a better position to decipher the relevant dynamics and implications affecting the value of a product, and innovators may be better positioned to understand the benefit minus the cost. The distinction that Adam Smith made in *An Inquiry into the Nature and Causes of the Wealth of Nations* (New York: Random House, 2000) between "exchange value" and "value in use" is worth noting here. Smith wrote: "The word value, it is to be observed, has two different meanings, and sometimes expresses the utility of some particular object, and sometimes the power of purchasing other goods . . . . The one may be called 'value in use;' the other, 'value in exchange.' The things which have the greatest value in use have frequently little or no value in exchange: and on the contrary, those which have the greatest value in exchange have frequently little or no value in use. Nothing is more useful than water: but it will purchase scarce any thing; scarce any thing can be had in exchange for it. A diamond, on the contrary, has scarce any value in use [yes, a bit dated, given the use of diamonds in precision cutting and polishing industries] but a very great quantity of other goods may frequently be had in exchange for it." To better coordinate and collaborate, marketers should concentrate on what makes for the exchange value, whereas innovators should concentrate on what make for the value in use. Effective introductions require the value equation is at least balanced—that the value in use (i.e., the benefit minus costs) equilibrates to the value in exchange—an equation that neither marketers nor innovators can escape.

143. E.M. Rogers, *Diffusion of Innovations*, 5th ed. (New York: Simon & Schuster, (1962, 2003).

144. rigteousness in the OT, George Arthur Buttrick, ed., *The Interpreter's Dictionary of the Bible*, vol. 4 (Nashville: Abingdon, 1962). 80.

145. John H. Lienhard, *Where Invention Begins: Echoes of Old Voices in the Rise of New Machines* (New York: Oxford University Press, 2006).

146. Richard N. Foster, *Innovation: The Attacker's Advantage* (New York: Summit, 1986).

147. Michael N. Kennedy. *Product Development for the Lean Enterprise: Why Toyota's System is Four Times More Productive and How you Can Implement It.* (Richmond: The Oaklea Press, 2003)

148. Jamee M. Morgan and Jeffrey K. Liker, *The Toyota Product Development System.* (New York: Productivity Press, 2006).

Chapter 9

149. David Packard, *The HP Way: How Bill Hewlett and I Built Our Company* (New York: HarperCollins, 1995), 57.

150. Jeffrey K. Liker, *The Toyota Way: 14 Management Principles from the World's Greatest Manufacturer* (New York: McGraw-Hill, 2004), 257ff.

151. Peter F. Drucker, *Innovation and Entrepreneurship: Practice and Principles* (New York: Harper & Row, 1985), 40-41.

152. Ibid., 46, 50.

153. Ibid., 57.

154. Massimo Piattelli-Palmarini, *Inevitable Illusions: How Mistakes of Reason Rule Our Minds* (New York: Wiley, 1994), 115-37.

155. Ibid., 133.

156. Peter F. Drucker, *Innovation and Entrepreneurship: Practice and Principles* (New York: Harper & Row, 1985), 28.

157. Transcript provided by National Public Radio, copyright © National Public Radio (July 17, 2009).

158. David A. Garvin and Lynne C. Levesque, "Emerging Business Opportunities at IBM," Harvard Business School Case Study (February 28, 2005), 10.

159. Matthew 7.2.

160. Robert C. Roberts, "The Blessings of Gratitude: A Conceptual Analysis," chapter 4, Robert A. Emmons and Michael E. McCullough, *The Psychology of Gratitude* (New York: Oxford University Press, 2004).

161. Richard N. Foster, *Innovation: The Attacker's Advantage* (New York: Simon & Schuster, 1988).

162. M. H. Meyer and J. M. Utterback, "Product Development Cycle Time and Commercial Success," *Engineering Management* (November 1995) and Eric H. Kessler and Paul E. Bierly. "Is Faster Really Better? An Empirical Test of the Implications of Innovation Speed." *IEEE Transactions on Engineering Management.* Vol. 49, No1, February 2002.)

Postscript

163. Rheinhold Neihbor. *The Irony of American History.* Chicago: The University of Chicago Press, 1952).

Index

CPSIA information can be obtained at www.ICGtesting.com
Printed in the USA
LVOW040715090212

267792LV00002B/2/P